Debates in Modern History

WEIMAR: WHY DID GERMAN DEMOCRACY FAIL?

Debates in Modern History

WEIMAR: WHY DID GERMAN DEMOCRACY FAIL?

Edited by
Ian Kershaw
Professor of Modern History
The University of Sheffield

Weidenfeld and Nicolson
LONDON

George Weidenfeld and Nicolson Ltd
91 Clapham High Street, London sw4 7TA

ISBN 0 297 82012 5

Printed in Great Britain at The Bath Press, Avon

Contents

Contributors

RICHARD BESSEL is a Lecturer in History at the Open University. His extensive publications on twentieth-century German history include a volume which he co-edited with Edgar Feuchtwanger, *Social Change and Political Development in the Weimar Republic* (London, 1981), and *Political Violence and the Rise of Nazism* (New Haven and London, 1984). He is currently completing a study of demobilization after the First World War.

DICK GEARY is Professor of Modern History at the University of Nottingham. He has published widely on Germany in the nineteenth and twentieth centuries, particularly on the history of the German working class. His works include *European Labour Protest* (London, 1981), *Karl Kautsky* (Manchester, 1987), and, together with Richard Evans, an edited volume of essays on *The German Unemployed* (London & Sydney, 1987). At present he is preparing a full-scale study of the impact of the slump on the working class in Germany.

CARL-LUDWIG HOLTFRERICH is Professor in the Abteilung für Wirtschaft of the John F. Kennedy-Institut für Nordamerikastudien in the Freie Universität, West Berlin, and is one of the foremost economic historians in the Federal Republic of Germany. His wide array of publications on the Weimar economy includes a study of the great inflation which has appeared in English: *The German Inflation 1914–1923: Causes and Effects in International Perspective* (Berlin/New York, 1986). He has been the most prominent critic of the 'Borchardt thesis' since the early 1980s.

HAROLD JAMES, formerly at Peterhouse, Cambridge, is now a Professor of History at Princeton University. His publications, notably his books on *The Reichsbank and Public Finance in Germany 1924–1933: A Study of the Politics of Economics during the Great Depression* (Frankfurt, 1985), and *The German Slump. Politics and Economics 1924–1936* (Oxford, 1986), have made him a leading international authority on the economy of inter-war Germany.

IAN KERSHAW is Professor of Modern History at the University of Sheffield. His publications include: *Popular Opinion and Political Dissent in the Third Reich. Bavaria 1933–1945* (Oxford, 1983), *The 'Hitler Myth'. Image and Reality in the Third Reich* (Oxford, 1987), and *The Nazi Dictatorship. Problems and Perspectives of Interpretation* (2nd edn., 1989).

Ian Kershaw

Introduction: Perspectives of Weimar's Failure

The collapse of democracy and establishment of authoritarian systems of rule was no rare occurrence in interwar Europe. By the outbreak of the Second World War liberal democracy in Europe was confined to Scandinavia, the Low Countries, Switzerland, France, and the British Isles. Of these democracies, the French Third Republic had appeared a shaky edifice indeed at times during the 1930s though it survived until the military defeat of 1940. In central and eastern Europe, especially, democracy was a fragile flower planted in infertile ground after the First World War and in most cases soon capitulated to authoritarianism. Of the new democracies, that of Czechoslovakia had the most solid foundations – until it was dismembered at Munich and crushed by German invasion six months later.

In the bleak catalogue of failed democracies in interwar Europe, Weimar Germany is a special case. No other failure of democracy has attracted remotely the attention paid to the collapse of the Weimar Republic. This is not only because Germany, even in its weakened condition after the First World War, remained the largest, most strategically significant, most economically highly-developed, most culturally advanced nation-state in central Europe but, of course, because of what followed the failure of Weimar democracy. The burial of the

Weimar Republic with the appointment, by the head of state of that Republic, Reich President Hindenburg, of Adolf Hitler as Chancellor and head of a coalition government of 'national concentration' on 30 January 1933, marked an event of world-historical significance, whose consequences were ruthless dictatorship in Germany, a new world war, genocidal barbarism on a previously unimaginable scale, and ultimately the reconstruction of Europe in a shape familiar to us today. The history of the Weimar Republic has inevitably, therefore, been overshadowed by its end and what followed. There has consequently been intense scrutiny of the causes of its failure, speculation and debate about its chances of survival, and analysis of its missed opportunities. Weimar continues to offer in many respects a paradigm of the failure of democracy in a modern industrial society and the dangers of such a failure.

Although the Weimar Republic is one of the most thoroughly researched periods of the history of any country, interpretations of the reasons for its collapse and replacement by Nazi authoritarianism have varied widely.[1] For obvious reasons, scholarly analysis of the Weimar Republic could only begin in earnest after the Second World War. Initially, historians concentrated mainly upon the period of the disintegration of the Republic between 1929 and 1933.

Early debate centred in particular upon the role of Heinrich Brüning, Reich Chancellor between 1930 and 1932, and whether his policies, carried out largely by decree under the aegis of an increasingly authoritarian presidential regime without the support of the Reichstag, could be regarded as a last-ditch attempt, under intolerable economic strain and in the face of mounting political difficulties, to salvage democracy, or as paving the way for its complete dismembering under Hitler. Though there was no full resolution of the debate at the time, subsequent research and wider availability of sources, including not least Brüning's own memoirs,[2] have largely vindicated the second and discredited the first of these positions.

As his memoirs make plain, while Brüning was certainly striving to block the possibility of a Nazi takeover of power, his aims were fundamentally anti-democratic. His hopes were for the restoration of the monarchy, and for government independent of political parties and freed of the interference of parliament. Essentially, he wanted a constitutional order of the type which had existed under Bismarck. To attain these aims, which were therefore clearly directed at the nullification of the Weimar constitution and the permanent exclusion of the Social Democrats from power, Brüning was prepared to by-pass parliament as far as possible, working with the support of powerful anti-Republican forces within the framework of the President's emergency powers under Article 48 of the constitution.[3] There is, therefore, now wide agreement among historians that the appointment of Brüning as Reich Chancellor in March 1930 marks a highly significant step in the process of the undermining of German democracy.

In a second phase, the main focus of research shifted from the end to the beginning of the Republic. Bracher's seminal work in particular had drawn attention to the structural weaknesses of the Weimar republican fabric and the important anti-democratic forces which had been present from the outset, extending their hold during the world economic crisis after 1929. It was a natural progression to consider whether the decisive juncture was not the very birth period of the Republic. One widely-held interpretation was that Friedrich Ebert and the Majority Social Democrats had little choice but to come to terms with the traditional elites in order to avoid Bolshevism in Germany, maintain order, and provide a possibility for democratic rule. The counter-position argued that crucial opportunities for consolidating democracy were missed in the revolutionary months of 1918–9, and that a total break with the reactionary forces of the old order was not even attempted. The implication was that the course of the Weimar Republic was doomed from inception. A great deal of detailed research, especially on the role of the workers' councils during and after the Revolution, has succeeded in discrediting the view that the choice in 1918–9 was only between parliamentary democracy, dependent upon Ebert negotiating backing from intrinsically undemocratic elites, and a soviet-style of government.[4] Debate continues about whether the 'councils movement' had itself the potential for systematic, radical change, or should be seen as a largely heterogeneous and transient protest movement without clearcut and realizable aims.[5] But research has made absolutely plain that the forces wanting a bolshevik-style solution were insignificant even within the 'councils movement' and that the basis of support for a Majority Social Democratic government introducing far wider measures of democratization than were attempted was, initially at least, a very considerable one. Historians came increasingly to the view, therefore, that Ebert and the Majority Social Democrats could indeed have 'dared' more democracy, that the choices and room for manœuvre were less curtailed than Ebert imagined, and that hasty and timid decisions did mean that significant opportunities for a more auspicious foundation of Weimar democracy were squandered.

This does not, however, amount to acceptance of the 'deterministic' view that Weimar was doomed from birth. After all, for all its instability and the enormous political and economic problems in its early phase, German democracy survived the postwar crisis. Unlike the situation in Italy, where in this period democracy caved in to the challenge of fascism, the new German Republic at this time proved capable of withstanding the threat from the Right. In fact, the attempt by counter-revolutionary forces to bring down the Republic in the Kapp-Putsch of 1920 was impressively fended off by a general strike and rapidly collapsed. Three years later, following French occupation of the Rhineland, the worst inflation in history, and full-scale political crisis, the Republic once more weathered the storm, and a strengthened currency and more settled political conditions seemed to augur well for the future. And even allowing for the absence in 1918 of a far-reaching social revolution which would have swept away the old reactionary, counter-revolutionary forces, Weimar's political changes and social legislation were far from negligible in significance and, it could be argued, might have paved the way for a gradual consolidation of democracy had not the world economic crisis totally undermined the Republic's hopes.

As historians have gradually moved away from treating the Weimar Republic simply as a prelude to the catastrophe of 1933, concentrating only on the drama of the beginning and end of the Republic under the perspective of failure and collapse, and have begun to undertake analysis of the fourteen years of German democracy seen as a whole, with increased emphasis on the middle 'stable' phase of 1924–9, they have tended to combine understanding of the very real weaknesses of the Republic with emphasis upon the achievements of Weimar and the 'openness' of developments down to the very end.[6] Seen from this perspective, there was nothing predetermined about Weimar's demise. Chances existed to put democracy on a firmer footing, and even in the crisis period after 1930 the road to total collapse and Hitler's triumph was by no means an unavoidable one. Rather, the argument continues, mistakes were made – particularly under Brüning – and wrong policy options adopted, leading to the undermining of the potential which had hitherto existed to save democracy.

The intensified research conducted on Weimar's 'middle years' has, however, had another side to it. While some historians have viewed this period as illustration of the potential for consolidation of a healthy democracy, whose chances of survival were then destroyed from outside by the world economic slump, others have unfolded evidence of severe structural weaknesses and strains even in the so-called 'golden years' which greatly restricted the Republic's options once Germany fell into the grip of the depression. Without returning to the 'doomed from birth' line, the chances of establishing a successful democracy were, in such a perspective, already slim by the later 1920s and became as good as non-existent once the depression set in. Particularly under the influence of the analyses of the Munich economic historian Knut Borchardt from the late 1970s onwards, the interpretation gathered ground that Weimar was incurably 'sick' and that lack of options in facing unmanageable economic problems, already present in Weimar's 'good years' and irredeemable in the world economic crisis, spelled the inescapable end of German democracy.[7]

During the last decade or so, Borchardt's reinterpretation of the failure of Weimar democracy, centring upon its lack of room for manœuvre in coping with its mounting economic problems, has dominated research and debate. The debate which it has unleashed indeed forms a cornerstone of the present volume. Borchardt's thesis is fully outlined in one of the contributions below, that of Carl-Ludwig Holtfrerich. It can be summarized here, therefore, in the briefest terms. The nub of the argument is that the Weimar Republic had no possibility of adopting Keynesian-type reflationary policies both because of internal structural economic weaknesses and because of the constraints of Germany's foreign policy position. A major internal weakness, in Borchardt's view, arose from excessive wage levels of German workers resulting in the main from government interference in the labour market through, for example, the introduction of compulsory wage arbitration and increased employer contributions to social insurance payments. And since Weimar governments seemed to have strengthened the position of organized labour and thus enabled it effectively to price itself out of jobs and markets, it was understandable that business should look with increasingly hostile eyes on the Republic and want to replace it with an authoritarian system. Germany went into the depression, therefore, seriously weakened economically – a fault in no small measure of a political system which had allowed wage settlements to get out of step with production and capacity levels – and with few political options.

In addition, the limits imposed by the capital market meant the fiscal room for manœuvre was non-existent. An expansionist economic programme, once the depression had descended upon Germany, was impossible. Such a programme would have depended upon credits, either from domestic or foreign sources, which could not have been provided because – among other things – of fears of renewed rampant inflation, legal restrictions on the Reichsbank, or because of intolerable strings attached to foreign loans. In any case, it is claimed, advocates of reflationary policies only became voluble at a late stage in the depression – far too late to be effective in saving a democracy which by that time had no chance of survival. A corollary of this economic analysis is the pointlessness of attributing blame to Chancellor Brüning for not undertaking policies which were not open to him in the first place. Brüning had had no alternative. A sick economy, to which excessive wage levels had made a significant contribution, had left Germany in no shape to face major economic crisis.

And once the depression gripped Germany, democracy was left with no way out.

Once again, the Brüning chancellorship has emerged as the main terrain of divergent interpretations. For while Borchardt and those who have essentially followed his line of argument have tended to see Brüning as a tragic figure carrying out the only economic policy open to him (and thereby worsening both the economic situation and democracy's chances of survival), diametrically opposed interpretations have been advanced, vehemently contesting the premises of Borchardt's thesis and claiming that alternative strategies to that pursued by Brüning had indeed existed. As Carl-Ludwig Holtfrerich forcefully argues in his contribution to this volume, exponents of such a position contend that policy miscalculation and wilful rejection of alternatives, rather than the inexorable logic of economic forces and lack of choice, played the key role. Human agency, therefore, reoccupies centre stage in the counterblast to Borchardt's emphasis upon impersonal economic forces.

On one level, the Borchardt debate has been about complex and technical matters of economic policy-making. The stir which the controversy has made is probably not, however, explicable purely on grounds of an academic dispute over economic policy in the 1930s. In the context of the frontal challenge to Keynesian principles in the late 1970s, and attacks on deficit financing, levels of public spending, welfare expenditure, and labour costs in industry, Borchardt's analysis of the weakness of Weimar democracy had an uncomfortably modern ring to it.

The impact of the Borchardt debate is the historiographical point of departure for the present volume. The book constitutes something of an experiment, aiming not only to offer differing perspectives and interpretations from four experts on the Weimar Republic from Britain, the United States, and West Germany, but also to provide a discussion forum for the participants. The dispute arising from Borchardt's thesis lies quite expressly at the heart of the papers by Harold James (Princeton) and Carl-Ludwig Holtfrerich (Berlin), which present completely contrasting analyses of the economic viability of the Weimar Republic. The other two contributions shift the focus from economic policy-making during the slump to further political and structural factors in Weimar's collapse. Here too, however, the issues raised by Borchardt are inevitably close to the surface. The juxtaposed highly contentious issues of the role of workers and their employers in what he significantly calls the 'overthrow' of the Weimar Republic are the subject of the analysis by Dick Geary (Nottingham). And Richard Bessel (Open University) completes the volume with a wide-ranging multi-causal explanation of Weimar's failure.

The Borchardt debate, as the above short summary has indicated, has led to something of a polarization in approaches, though with much nuance and differentiation. One group of interpretations takes a basically pessimistic view of the Weimar Republic's chances of survival, and emphasizes both the magnitude of the problems facing democracy even before the onset of the depression and the lack of room for manœuvre after 1930. Another set of interpretations is more optimistic about possibilities of establishing a viable democratic system, disinclined to see foreclosed options until the very end, and prepared to stress human agency, anti-democratic strategies, and policy blunders. It is possible to see the four contributions to the volume ranged along a spectrum covering these positions.

The most pessimistic assessment presented here is made by Richard Bessel. While Bessel is at pains 'not to throw the idea of human agency out of the window',[8] the weight of his interpretation is placed upon impersonal, structural factors in Weimar's demise. At the very outset of his paper, he suggests that it might be mistaken to regard the Weimar Republic as 'a brave experiment gone wrong' and cites approvingly Gerald Feldman's recommendation 'to consider Weimar as a gamble which stood virtually no chance of success'.[9] If this is not the 'doomed from the start' argument, it certainly appears to be pushing in that direction. More than any of the other contributors, Bessel incorporates in his argument the problems which plagued Weimar from the beginning. He devotes considerable attention to the major handicaps which arose from Germany's participation of the Great War, let alone from losing it, and the problems – outlasting the wave of crises which ended with the stabilization of 1924 – which prevented the establishment of a solid base of support and popular legitimacy for the new state system. He is more than sceptical about arguments that the Left could have effected a far-reaching social transformation and democratization at the beginning of the Republic. He doubts that the potential for such a radical break in the socio-economic system existed, given the absence of clear-cut and agreed programmes among the socialists, the urgency of the need to pick up the pieces left by the bankruptcy of the old political order, and, above all, the overriding demands of a rapid demobilization of the armed forces and the huge economic problems of the imme-diate postwar period. The impossibility, given the objective lack of manœuvrability, of remotely fulfilling the utopian expectations placed in the new Republic again diminished support and enthusiasm for the democratic experiment before it was even able to establish itself securely.

Bessel is equally pessimistic about the 'golden years' of 1924–8. Here, too, the Republic was unable to create and consolidate an extensive base of popular legitimacy. And rather than providing a source of strength, the impressive advances of the social welfare system in this period, argues Bessel in a political counterpoint to Borchardt's economic evaluation, raised demands which could not be met, increased taxation and social insurance levels, intensified areas of con-flict between state and citizen, and proved 'a time bomb with a rather short fuse'.[10] As a symptom of the mounting political difficulties of Weimar, even in its best era and before the onset of the depression, Bessel points to the increasing frag-mentation of bourgeois party politics – the diminishing sup-port for precisely the parties which had been running the Republic during its 'good' years. It was a fragmentation which, during the depression, was to benefit only the Nazi Party.

Given this analysis, it is scarcely surprising that Bessel holds out no hope of democratic survival once the world economic crisis had struck. Democratic politics, in this view, were bank-rupt from 1930 onwards.[11] The lack of a popular legitimating base for any set of policies aimed at a salvage operation for democracy was painfully apparent. By this time, Germany's economic and military elites were patently scouting around for an alternative political system. But they were in themselves capable only of destroying Weimar, not of offering a popular alternative. Only one person came ultimately to be in a position to provide the populist backing the elites needed: Hitler.

Bessel attaches great importance in his analysis, therefore, to the absence of legitimacy which long predated the depression crisis. When the depression hit, Weimar democracy was in no shape to sustain itself and eventually succumbed to a peculiar combination of long-term and short-term pressures which coalesced with terrible destructive force.

Harold James's assessment of Weimar democracy's survival chances is also highly pessimistic. Though, unlike Bessel, he confines his analysis to the depression era, he emphasizes long-term structural economic weaknesses which were not simply imposed on Germany by external circumstances arising from the turmoil in the international economy. These weaknesses, he argues, were rooted in Weimar's political and institutional structures. He stresses the combination, arising from the war, of great social upheaval, exaggerated hopes and expectations of a postwar economy which was in no position to deliver, and the way in which clashes over sharing out the meagre economic cake were fought out in directly political fashion, since the state itself had centralized the institutional arrangements for determining important issues of economic distribution such as wage levels and prices of crucial commodities like coal. In each of the seven key areas of economic weakness which he analyses (impact of world economic conditions, investment rates, misinvestment, falling profitability, instability of public finance, and excessive protection of agriculture), unfavourable demographic development, low savings and he sees the problems as more than simply a phenomenon of the depression itself, and not merely 'accidental' repercussions of external economic crisis. Reduced trade and loss of an important part of the industrial base provided constraints on German economic growth from the outset. Demography worked against the Republic in bringing a larger labour pool to be accommodated by the mid 1920s, adding substantially therefore to the task of coping with mass unemployment long before the depression struck. As savings rates fell, especially following the inflation, investment had to depend upon foreign sources of capital. But foreign investors were finding Germany an unattractive proposition already before the Wall Street Crash. So, for that matter, was German business itself, argues James, as declining profitability, largely a result of excessive wage rises, affected the business climate already by 1927–8. Supporting Borchardt's interpretation, James agrees that there was an 'economically damaging wage push'[12] in the critical period of the later 1920s, which led to a scaling down of investment and encouraged a negative attitude towards the Republic among business men. In the sphere of public finances, too, James adjudges the central government's room for manoeuvre to have been extremely constrained even before the depression as a consequence of increases in public spending in the later 1920s. Finally, the collapse of world food prices after 1926 and the onset of the agricultural crisis again left Germany in a peculiarly exposed position, as Weimar governments, buffeted by unrest from the countryside, tried to buy off agriculture at the expense of the rest of the economy and ended by pleasing nobody.

In each case, therefore, James points to problems inherent in the position of the Republic, even in its apparently 'healthy' phase of the mid 1920s. Indeed, it is precisely in this phase that the problems begin to mount on all fronts, with major difficulties looming long before the Wall Street Crash sent the German economy reeling out of control. In economic terms, the 'points were set to depression'[13] already in 1927–8; 'Weimar's economy suffered from an inherent instability, and ... required only a relatively small push to bring down the whole structure'.[14] The consequence of Weimar's weaknesses was a lack of alternatives for governments during the depression and corresponding discrediting of the political system itself. James's evaluation of the Brüning government, following upon his analysis of the pre-depression structural failings of Weimar, emphasizes, therefore, the lack of policy options and the near inevitable erosion of democracy in favour of an authoritarian (though – he is at pains to add – not necessarily a Nazi) solution.

The counter to Harold James's pessimistic assessment of

Weimar's economic chances is provided by Carl-Ludwig Holt-frerich, who since the early 1980s has published a number of important articles in Germany which have placed him at the forefront of those historians who reject the Borchardt thesis.[15] In the paper below, Holtfrerich, after outlining Borchardt's argument and examining the evidence on which it rests, posits a hypothesis in which the Weimar Republic could both have developed a long-term strategy offering consolidation and viability, and in which genuine policy options as alternatives to Brüning's deflationary course remained open even as late as 1931–2. Rather than accepting Borchardt's contention that there was no choice but deflationary policy, and no substantial pressure for reflation, Holtfrerich speaks of 'an avoidable failure in political leadership', and sees the problem even in 1931–2 as less a lack of options than a 'lack of determination'.[16]

Holtfrerich is keen to dispel what he regards as an exaggerated impression of the 'sickness' of the pre-depression Weimar economy, and particularly concerned to attack the notion that excessive wage levels were to blame for Weimar's economic ills. He argues that investment levels were less unsatisfactory than has been claimed, that by no means all foreign observers before the slump were pessimistic in their prognostications of the future development of the economy, and that industrial wage increases in the later 1920s were not out of step with the rise in labour productivity. If by then the German economy was indeed 'off the rails',[17] this had far more to do with low profits ensuing from lack of dynamic competition – itself a product of the growing cartellization and concentration of huge business concerns – than with trades union power and pressure for wage increases. He sees the main problem of the pre-depression Weimar economy as residing in the level of German interest rates – the high price of capital – which served as a deterrent to domestic capital formation. One major fiscal effect of the hyperinflation, on which Holtfrerich has written the most authoritative study to date,[18] was drastically to reduce the level of unearned income from the financial assets of the propertied classes and to redistribute it, seen as a proportion of national income, in wages and salaries. The consequence of this was an increase in consumption, but a decline in savings, and, as a result, low levels of capital formation, investment, and economic growth, and scant prospects therefore of full employment.

This is where Holtfrerich sees vital errors being made which obstructed the possible economic salvation of the Weimar Republic. What, in his view, the Weimar governments should have done, according to modern theory, in the immediate post-inflation phase of the mid 1920s in order to solve the Republic's economic dilemma and put democracy on a sounder footing, was to have stimulated savings and diverted, through collective bargaining agreements, parts of wage income into investment in capital formation funds owned by employees – a strategy successfully deployed after the Second World War and contributing to the growing solidity of the Bonn Republic. The emergence from the hyperinflation of 1922–3 was, in this view, a critical time. An investment and capital formation policy along these lines would, according to Holtfrerich, have made the economic system and social compromise of the Weimar Republic viable, and would have given German democracy a future.

Accepting the economic weaknesses before the onset of the depression, Holtfrerich nevertheless refuses to see the Weimar Republic as doomed through lack of alternatives to Brüning's deflationary policy. Even after the banking crisis of the summer of 1931, Holtfrerich contends that options remained open but were rejected on political, not economic grounds. He suggests several significant advocates of a reflationary strategy in government circles. The hypothesis that Brüning was faced with no alternative other than deflation cannot, in his view, be sustained. The answer to the question of why no alternatives were tried lies, therefore, in the political, rather than the economic, field. Well aware that his policies would worsen rather than improve the depression, Brüning made a conscious choice of strategy with the overriding aim of ridding Germany of the burden of reparations through demonstration to the allies of Germany's patent economic weakness and inability to pay. At the same time, the rolling back of Weimar's welfare state and drastic cuts in public expenditure were consciously intended to destroy permanently the economic and social compromise of the Republic. Through the removal of reparations, reordering the economy along the lines which business favoured, and the establishment of 'balanced budgets' under conservative-authoritarian 'strong' government, Brüning hoped in the long run to put Germany's economy on an entirely different and sounder footing. Unfortunately for Brüning, and even more unfortunately for Germany, there was no long run. Brüning's chosen policies therefore killed Weimar's chances of survival, paved the way for authoritarianism, and drove voters into the hands of the Nazis.

Dick Geary does not enter directly into the debate about the survival chances of Weimar democracy. His analysis of attitudes of workers and their employers towards the Republic mitigates, however, against attempts to claim any long-term inevitability about the demise of German democracy. He points out at the outset Weimar's capacity to survive its initial crises, when the aftermath of defeat and the imposition of reparations were most keenly felt. He suggests that the experiences of depression differed sharply from those of inflation and provided the key to the puzzle of Weimar's failure. Since the responses of both sides of industrial relations differed so acutely in the two different periods, the reasons for the collapse of democracy must, according to Geary, be located in the conditions and experiences of the slump, rather than in any predetermined long-term 'inherited' difficulties of the Republic.

A factor of central importance to Geary's argument is the behaviour and attitude of German industrialists. While in the early period of the Weimar Republic, industry showed a considerable willingness to cooperate with organized labour, this cooperation was not forthcoming in the late 1920s and early 1930s. Geary is concerned not to reduce Weimar's failure to the antagonism of industry. At the same time, he points out how the alienation of important sectors in economy and society helped to foster a climate of crisis and instability. Moreover, the growing hostility from the mid 1920s of large sections of the business community to Weimar labour law and welfare legislation – an integral element, as Geary stresses, of the Weimar system – played its part in helping to deprive the Republic of legitimacy. In this argument, therefore, the problems facing the Republic in the depression were all the more serious since one side of industrial relations was increasingly determined to countenance, and then openly work for, the end of democracy and an authoritarian solution. This shift in business attitudes had set in during the restabilization phase, once the profitability which business had enjoyed in the inflation era was put in question, once the fears of left-wing instigated social revolution had passed, and once business interests saw themselves threatened by the extension of welfare provision and labour legislation. From the late 1920s, heavy industry leadership in particular was prepared to take the offensive against organized labour. The democratic system was now plainly under threat. But, despite an ingrained distaste for the Weimar Republic in much of industry's leadership, the death-knell of democracy was sounded only under the severe impact of the depression. In this interpretation, the possibility of another path is not ruled out. 'Had capital and labour united' (as they had done in the early 1920s) 'in support of the political order', claims Geary, 'it would certainly have been in a better position to survive'.[19]

At the same time, his own analysis makes plain why such unity between capital and labour in support of the Weimar system was a non-starter long before the depression struck. It was not simply that many German employers carried into the Republic the authoritarian, anti-democratic attitudes which they had held under the Kaiser, and voiced with new vigour once the time for necessary compromise with organized labour in the first Weimar years was past. It was also that the Republic produced a new arena of industrial relations where, for the first time, German employers had to compete with unions in a state system which underpinned collective bargaining with compulsory arbitration, provided new labour law favouring employees, and extracted contributions for a more extensive welfare state. Geary is suggesting, therefore, that a sharpening of industrial conflict from the employers' side, coupled with a keenness to overthrow the Weimar settlement, was inescapable even before the depression intensified the employers' anti-democratic stance. Cooperation with organized labour, such as had occurred at the beginning of the Republic, was consequently out of the question. To this extent, Geary's prognosis of the survival chances of the

Republic appears distinctly more gloomy than that of Holtfrerich.

A view Geary emphatically shares with Holtfrerich, nevertheless, in opposition to Borchardt's interpretation, is that the failure of the Weimar Republic cannot be attributed to the high price of labour during the 1920s. He points out that other societies have been able to tolerate without undue strain higher levels of wages, public spending, and taxation for social welfare, and that Weimar Germany was far from being a high-wage economy. The failure of Weimar can in no sense, therefore according to Geary, be attributed to the demands of organized labour. The danger for democracy lay rather in the refusal of Germany's economic elites to countenance the inroads which it had made into their privileged position, and their keenness to destroy the political order and the social welfare provisions on which it rested.

Geary does not absolve organized labour from all responsibility for Weimar's failure. The gulf between expectation and performance in the 1920s – a point which Richard Bessel and Harold James also stress – had alienated increasing numbers of industrial workers from the Republic. This alienation deepened drastically during the depression and was reflected in the losses of support suffered by the SPD, the main prop of the system, which flowed mainly to the anti-republican Communist Party. And gross errors of evaluation and strategy were made, particularly by the KPD but also by the SPD, in the critical years after the seemingly promising result of the 1928 election. But arguments suggesting that democracy was destroyed as much by the Republic's communist as by its right-wing enemies are entirely misleading, and ignore or distort the realities of power in Weimar Germany. The Communist Party, with about ninety per cent of its 300,000 strong membership unemployed in the early 1930s, had no leverage at all on power. Like the SPD in this respect, the KPD could do little other than react to policies shaped by small but powerful circles, keen to eradicate parliamentary democracy and with access to and influence upon the Chancellor and President.

Geary stresses how limited the chances would have been for even a united working-class party to have saved the democracy given the strength of the anti-democratic forces in Germany, and given, especially, the impact of the slump upon the working class itself. Compared with the successful defence of the Republic in the post-war crisis, the divisive and demoralising experiences of the unprecedented levels of unemployment after 1930 left the pro-democratic forces in the working class gravely weakened and exposed. Though the backbone of support for the largest and most vicious of the anti-democratic movements, the Nazi Party, was provided by sections of society other than the industrial working class, many workers had long before end either lost faith entirely in the Weimar Republic and the party which was its last loyal prop, the SPD. During the slump, organized labour found itself without friends. Its political isolation reached back to Bismarck's time. Now, enfeebled through the depression, it lay wide open to the destructive assault of its sworn enemies.

Geary's assessment of the viability of the Weimar system seems in good measure compatible with, though less pessimistic than, those of Bessel and James. The implication of his analysis is that Weimar democracy was threatened, though by no means doomed, before the onset of the depression, but that from about 1930 onwards its chances of survival diminished sharply to the point where they rapidly became as good as non-existent.

Although the four historians represented in this volume provide varying perspectives, and at times sharply differing interpretations, of the failure of Weimar democracy, it is also possible to indicate a good deal of common ground between them. While there is no likelihood of consensus on many central issues, particularly as regards Brüning's chancellorship, the following points suggest a minimal framework of agreement among most historians of the Weimar Republic.

1. The economy was facing extremely serious problems even before the depression. Certainly there is a significant difference in whether, following Borchardt, the state of the economy is regarded as chronically 'sick' or merely, as Holtfrerich sees it, as temporarily 'off the rails'. Clearly, too, there is no agreement about the contribution of wage settlements to Weimar's economic difficulties. But there seems acceptance

that the Weimar economy did face such major obstacles as the gathering agricultural crisis, the costs of financing the welfare programme, a worryingly low level of capital formation, and an unhealthy dependence upon the vagaries of foreign lending. How things would have developed without the onset of a world economic crisis can only be a matter for speculation. But what can be said is that the Republic's already existing economic weaknesses left it peculiarly vulnerable to the worst effects of the slump, when the crash in the international economy did occur.

2. How successful anticyclical reflationary policies involving work creation schemes would have proved in shoring up support for the Republic had they been adopted in 1931–2 can again only be a matter of speculation, though most historians would be very sceptical about the chances of democratic survival by that time. Certainly, the political circumstances could hardly have been less propitious for a successful salvage operation of pluralist democracy. Nevertheless, a Nazi takeover might have been avoided. Until the bank crash, the moratorium on reparations, and the general desperation of the situation, proposals for alternative reflationary policies were not numerous. By the time they emerged, the warning lights for Weimar democracy were burning with a glaring intensity.

3. It is generally accepted that the anti-democratic stance of the traditional political elites (or ruling class) was a serious hindrance to the long-term prospects of the Republic. Already during the 'good years', the elites were looking to challenge the political and social compromise of the 1918 settlement, and they used the depression to attempt a restoration of the power relations which had prevailed before 1914. It was not, therefore, as if the economic crisis, when it struck, rocked a country whose ruling groups strongly supported the existing political system (such as was the case in Britain in the early 1930s). Rather, the sections of society with the greatest influence on the levers of power – many business leaders, landowners, military top-brass, and some figures in prominent positions in the civil service – were increasingly determined to exploit the crisis in order to overthrow Weimar democracy at the earliest available opportunity and restore some form of authoritarian rule.

4. There is much agreement that the Weimar system was inherently unstable, even in its 'healthiest' phase. This was reflected not only in the declining tolerance level of the elites, but in the fragmentation of party politics to the right of the Catholic Centre Party. The discontent with the conventional rightist parties, which was reflected even in the 1928 election results, when translated into bitter protest from the 1930s onwards, turned in only one direction. Despite the drift further to the right of all the 'bourgeois' parties, it poured into the reservoir of the Nazis – the most radical anti-left party, and the one which, at least at Reich level, had kept completely out of Weimar government. Whereas in Britain the depths of the economic crisis in 1930–1 produced a strengthening of conservatism through the resounding victory of the National Government in the 1931 elections, the conservative-liberal spectrum of voters in Germany disintegrated. The traditional 'right-wing' (though very different to and harsher than the British variant) was divided before 1914, split still further after 1918, fragmented yet further after 1928, and collapsed almost totally into the hands of the Nazis by 1932–3. The perceived (and real) weakness of the 'orthodox' right provided the 'political space'[20] which the Nazi Movement needed in order to take off.

5. This brings us to the culminating point on which a broad degree of consensus exists among historians: that the Weimar Republic suffered throughout its lifespan from a serious, and ultimately a critical, loss of legitimacy. This lack of legitimacy, which the contributions to this volume have all stressed in different ways, is the underlying key issue to the failure of the Weimar Republic. 'Democratic legitimacy', it has been said, exists on the basis of widespread acceptance that 'no other type of regime could assure a more successful pursuit of collective goals'.[21] Again, an international comparison is instructive. During the economic crisis in Britain in 1930–1 no alternative to parliamentary government was contemplated by any political grouping of more than fringe importance or by any influential grouping in the political 'establishment'. Even in the French Third Republic, where governmental instability was endemic, the forces rallying to democracy were far too strong for the fascist leagues, and

neither the vast bulk of the electorate nor the key sectors of the elites looked to an alternative system of rule. By contrast, the only political party in Germany still by 1931 giving unreserved support to the Weimar Republic was the SPD. And this party was compromised in its own ranks by its support for unpopular policies, was losing votes to the Communists, had many other adherents who had lost faith in the Republic, and was detested in bourgeois circles. The Republic's only friends were themselves friendless. The economic crisis in Germany triggered off, therefore, a withdrawal of support, not just from the government of the day, but from the political system as a whole, on the part of wide sections of the electorate as well as the power elites. It was not just a crisis of government, but a comprehensive crisis of the state itself.

Once more, it is impossible to claim that had the Wall Street Crash not plunged the world economy into depression the Weimar Republic would nevertheless inevitably have collapsed because of its problem of legitimacy. It certainly did not look that way when the Reichstag election results were announced in May 1928. But a growing disenchantment with the Republic was visible before the effects of the Wall Street Crash made themselves felt. On the far right, municipal and regional elections in autumn 1929, in the wake of the Young Plan campaign, brought sizeable increases in the Nazi vote. Seen in this light, the crucial electoral breakthrough of the Nazi Party in the September elections of 1930 did not come out of thin air. At the other end of the political spectrum, the communists, too, increased their vote significantly in 1930. Since an election had not been necessary in 1930, Brüning's request for a dissolution of the Reichstag proved a calamitous and culpable misjudgement. From this date, with the Reichstag virtually unmanageable, it is difficult to see how the Republic, in conditions of economic crisis, could have avoided further diminution in its popular support, and therefore in its basis of legitimacy. Even in 1928, substantial sections of the electorate had voted for parties hostile to the Weimar system. The legitimacy of the Republic rested on no strong base even in the 'good years'. This hardly augured well for a time when the Republic might be faced with renewed political strains. When the depression set in, the fabric of the political system was too weak to hold and its remnants of legitimacy fell apart in shreds.

A low level of legitimacy had been a feature of Weimar since its earliest days. For important sectors of the elites, the Republic was only tolerated, not accepted. Intellectual and church leaders also frequently made no bones of their disdain for the new political order. And when the Weimar supportive parties suffered major losses already at the 1920 Reichstag election, it was said that Germany had a Republic without republicans. In its attempts to consolidate its basis of popular support, the Republic faced a vicious circle: insurmountable problems, performance gap, loss of support, new problems. The unenviable inheritance – consequences of a lost war and a detested peace settlement – was of course in itself far from fatal. Otherwise the Republic would have collapsed between 1919 and 1923. But the taint attached to the Republic by its enemies never went away, and returned to strike with unremitting cruelty when democracy was on the ropes in the early 1930s. Moreover, the economic problems which the Republic had to encounter from the outset meant it always faced difficulties of effective implementation of policy aims. This in turn led to disappointment in its supporters in the ability of the Republic to fulfil expectations, a point stressed in most of the contributions to this volume. The perceptions of failure were, not surprisingly therefore, widespread even before the onset of the depression, and rapidly deepened into a comprehensive lack of confidence in democracy. This extensively perceived failure of the democratic system and of all the political parties which had participated in it cleared the way for the rapid growth of the Nazi catch-all protest movement. As Weimar lurched into its multi-dimensional crisis - scant legitimacy, instability, ineffectiveness, perceived failure all interacting and reinforcing each other in conditions of acute economic disarray – a clear alternative began to present itself to increasing numbers of voters, and gradually, too, to the brokers of power.

In the light of the above discussion, the survival chances of Weimar democracy might be regarded as fairly poor by the end of 1929, very low by the end of 1930, remote by the middle of 1931, and as good as zero by spring 1932. Viewed in an international comparative perspective, the prospects for the Republic on entering the world economic crisis might be equally unfavourably assessed. The European democracies which survived the depression and did not succumb to either a conservative-authoritarian or fascist-type takeover from within – the United Kingdom, France, the Netherlands, Belgium, Sweden, Denmark, Norway, Switzerland, and Czechoslovakia – had either been neutrals or had fought on the victorious side in the First World War; with the exception of Czechoslovakia had been long-established state systems enjoying scarcely questioned legitimacy; had no serious border problems giving rise to deeply-felt irredentist demands favouring extreme nationalist movements; had faced no revolutionary threat from the left; and (with the partial exception of Belgium and Czechoslovakia) had experienced no major problems of cultural identity.[22] All of these factors combined to weaken the survival chances of democracy in Weimar Germany. From every perspective, one would have to conclude, the German experiment in democracy was particularly poorly placed to cope with the scale of crisis which engulfed it after 1929.

There is no disagreement among the authors of this volume that the Nazis were the beneficiaries of Weimar's failure more than they were its cause. Certainly, the electoral break through of the NSDAP in September 1930 and subsequent remarkable growth of the Nazi Movement both symptomized in the clearest fashion the crisis of the democratic system and helped to paralyse it still further. But, as is abundantly clear in the pages to follow, the decay of parliamentary government preceded the Nazi rise. This is true not only in the sense that the fragmentation of the bourgeois parties had been visibly in progress before the Nazis could capitalize on the disorientation of middle-class voters, but also in the sense that the initiatives to replace the parliamentary government of Müller's 'Grand Coalition' by a presidential regime under an authoritarian 'Hindenburg Cabinet' reach back to spring

1929, six months before the Wall Street Crash, a year before Brüning was installed as Chancellor to replace Müller, and almost a year and a half before the startling Nazi advance in the 1930 Reichstag election.[23]

The four contributions which follow quite rightly, therefore, concentrate their attention on explaining the complex combination of factors which resulted in the failure of Weimar's democracy, rather than the interlinked and in many respects consequential, but nonetheless separable, reasons for the rise of Nazism.[24] As Harold James clearly points out, it is important to separate analytically the reasons for the collapse of the Weimar Republic from the reasons for Hitler's triumph in January 1933: while the replacement of German liberal democracy by some form of authoritarianism was as good as certain by 1930, or at the latest by the summer of 1931, there was nothing at all predetermined about the appointment of Hitler as Reich Chancellor.[25] James stresses the role played by chance events in the developments leading up to Hitler's takeover of power. The role of personality and chance was itself a reflection of the corrosion of democratic rule. As the normal organs of parliamentary government were increasingly by-passed after Brüning had become Chancellor in March 1930, and were replaced by a presidential regime in which access to Hindenburg was vital, the role played by the intrigue of those in the President's inner circle greatly expanded. The diminution of institutional constraints and the resulting power vacuum left the field wide open for individual 'initiatives' and ambitions to play a disproportionate part in power-brokerage. Out of the complex web of intrigue and counter-intrigue centred upon the President's palace, Hitler eventually emerged the winner. But despite the Nazi Party's massive electoral gains in the summer of 1932, a Hitler chancellorship was at no stage a foregone conclusion until it actually happened.

Of all the ways, threatening since 1930, in which the Weimar Republic might have met its end, the handover of power by Hindenburg to Hitler on 30 January 1933 was the worst of all. Before that time, other possibilities had been seriously contemplated by those controlling the levers of power. In the months before his dismissal, Brüning had attempted to persuade Hindenburg and von Schleicher of the virtues of restoring the monarchy under the Crown Prince August Wilhelm. He thought a constitutional monarchy would gain the support of the working class as a bulwark against a Nazi dictatorship.[26] But he found little positive support from either the President or von Schleicher. In late 1932, Reich Chancellor von Papen was prepared to risk civil war by using the army and police to suppress political parties and organizations and introduce a new authoritarian constitution.[27] But the dangers of the involvement of the Reichswehr in a civil war, particularly if problems arose on the eastern borders, were regarded by the Defence Minister von Schleicher as too great. When, in December 1932, von Schleicher himself succeeded von Papen as Chancellor, he sought to find mass support for his authoritarian rule in a 'diagonal' solution incorporating the trades unions and the Nazi Movement under Gregor Strasser as his Vice-Chancellor. But the conflict about strategy within the Nazi Party was won by Hitler. Strasser resigned all his offices and left the country.[28] Von Schleicher's hopes of building a basis of popular support had evaporated. More than that, his opening to the working class had frightened and alienated leaders of big business and, even more importantly, the agrarian lobby of the major landowners. As the mounting anxieties about von Schleicher were conveyed to Hindenburg by representatives of the agricultural lobby of the big landowners, a group whose sympathies he shared, the days of the last Chancellor before Hitler were patently numbered.

By January 1933, therefore, a number of possible authoritarian solutions had been contemplated. They had all foundered on the absence of a mass base of support. It was in such circumstances that von Papen and his cronies were prepared to gamble with Hitler as Reich Chancellor, in the belief that Hitler would be 'tamed' by his participation in government and the Nazi bubble would burst. By January 1933, therefore, it could be argued that the power-broking elites had run out of alternatives which excluded the Nazis. Their central problem was their lack of mass support. The only person who could deliver them this was Hitler. On 13 August 1932, after Hitler had won a major electoral triumph, Hindenburg had flatly refused to appoint him to the Chancellorship. Now, in January 1933, when the last election, in November 1932, had seen the Nazi Party lose three million votes, Hindenburg installed Hitler in the Reich Chancellory. Elections had placed Hitler in a position where he could not be ignored in the power-brokerage game. But he was not 'elected' Reich Chancellor. Nor was there any greater compulsion to place him in power in January 1933 than there had been four months earlier. He was appointed by Hindenburg following intrigues of the sort which had made and then unmade his immediate predecessors – Brüning, von Papen, and von Schleicher. Hitler needed the brokerage of the camarilla around Hindenburg in order to get to power; the conservative elites needed Hitler's control of the masses in order to bring off a lasting return to authoritarian rule. It sounded a good deal. It formed the basis of the fateful 'alliance' of interests which put Hitler in the Chancellor's seat at the end of January 1933.

Hitler's triumph on 30 January 1933 was at no stage an inevitable outcome of the failure of Weimar democracy. As the eminent German historian Friedrich Meinecke commented on hearing the news of Hitler's appointment to the Chancellorship: 'this was not necessary'.[29] After the losses suffered by the NSDAP in the Reichstag election of November 1932, many had drawn the conclusion that the Nazis' advance was over, and that Hitler would never gain power.[30] And indeed, had Hitler not been jobbed into office in January 1933, it is not inconceivable that the unstable Nazi Party would have faced growing internal rifts and begun to disintegrate. With the beginnings of an improvement in the economy becoming visible by mid 1933 (and owing little or nothing to the initial policies of the new Nazi government), it is possible that January 1933 might have been Hitler's last chance of becoming Chancellor. But the bankruptcy, not only of democratic politics, but also of elite strategies, had made the nomination to the Reich Chancellorship of a rank outsider to the conventional power circles acceptable to those who controlled the access to power. In Hitler, with an enormous political army behind him, they had a man who, they thought, could do a job for them. They had not reckoned with the fact that once he had the opportunity he might be able to do more than that.

More than half a century after it met its end, the Weimar Republic continues to exert an enigmatic fascination over all who ponder its fate. It continues to pose serious problems of interpretation. Modes of thinking and debates about Weimar have, however, altered considerably over this period of time. The founding fathers of the West German Federal Republic initially looked to the 'lessons' of Weimar to provide constitutional guidance. The 'flawed' structures of the Weimar state dominated early considerations. Much blame was attached to the mechanisms of democratic government constructed in the 1919 constitution, such as the weaknesses of the proportional representation system used, and in particular the fateful role of the notorious Article 48, which provided the basis of Hindenburg's rule by presidential decree after 1930. This rather narrow attention to constitutional form gave way to deeper analysis of the anti-democratic power-elites who were working consciously to destroy the Republic. In turn, this opened the path for concentration on the socio-economic continuities in German history providing a barrier to the establishment of solid foundations for democracy. Whereas East German scholarship retained its emphasis on Weimar as a bourgeois state founded on the betrayal of the working-class interests by Social Democracy and undermined by the hostility of big capital, West German research turned towards the continuing dominant role of traditional, pre-industrial elites in blocking, opposing, and then overthrowing democracy. The key questions which seemed to need answering were why the peculiarly German path to 'modernity' deviated from the 'normal' pattern of western countries towards democracy leaving 'pre-modern' power elites intact, even after the 1918 revolution, and able, therefore, to be in a position to overturn the democratic experiment and return to authoritarianism by the early 1930s. More recently, this type of interpretation has also been found inadequate. Notions of a 'normal' path to modernization, equatable with liberal democracy, have been seriously doubted. How far Germany's power elites can realistically be labelled 'pre-industrial' or 'pre-modern' has been rigorously questioned. The view that traditional patterns of authoritarianism led inexorably towards 1933, interrupted by an inevitably doomed experiment in democracy, no longer carries the conviction it once did. Without reverting to orthodox Marxist–Leninist theories of class struggle, the answer to the question: 'what produces fascism: preindustrial traditions or a crisis of the capitalist state?',[31] has swung back towards the latter alternative. There has correspondingly been a new emphasis upon Weimar as a highly modern, highly industrialized society in crisis – a crisis which ran to the roots of all its political, economic, and cultural developments in a way unparalleled by any other contemporary society. In this perspective, Weimar is seen as an experiment in modernity, taking place in the most difficult conditions imaginable. During the fourteen years of the Republic, it has been said, 'nearly all the possibilities of modern existence were played out', and in a whole number of scientific, technological, and cultural spheres 'the features of the world in which we live today arose'. Yet at the same time, the powerful expression of this modernity 'was accompanied by its being called into question, by reversals, and disaster'.[32]

The understanding of Weimar as a modern society, beset – though incomparably more acutely – with many problems which are still familiar today is implicit in all the following contributions. It provides the study of Weimar with wider relevance than simply as a period of German history. Weimar Germany will continue to be an important topic of debate, since there is no likelihood that all the significant issues on which historians disagree will ever be completely resolved. But, as Richard Bessel has written elsewhere, 'the debates about Weimar Germany are not just arcane disagreements among historians. They involve fundamental questions about the viability of democracy, the relationship of economics to politics, the degree to which a society and economy can bear the costs of social-welfare programmes, the relationship between state and society, the stability of modern industrial society'.[33] The 1980s have shown that these are by no means bygone issues.

Notes

1. For an excellent historiographical survey, see Eberhard Kolb, *The Weimar Republic* (London, 1988), pp. 127–96.

2. Heinrich Brüning, *Memoiren 1918–1934* (Stuttgart, 1970). For the debate about Brüning, see Kolb, pp. 179–82.

3 This was the position adopted in his brilliant early study by Karl-Dietrich Bracher, *Die Auflösung der Weimarer Republik. Eine Studie zum Machtverfalls in der Demokratie* (Villingen, 1955). He reasserted his interpretation, following the publication of Brüning's memoirs, in his article 'Brüning's unpolitische Politik und die Auflösung der Weimarer Republik', *Vierteljahreshefte für Zeitgeschichte*, 19 (1972), pp. 113–23.

4. See Kolb, pp. 138–47, and, for a balanced evaluation of the possibilities facing Social Democratic leaders and the limits on their freedom of action, the excellent study by Heinrich August Winkler, *Von der Revolution zur Stabilisierung. Arbeiter und Arbeiterbewegung in der Weimarer Republik 1918 bis 1924* (Berlin/Bonn, 1984).

5. For this latter position, see Wolfgang J. Mommsen, 'The German Revolution 1918–1920: Political Revolution and Social Protest Movement', in Richard Bessel and E.J. Feuchtwanger (eds.) *Social Change and Political Development in Weimar Germany* (London, 1981), pp. 21–54.

6. A recently published excellent analysis, which consciously seeks to break away from a teleological approach to Weimar's collapse, is Detlev J.K. Peukert, *Die Weimarer Republik. Krisenjahre der Klassischen Moderne* (Frankfurt am Main, 1987). An English translation is in preparation.

7. Knut Borchardt's 'Zwangslagen und Handlungsspielräume in der großen Wirtschaftskrise der frühen dreißiger Jahre: Zur Revision des überlieferten Geschichtsbildes' (1979), and his 'Wirtschaftliche Ursachen des Scheiterns der Weimarer Republik' (1980), both reprinted in his *Wachstum, Krisen, Handlungsspielräume der Wirtschaftspolitik* (Göttingen, 1982), are the key essays.

8. Below, p. 121.

9. Below, p. 121.

10. Below, p. 135.

11. Below, p. 137.

12. Below, p. 39.

13. Below, p. 38.

14. Below, p. 32.

15. See especially Carl-Ludwig Holtfrerich, 'Alternativen zu Brünings Wirtschaftspolitik in der Weltwirtschaftskrise, *Historische Zeitschrift*, 235 (1982), pp. 605–31; and 'Zu hohe Löhne in der Weimarer Republik?', *Geschichte und Gesellschaft*, 10 (1984), pp. 122–41.

16. Below, pp. 73–4.

17. Below, p. 77.

18. Carl-Ludwig Holtfrerich, *The German Inflation 1914–1923. Causes and Effects in International Perspective* (West Berlin and New York, 1986).
19. Below, p. 105.
20. For the concept of 'political space', see Juan J. Linz, 'Political Space and Fascism as a Late-Comer', in Stein Ugelvik Larsen et al. (eds.), *Who were the Fascists? Social Roots of European Fascism* (Bergen, 1980), pp. 153–89.
21. Juan J. Linz and Alfred Stepan (eds.), *The Breakdown of Democratic Regimes* (Baltimore and London, 1978), vol. 1, p. 18
22. These factors are emphasized by Linz, 'Political Space', pp. 158–67, in his multi-causal explanation of opportunities for the successful breakthrough of fascist movements.
23. See Kolb, pp. 111–12.
24. The literature on the rise of Nazism is extensive. Some of the key studies in English are included in the guide to further reading below. A recent good, concise survey is provided by Martin Broszat, *Hitler and the Collapse of Weimar Germany* (Leamington Spa, Hamburg, and New York, 1987).
25. Below, p. 30.
26. Brüning, *Memoiren* (dtv edn., Munich, 1972), vol. 2, pp. 542–3, 612.
27. See Kolb, p. 122.
28. On the crisis within the Nazi Party culminating in Strasser's resignation, see Peter D. Stachura, *Gregor Strasser and the Rise of Nazism* (London, 1983), pp. 103–20.
29. Friedrich Meinecke, *The German Catastrophe: Reflections and Recollections* (Cambridge, Mass., 1950), p. 63.
30. The mood in an upper-middle-class Jewish family at the end of 1932 is captured brilliantly in Lion Feuchtwanger's novel, *Die Geschwister Opperman* (paperback edn., Frankfurt am Main, 1981). On the last day of 1932 the family, certain that Hitler would never get to power, discuss whether he will end his days as a market tout or an insurance salesman (p. 116).
31. Geoff Eley, 'What produces Fascism: Preindustrial Traditions or a Crisis of the Capitalist State?', *Politics and Society*, 12 (1983). pp. 53–82.
32. Detlev J.K. Peukert, 'The Weimar Republic – Old and New Perspectives', *German History*, 6 (1988), p. 139.
33. Richard Bessel, *Weimar Germany. The Crisis of Industrial Society, 1918–1933*, Open University Study Guide (Milton Keynes, 1987), p. 5.

Harold James

Economic Reasons for the Collapse of the Weimar Republic

In analysing the collapse of Weimar and the rise of National Socialism, we should distinguish two logically separate processes: the failure of democracy *and* the growth of Nazism. In the following essay, I shall show how economic strains at the end of the 1920s eroded democracy and prepared the path for an authoritarian solution. That does not, however, mean that the specific outcome of Germany's interwar political crisis – the appointment by Reich President Marshal Paul von Hindenburg of Adolf Hitler as Reich Chancellor on 30 January 1933 – was historically necessary, determined, or inevitable. In the latter process, chance events played the major role. Germany could have moved towards military dictatorship, the restoration of monarchy, autocratic rule through the Reich President, imitation of Italian fascism (as Chancellor Brüning sometimes appeared to be doing), or a continuation of von Papen's experiment with a reactionary and aristocratic 'new state'. Only a restoration of 1920s democracy was unlikely.

Another way of making this point is comparative: the transition from liberal democracy to authoritarian state was a common one in the interwar period and generally involved a response to economic crisis. Poland turned towards authoritarianism) in 1926 (under Pilsudski); and the Hungarian regime became more repressive in 1931 (under Gömbös). In 1934, the Austrian government launched a civil war against the Socialist Party and instituted a clerical fascism. In 1936 the Metaxas dictatorship in Greece began. Military coups in Portugal and Spain destroyed constitutional republics. In all these cases – as with similar developments in Latin America – economic depression and collapses of democracy stood in a close relation with each other. By the end of the 1930s, it had become a truism that – at least outside the Anglo-Saxon world of Great Britain and her former colonies – democracy could only survive as a 'fair weather system'.

Weimar's Economic Weakness

The crisis of Weimar democracy was preceded by economic problems. Profits in agriculture fell from 1926. In May 1927, the German stock market collapsed as a result of a deliberately designed policy on the part of the central bank to reduce the attractions of Germany to foreign investors. Construction reached a peak in the summer of 1927, and after that suffered as public authorities cut back their spending on building. According to the Institute for Business Cycle Research (Institut für Konjunkturforschung or IfK), the output of consumer goods fell from February 1928 (though for producer goods the cyclical peak came much later, in 1929, and German industrial production overall was slightly higher in 1929 than in 1928). In the summer of 1928 unemployment rose above its level of the previous year, and continued to increase until the beginning of 1933. The IfK index of industrial production shows the trough of the depression occurring in August 1932 (for producer goods already in January 1932, for consumer goods only in August).[1]

   In March 1930 the coalition government under the Chancellorship of the socialist Hermann Müller collapsed. Müller's was the last democratic government in interwar Germany in the sense that it was the last to be supported by a majority of deputies in the Reichstag. By this time the economic problem had become acute, and an international depression increased Germany's vulnerability. Müller's successor,

Heinrich Brüning (1930–32), was unable to construct a parliamentary basis and instead depended on the emergency presidential powers laid down by the Weimar constitution.

Germany's economic crisis preceded both the world depression and the political collapse. Weimar's economy suffered from an inherent instability, and like any unstable structure required only a relatively small push to bring down the whole structure. Some of the causes of Germany's problems stemmed from the world economic setting, but many of them were endogenous.

They had their roots in Weimar's institutional and political arrangements, and were discussed and analysed, both at the time and by subsequent historians, in a highly political way. The First World War had resulted in tremendous social upheaval and shifts in income and status which some believed should continue and others thought should be reversed. In consequence, the Weimar economy provided a focus for all manner of hopes and expectations. Workers believed that their pay would rise, employers sought government subsidies, farmers called for tariff protection and interest rate support, civil servants demanded better remuneration and a return to their prewar status. All these distributional demands, and the resulting clashes, were fought out in a highly centralized manner, through institutions set up by the state in the hope of defusing conflicts.[2] Coal prices were set by a newly created Reich Coal Council. The Labour Minister played a critical role in wage determination. But mechanisms such as the labour arbitration created under the 1916 Patriotic Auxiliary Service Law, and established anew by a decree of 1923, merely transferred wage and labour conflicts from the factory to the level of the state. Rather than resulting from the decentralized operation of local forces and markets, distributional outcomes now stemmed from political decisions. The central institutions in consequence became the subject of a political tug-of-war, as they became overloaded with expectations.

Such an expansion of the state's political and economic role has been a characteristic of much of twentieth century experience. But in Weimar Germany, the circumstances were highly unpropitious. In addition, the rapid expansion of the state itself contributed to the difficulties.

Weimar's economic problems may be summarized as follows:

1. World economic conditions
2. Unfavourable demographic developments
3. Low savings and investment rates
4. Misinvestment
5. Falling profitability
6. The instability of public finance
7. Excessive protection of agriculture

1.   The *world context* of the 1920s was much less favourable than had been the pre-1914 period. Germany had traditionally depended on exports as an engine of growth. In the 1920s, world trade recovered from the impact of the War far less quickly than world manufacturing output. Despite efforts to promote exports, foreign trade now played a smaller role in German economic life than it had under the old Empire. Before the First World War, German exports had accounted for 17.5 per cent of Net National Product (NNP) (1910–13); while from 1925–9, at the height of Weimar's prosperity, this ratio was 14.9 per cent.[3] (Since Germany's territory was smaller in 1920 than in 1914, if her economic activity had remained at exactly the same level as before the War, her export share should have risen.)

Germany suffered economically because of the terms of the Paris peace settlement. The territorial clauses of the treaty deprived her of part of her coal resources (in Silesia), but above all of the rich phosphoric iron ore fields of Lorraine – a key resource for the steel industry of Imperial Germany. Before the War, one of Germany's most dynamic industries had been the giant chemical and pharmaceutical business: in the 1920s, it experienced new competition since the Allied powers had confiscated German patent rights.

Reduced trade, confiscated patents, and a permanent loss of an important part of the industrial base: such constraints limited the room for possible German economic growth.

2.   Within Germany, *demographic developments* pointed to higher levels of unemployment. German population – and thus overall demand – had fallen because of wartime military casualties, and also because malnutrition and epidemic disease

attacked the rest of the population and reduced the number of live births. There were also fewer conceptions. But during the 1920s, the large cohorts born before 1914 were moving onto the labour market: it was not until 1931–2 that the pressure eased as the much smaller cohorts born after 1914 sought employment. In 1925, the labour pool was some 5 million larger than it had been at the time of the last census, 1907. The swelling of the population available for employment continued through the decade. According to the IfK, the number seeking employment (available work force) rose from 32.4 m in 1925 to 33.4 m in 1931.[4] Even without a major depression, there was likely to be higher unemployment, as a larger labour force confronted a diminished population and lower demand.

3. Rates of *saving and investment* were lower than they had been before the War. In 1910–13 investment accounted for 15.2 per cent of NNP at market prices, but for 1925–9 only 11.1 per cent. After 1930, as replacements were no longer made, there was net disinvestment (amounting to 5.4 per cent of NNP in 1931, and 4.1 per cent in 1932). Even for the good years of the later 1920s, the figures may be misleading in that over two fifths of total investment in industry and commerce ('*Gewerbe*') is accounted for by inventory investment rather than investment in new plant: there was a massive restocking on the part of business at the end of the inflation period.[5]

The lower level of investment in the later 1920s (when the Weimar Republic is generally supposed to have been most prosperous) may in part have been due to the cost of investment funds. Interest rates were appreciably higher in Germany than in Britain or USA, and long term funds were particularly scarce and dear. This reflected the reaction of the financial system to Germany's postwar inflation: savers had lost a great deal of money and suffered a major blow to their confidence. Subsequent savings rates fell. Starved of savings, Germany came to depend on foreign sources of investment. When foreign capital flows slowed down (as in 1925, or after 1928), the level of German economic activity also dropped.

It would, however, be unwise to explain Germany's investment problems solely from the supply side, and from a dimi-

nished propensity to save resulting out of the aftermath of inflation, the inavailability of funds, or even from the mentality
of German investors. If the German economy had been sound
and business prospects alluring, the impoverishment of German savers and their nervousness would not have mattered
very much. Foreign capital would simply have stepped in and
filled the gaps left by the shortages of German funds.

Would this have been an inadequate or unsatisfactory solution to Germany's problems? Certainly foreign investors,
operating at a distance, are not always good at making sound
economic choices. In addition, the dependence on foreign
money might (and indeed actually did) link German to world
wide trends in a decade marked by extreme volatility in capital
markets, with catastrophic results. Some analysts – notably
Carl Schmidt, David Landes and Malcolm Falkus – have
argued that the attractions of the feverish speculative boom
on Wall Street made German investments seem less attractive
to Americans, and slowed down the rate of capital flow.[6]
If this were true, it would be exogenous shocks (and in particular the Wall Street boom), rather than internal weaknesses,
that produced the first signs of depression in Germany in 1928
and 1929. The volume of foreign lending to Germany fell
off in 1928 and during the first part of 1929, and recovered
slightly after the Wall Street crash (October 1929) destroyed
confidence in the domestic American economy, before international loans dried up completely in 1931.

It is, however, rather difficult to sustain the Schmidt-Falkus
case about the foreign determination of Germany's economic
problems in the light of the chronology of depression set out
above (which sees the first weaknesses in 1927). In general,
the calculation made by foreigners when contemplating the
allures of Germany depended on a relative assessment of the
risks and likely gains in Germany and outside: it implied an
investment 'view' of Germany's attractions relative to those
of the rest of the world. By 1929, many Americans had come
to the conclusion that Germany was – for her own domestic
reasons – exceedingly unattractive. Germans, so the bearer
of Wall Street's most prestigious name J. P. Morgan opined,
were 'second rate people'.[7] He did not want to risk his house's
money in such a dubious case. After the crash of 1929, though

American activity in Germany picked up once more, the larger and reputable houses knew they should stay out. German business instead went to the buccaneering houses – such as the Boston firm of Lee Higginson, which was heavily involved with the speculative and probably fraudulent activities of the Swedish 'Match King' Ivan Kreuger, which collapsed in 1932. In 1930–1 it was Lee Higginson which played the central role in funding the German government and channelling new money to Germany.

Americans now spoke of Germany in withering terms. They saw economic instability and political uncertainty. One memorandum of the Federal Reserve Bank of New York tried to depict Germany as a giant version of New York City's Tammany Hall: 'they put coal in the German Mrs Murphy's cellar by furnishing social aid out of the budget and in addition providing jobs in the government for Mrs Murphy's boys. All this makes Germany the most highly taxed nation in the world.'[8] Perhaps this statement exaggerated: but it contained an element of truth. This was why foreign investors were so sceptical about Germany.

4.   The *quality* as well as the quantity of *German investment* was low. This statement may seem surprising in view of the widely held belief that the German economy modernized rapidly during the 1920s. In the later part of the decade, discussion of American methods permeated German life: rationalization, assembly line production ('*Fordismus*'), or scientific management involving time controls ('*Tayloris-mus*'). Rationalization was said to involve destroying jobs through the application of new methods of production, and destroying character through the subordination of man to the machine. A cultural obsession with modernity and with Americanism reached fever pitch as film directors such as Fritz Lang and artists such as George Grosz saw in America a vision of Germany's future.

In fact – for all the talk about rationalization – the extent of technical change was surprisingly limited. Modernity took place on the cinema screen and in the novel, but on the whole not in the German workplace. Only two industries provide an exception: coal-mining, which in the Ruhr field at least became almost completely mechanized; and automobile manufacture, where Ford and General Motors/Opel did indeed build new assembly lines. The steel industry saw little change in the later 1920s: the most important innovations had come earlier and been concerned with economizing energy in the postwar coal shortage. Hourly productivity in the textile industry often lay below prewar levels. In clothing, there could be little streamlining because the vagaries of fashion made it senseless to introduce large-scale production. In the electro-technical industry, 'rationalization' meant organizational simplification, new products, and new ways of calculating wages, but not fundamentally labour-saving technology.[9]

Where rationalization was carried out, it usually meant a cult of bigness, regardless of the consequences. Germany's leading business economist, Eugen Schmalenbach, wrote retrospectively: 'Many expansions were carried out only for prestige reasons. Managements could not resist the drug of expansion, although their firms were operating well in the market and did not need to fear a serious competitive battle. But they desired a monopoly position. This was enough to produce a clamour for unprofitable investments and acquisitions.'[10] The result was massive capacities with little technical advance.

A major part of the problem came from the way in which industry was financed. A relatively small share of investment funds came from profits generated internally by German companies: most was externally financed, and came from banks rather than from a stock market. Dependence on bank lending meant a preference for conservative investment, for staid old favourites. Banks no longer led the way in modernizing Germany's business structure, as they had done in the nineteenth century. A Bank Inquiry in 1933–4 set up in the aftermath of the dramatic bank collapses of 1931 to examine retrospectively the weaknesses of the 1920s – demonstrated how little bank credit went to dynamic industries such as chemicals or engineering or automobile construction. The electro-technical industry, which before the War had been a major area of bank involvement, accounted for only 2.3 per cent of bank credits (less than the wood trade). The major recipients of bank loans were the rather uninnovative food industry (11.2 per cent) and textiles (11.8 per cent).[11]

Why was investment so low, and why were investors – especially the banks – so conservative? Investment depends on calculations about future returns, and in the 1920s, such reckoning produced gloomy results, and expectations of profitability began to fall.

5. *Expectations of future profitability* fell at the end of the 1920s, in part because of the weakness of German productivity growth, but also because of the level of wage settlements, and because of the political strength of the labour unions and their influence within the Reich Labour Ministry. Again, these are developments quite independent of the problems of the world economy, and represent specifically German obstacles to economic growth. In 1927 hourly wages rose 9 per cent (correcting for price rises, this represented a real increase of 5 per cent, while labour productivity rose 5 per cent). In 1928 nominal hourly wages rose 12 per cent (real by 10 per cent), while hourly productivity actually fell (by 4.8 per cent).[12] It was at exactly the time when the economic points were set to depression, in 1927–8, that a decline in profitability, attributable mainly to wage rises, left its mark on the business climate.

Over the last ten years this argument has become one of the most fiercely contested areas of Weimar historiography. In 1978 in a lecture to the Bavarian Academy, the economic historian Knut Borchardt made the claim that the wage position of Weimar constituted one of the major economic weaknesses by looking at data in the framework of a long run comparison. This opened a new way of looking at Weimar's economic history. He showed how labour's distributive position was far better in the 1920s than it had been either before 1914 or than it would be in the post-1945 recovery (in other words, than in periods when economic growth was much more vigorous). In criticizing this argument Carl-Ludwig Holtfrerich has focused attention on the methodological problems presented by long term statistical comparisons, and has explained the favourable wage developments in the Weimar Republic in terms of shifts in employment structure (towards more skilled and more tertiary sector – service – employment).[13]

The issue of the suitability of long run comparisons may

actually make little difference when it comes to the timing and the origins of Germany's depression: here the wage data (as recalculated by Holtfrerich himself) show quite clearly how a worsening relationship between wages and productivity cut profitability. When it comes to explaining depression, it may be appropriate to look at *short run* developments in the period immediately before the onset of crisis. For the critical period of the later 1920s, the evidence—as presented in different ways by Borchardt, by Jürgen von Kruedener and by Theo Balderston – bears the hypothesis of an economically damaging wage push. (It should be added that the picture may not yet be complete: German workers were rarely paid the negotiated rates, but the supplements they received did not remain constant. It is quite conceivable that a new study using actual rather than negotiated wage rates would show the upward movement of the 1920s even more dramatically.)[14]

Furthermore, the actual developments of 1927–8 may well have been interpreted by the historical actors as heralding a long run trend. Investment decisions are of course made by business men, who saw Labour Ministers such as Heinrich Brauns and Rudolf Wissell openly boast of the Labour Minister's role in raising wages. Wage arbitration, with the possibility of making the awards of an arbitrator legally binding on all parties to a dispute, had been imposed in 1923. This had been an explicit attempt to hold out a carrot to a labour movement whose real wages were to be attacked as part of the stabilization of the Mark. Arbitration, and the principle of a fair wage that could be politically determined, appealed to socialists. The SPD politician Rudolf Hilferding, for instance, spoke with pride of the 'political wage' that his party could influence.[15] State policy also contributed to the wage push of the late 1920s by the demonstration effect of public sector settlements. In the course of 1927, civil service incomes increased dramatically (some by almost a third). These awards found an echo in private sector pay demands in the next year, as unions pushed for parity with state employees. On the basis of statements and claims of the politicians involved in wage determination, industry could conclude that the political framework of republican Germany stood at odds with what they held to be the legitimate requirements of the economy.

There are two major consequences of the employers' interpretation of the wage rises of 1927–8. In political terms business men began to take a more hostile view of a republic they saw as undermining their economic interests. They financed institutions and associations, such as the League for the Renewal of the German Reich, dedicated to authoritarian constitutional reform. Such political involvement produced results: industrial intrigues and pressure on the right-wing liberal party DVP played a major part in the downfall of the Müller coalition.

In economic terms, their actions had consequences that were much more striking and immediate. Industrialists concluded that – in the absence of far reaching political changes which they sought – the position of labour would go on improving. It is expectations of profitability, rather than current profitability, that determine investment decisions: on these grounds Germany's future looked bleak by 1928 and business men scaled back their investments. Such decisions in turn affected output and employment: in short, determined the destinies of all Germans.

6.   Another weakness – again frequently commented on by foreign observers – was *the instability of Germany's public finances*, and their vulnerability to political pressures. Here again there was an obvious legacy of the inflation era: confidence in the state as a debtor had been destroyed by the events of 1918–23. After the stabilization of the currency (1923–4) taxes had been put up and public spending radically pruned: with the consequence not simply that the Weimar Republic produced its first balanced budget, but also that it accumulated surpluses. These surpluses disappeared as the government dealt with the short but intense economic crisis of 1925–6 with a contra-cyclical strategy of tax cuts and spending increases, and as political pressures to reduce taxes and to spend more mounted. By the end of the 1920s, a series of catastrophes indicated how limited had become the central government's room for manoeuvre in fiscal affairs.

Attempts to fund the swelling short term debt domestically through major government bond issues in 1927, and again in 1929, failed humiliatingly. International loans did not fare much better, and opened the government to political pressures. At the end of 1929 the German government looked for an American loan (from the firm of Dillon Read): but the President of the German central bank, Dr Hjalmar Schacht, staged a political scene, destroyed the loan, and forced the resignation of the socialist Finance Minister Hilferding. In the aftermath of this affair, the political price for foreign money looked as if it might be too high.

Yet the fiscal problem grew more acute. State spending and revenues were both at this time already reacting to the impact of the depression. Tax yields fell, at the same time as spending rose involuntarily as the state needed to subsidize an inadequately funded unemployment insurance scheme. The total spent on unemployment relief rose from 1.2bn RM in 1928 to 1.8bn RM in 1929, 2.7bn RM in 1930 and 3.2bn RM in 1931. As a consequence of falling revenues and greater spending pressure, government deficits widened further: in 1928/9 new debt amounted to 4.0 per cent of Gross National Product (GNP), in 1929/30 3.6 per cent, and in 1930/31 3.4 per cent, before the deflationary axe of the Brüning Chancellorship (March 1930–May 1932) finally swung down on its target.[16]

Like the wage rise, this increase in public debt had dangerous consequences both in political and economic terms. It made the German government highly dependent on external financing and as a result vulnerable to political pressure from the financial community – of just the sort Schacht had applied in 1929 in order to remove Hilferding. In addition, Germany made herself vulnerable to pressures from foreign countries: what the international financial community thought of Germany mattered if new credits were to be needed to save her. This in fact was the story of the first half of the German depression, until the financial crisis of 1931. Deflationary budgets represented on the part of the German government a desperate bid to regain fiscal autonomy from domestic lenders and to put a respectably orthodox face to prospective foreign lenders.

Brüning's austerity measures of October and December 1930 raised unemployment insurance contributions, cut civil service pay by means of a special tax, and reduced central government tax transfers to state and local level government.

Without this deflationary package, it would have been impossible to secure enough foreign confidence to obtain the Lee Higginson loan. Again in the early summer of 1931, as Germany's position became ever more desperate and she looked for foreign assistance (this time from foreign governments and central banks), she found a choice of conditions for lending. While the French wanted political concessions on the proposed customs union with Austria and on the construction of battleships, the British and Americans stated that balanced budgets were needed as a way of dealing with the depression.[17]

The tie with foreign markets now had a major significance: it provided the mechanism through which a global doctrine about economic management could be propagated. An international consensus on budget stabilization – in practice deflation – as propagated from the grim unsmiling lips of US President Herbert Hoover, British Chancellor of the Exchequer Philip Snowden and Montagu Norman, the Governor of the Bank of England, decided Germany's destiny during the world crisis.

Politically, therefore, German governments had lost what Knut Borchardt terms their 'room for manœuvre' during the depression. They faced an impossible dilemma: they could only ease deflation, spend more, and encourage capital inflows by showing the world that they were imposing deflation and spending less.

The economic consequence of this dilemma was that, because of the political volatility of public debt, even small deficits could lead to financial instability. Without external help and with laws preventing the central bank from simply monetising public debt, or 'printing money' in conventional parlance, German banks could only lend more to the government by reducing loans to private corporations. In the circumstances of the depression, such a cut in credit might well bring down many firms. In this way, a crisis could spread from the public sector to the rest of the economy.

In July 1931 it did. A banking crisis in which two of Germany's major commercial banks (the Darmstädter and the Dresdner) failed made the depression worse, and ended any hopes that 1931 might be the bottom of the depression trough. In the course of the spring, there had been signs of recovery;

but after the banking crash, Germany's economy began a new phase of the downward spiral. The crisis arose when a relatively small government deficit could not be funded by the banking system, and when at the same time major cities in the Rhineland approached illiquidity and brought down the financial institution which had supported them (the Landesbank der Rheinprovinz). These origins of the German banking crisis deserve at least as much emphasis as the traditional account offered in the historical literature, which places at the centre of the story the difficulties of the textile firm of Nordwolle and their impact on the weakest of the German banks, the Darmstädter.

Even after 13 July, when the government responded to the bank collapse by decreeing a general bank holiday, the link between fear of renewed financial crisis and fiscal rectitude remained a crucial determinant of policy. Brüning often referred to the need to avoid a repetition of the banking crisis. High civil servants, such as the State Secretary in the Finance Ministry Hans Schäffer, feared that an increase in government spending (for instance to finance work creation projects) could bring few gains and risked setting off a new round of financial instability.

Politicians, even in the deflationary Brüning government, would have liked to have been able to spend more on work creation. By the beginning of 1932, both the Labour and the Finance Ministers had become enthusiastic advocates of reemployment projects: but they were consistently obstructed by the senior civil servants, who argued against the political pressure that Germany simply could not afford to run the risk of a repetition of the financial crisis.

Schäffer, the most prominent and also the most perceptive of these civil servants, resigned in March 1932 (though he stayed in the Finance Ministry until May) because the government's budget had become too unbalanced, the deficit too large. In January, he had commented on the plans for stimulating and reflating the economy: 'It is impossible to pay for work creation out of the budget – which is already excessively strained – but the alternatives suggested by [Finance Minister] Dietrich are even more damaging: the use of central bank financing, as suggested in the drafts, is under no circumstances possible [because it was illegal, under laws that had been incorporated into international treaties after the Dawes and Young reparation plans]'. He later wrote to Brüning: 'After my attempts – which according to my conception of duty were essential – to stabilize the budget and the government's cash-flow have produced no satisfactory results, I can no longer take responsibility for the central state's capacity to make payments ... Two things for me are impossible: to carry the responsibility for the central state's credit and cash-flow in the face of measures which jeopardize them; secondly, to express the opinion that we can survive until spring of next year, although I know that as things stand we are approaching the limit much sooner.'[18]

The political impetus to spend Germany out of the depression thus ran into objections that such a strategy would be economically counter-productive and would only lead to further destabilization. On purely economic grounds (the nervousness of markets) a Keynesian strategy to deal with the crisis was ruled out. The logic of Keynesianism involves the state stepping in to borrow in a climate in which private borrowers hesitate. In this way the state creates a market for stable and secure debt (since public debtors, which can always raise revenue by taxing, are regarded as being most secure). The state's spending at the same time augments demand. But such an approach can only work if investors have sufficient confidence to buy public debt. In the early 1930s in Germany such confidence was lacking. Keynesianism failed, not through the absence of a political will, but because it did not represent an economic viability.

7. Another weakness of Weimar's economy lay in *the politically privileged position of agriculture*. All the major parties believed that they needed agricultural votes. Even the socialist party (SPD) cultivated the peasant vote.[19] These calculations meant that governments adopted expensive measures to shield agriculture from the depression at the expense of the rest of the economy. Almost inevitably the result was a catastrophe for all sides: farmers believed they had not received enough support, and became politically more militant, and the rest of Germany still had to pay a substantial price.

From 1926, world food prices collapsed, and German

governments reacted with tariff increases in order to isolate Germany from the world market. By 1932 the tariff on wheat, rye and barley amounted to 3.7 per cent of NNP – constituting a significant burden for the German economy.[20]

In addition, highly indebted areas were provided with funds for debt relief. A scheme called 'Eastern Help' (*Osthilfe*) was subsequently expanded until by 1933 the whole of Germany had been covered by some sort of agricultural debt relief programme.

In the last three explanations for German weakness (5, 6 and 7) political calculations played a major role: in pushing up wages in the later 1920s, in the interpretation of that increase, in prompting increases in public spending through the later half of the 1920s, and in the story of subsidization of agriculture. Political calculations also made it difficult to resolve conflicts or create consensus about economic management.

Economics and Politics

There appears to be a quite simple correlation between the severity of the economic crisis and the emergence of despondency and political disaffection. From 1928, tax strikes, bombings of tax offices and disruptions of bankruptcy auctions swept the North German countryside. The rural agitation was graphically described in Hans Fallada's novel of 1931 'Peasants, Bosses and Bombs' (*Bauern, Bonzen und Bomben*): he based the book on his experiences as a court reporter in Neumünster. Unemployed workers felt disillusioned with labour unions and a socialist party which had failed to prevent their personal catastrophe. Government employees after 1930 suffered from round after round of pay cuts.[21] Small shopkeepers and artisans saw their business decline, and also felt the competition of unemployed workers who moved into casual trades: peddling, or house painting and repairing.

Yet none of this actually *explains* a political reaction. We should be cautious about establishing overly simple linkages between economic misery and political radicalism.

Unemployment has frequently led to political passivity, disenchantment and demobilization. The radical peasants of 1928 formed their own movements and expressed themselves through a specifically peasant protest against the big town, the financier, and the tax collector. At first they also protested against the major political parties. It was 1930 before the NSDAP embarked systematically on rural propaganda and had a major impact on the German countryside.[22] Economic problems helped to prepare the ground for a large scale rejection of capitalism and the market order. The banking crisis of 1931 accelerated this process: it had meant recalled credits, reduced loans, high interest rates and state subsidies for banks but not for their badly affected customers.

Not only did anti-capitalist and anti-liberal feeling swell as a consequence of the depression. The peculiar nature of Germany's highly politicized economy was that anti-*anything* sentiment grew. A picture of the world populated by enemies emerged: there was a proliferation of what Germans call *Feindbilder* (images of the enemy). As in Britain in the 1970s, a failed economy resulted in bitter and unbridgeable political clashes, and altered the operation of the political system.

In the context of economic stagnation, there sometimes emerges the following vicious circle: political polarization, inability to solve economic problems by consensual means, a worsening economic performance, and then further polarization. Economic and political systems lock themselves in this way into a stalemate.

In Weimar Germany, employers believed that they had been obstructed by over-powerful trade unions. Unions believed that employers had embarked on a combination of economically senseless investment projects and political counter-revolution. The state's fiscal crisis led to farmers thinking that they paid high taxes to subsidize unemployed (and idle) workers and bankers who needed state bail outs when they failed as a result of their own mistaken policies. Workers thought that their real wages were so low because of the limitless greed of German agriculture.

This culture of blaming anyone and everyone else dominated political debate. It helps to explain the context of the rise of political anti-semitism in the depression period. It also determined the way in which political alliances and coalitions could be shaped in late Weimar.

The political reaction to depression can be accounted for partly by examining electoral shifts, and partly by reconstructing how political parties reacted to those shifts – in other words by looking at how high politics faced the problems of economic crisis. Throughout the 1920s, voting patterns had been highly unstable. Traditional patterns of voting, or deferential voting, belonged to the past.

Liberal parties lost votes: first to special interest parties, appealing to highly fragmented and sectionalized groupings: such as the Reich Party for People's Rights and Revaluation (of savings that had depreciated during the Great Inflation), or regional parties (the Hanoverian Guelphs), or peasant parties (the *Landbund*, the *Deutsche Bauernpartei*, and the *Christlich-nationale Bauern und Landvolkpartei*). These so-called 'splinter parties' had their best performance in the Reichstag elections of 1928, when a staggeringly large one quarter (24.6 per cent) of the total vote went to parties whose individual share lay below 5 per cent. After that the voters went to the NSDAP (in the elections of September 1930 and July and November 1932).[23]

The SPD gained votes while it was out of power in central government (between 1924 and 1928), but lost heavily after its participation in the coalition government of Hermann Müller (SPD) from 1929 to 1930. In the 1928 election, the party had scored a substantial success (29.8 per cent of the vote), while in 1930 the share dropped to 24.5 per cent. A 5 per cent loss represented the price the SPD had to pay for having taken responsibility for unpopular measures.

The obvious lesson, that almost all the political parties drew from these developments, was that participation in government led to electoral losses. During the depression the paradox that political power turned out to weaken its possessors became even clearer. Politics is about making choices. But the constraints of the depression era – in particular a falling tax base and the inability to borrow on domestic German or on foreign markets – ensured that politicians who remained in power had few choices. They were bound to alienate voters. Politicians in opposition on the other hand had plenty of choices about what to oppose, and plenty of opportunities to denounce the government. In consequence, there exists a direct link between the fiscal crisis of the state and the shift of politicians and voters to opposition.

The politicians faced competition for votes, since they could not rely on a stable and loyal electorate. The liberal parties had to deal with the alternative on the right. Socialist voters might be lured away by the communist party. It is significant that the Centre Party, which because of its loyal Catholic base had by far the stablest vote, was also the most 'responsible' in terms of remaining in office and taking on its self the task of putting through unpopular measures. It could afford to be.

After 1928, two parallel processes set in. First, voters abandoned governmental parties. Second, previously governmental parties abandoned government. At the end of 1929, the small Bavarian People's Party refused to support the Great Coalition over the proposal to increase beer taxes by 50 per cent – since this would alienate brewers and drinkers in Bavaria, where beer famously played a major role in the economy and in social life. In consequence, it voted against the fiscal package of December 1929, and thus set in train the events that led to Müller's fall. The Great Coalition, Weimar's last democratic government, finally collapsed in March 1930 when the left wing of the SPD refused to tolerate proposed cuts in the rate of unemployment benefit. At the same time the right wing liberal party DVP demanded such cuts: and compromise was impossible.

The DVP recognized that it was losing popular support, and feared that its association with the austerity measures of Müller's successor Brüning (previously the parliamentary head of the Centre Party) would damage its position further. In particular civil servants would be hit by the pay reductions and the special tax on those with security of employment proposed by Brüning. Civil servants would pay 4 per cent of their incomes, and other white collar workers 2¼ per cent. The Finance Minister who took responsibility for this measure – Paul Moldenhauer, himself a DVP member – was attacked by his own party and in June 1930 forced to resign. The opposition of the DVP contributed to the defeat of Brüning's tax decrees in the Reichstag on 16 July 1930, the dissolution of parliament and the calling of the September elections – in which the Nazi vote rose so dramatically (and the DVP's support fell). However, the party merely drew from this the conclusion that only a more radical distancing from government could produce a revival of electoral confidence; particularly since in December 1930 Brüning made a further cut in civil service pay. In the summer of 1931, the DVP again intensified the political crisis by demanding the reconvening of the Reichstag – which would lead to the passing of a new no confidence motion in Brüning. Only at the very last moment in June, as the banking and financial situation worsened, did the DVP withdraw its demand.

In public, the SPD opposed Brüning. At the same time, it saw that the only alternative to Brüning lay in a more reactionary government, and for this reason the party refused to join Nazi or communist no confidence motions: a strategy known as 'toleration policy' (*Tolerierungspolitik*) which in fact allowed Brüning to remain in office for two years. Many of the SPD's leading politicians could only hang their heads in helplessness. In a private letter Rudolf Hilferding wrote: 'There is no socialist solution to the crisis, and this makes the situation unprecedentedly difficult and allows the Communists and National Socialists to grow stronger.' Wilhelm Keil, one of the SPD's financial experts, commented after a member of his party had attacked the fourth and most deflationary of Brüning's decrees (December 1931) which cut everything: civil service pay, wages, government spending, 'What is Naphtali's programme? I can see none. One should not overlook that the Emergency Decree contains, besides unsocial measures, also price cuts, rent cuts and an interest reduction on the 50 billion [Marks] borrowed capital. Above all – would the Decree be cancelled if we vote against it? Not at all. No government today would cancel the Decree.'[24]

Some members of the labour unions (Woytinsky, Tarnow, and Baade) tried hard to create a socialist alternative – at a rather late stage in the depression (1932) – as a political way out of Weimar's dilemma. Their plan for work creation involving one million new jobs was taken up at an Extraordinary Congress of the Free (Socialist) Trade Unions Federation in April 1932; but it quickly ran into hostility from important parts of the labour movement which believed that a reformed capitalism could not work. Was not after all the magnitude of the depression the final sign of the demise of capitalism? In a famous metaphor, Tarnow described the dilemma of the labour movement: they were the heirs at the sickbed of capitalism, and yet at the same time were trying to be the doctors.[25] By June the trade unions had formulated a more ambitious programme calling for the nationalization of key industries and banks – a programme whose chief charm was that it could not be realized, and thus represented the ideal political platform for a socialist party in a depression, a message of out and out opposition to the existing system. Opposition seemed better than reform or than 'toleration policy'.

In this the behaviour of the unions was also representative of the general behaviour of Weimar parties. One of the standard political manœuvres involved shifting the blame to other parties and agents – in the manner of the SPD's or the DVP's half-hearted distancing of themselves from the Brüning regime. The withdrawal of socialists and of right liberals left the parties of the middle weak and isolated.

From the point of view of government, the problem appeared the other way round: it lay in distributing responsibility for political decisions more widely. One way was constitutional and administrative change: the Brüning decrees forced local and state governments to bear a great deal of the brunt of unpopularity. They had to put up local taxes, lay off employees, and above all cut back on their welfare payments and spending projects.

At the level of central politics, Brüning tried to involve other parties as a way of emasculating the political opposition. The most interesting example is the story of Brüning's relations with the NSDAP. In October 1930, after the September elections which had brought such large Nazi gains, and then again one year later Brüning held discussions with Hitler about participation in the cabinet. Since it was unlikely that Hitler would have been able to do much apart from follow a course rather similar to Brüning's, such involvement would simply call the Nazi's bluff and show up their movement as politically ineffective, and unable to 'do something' about the depression. By the second half of 1932, the strategy of allowing the NSDAP to commit political suicide by wearing itself out in government (*abregieren*) found advocates across the democratic spectrum: from socialists (Hilferding) to businessmen (the brown coal industrialist Silverberg).[26] In November 1932, 1500 Rhineland-Westphalian businessmen met to discuss the political situation: some 'felt it was advisable to appoint Hitler as soon as possible. The observer found among those who held such views no expectation that Hitler would succeed in solving Germany's problems. He also added that sceptics among them assumed that a cabinet formed by the Nazi leader would last only a few weeks.'[27]

Hitler recognized the goal of this operation and the motives behind it, and remained resolutely outside the government. Nevertheless, the Nazis still faced a political problem. The big election victories – the party had 107 seats in September 1930, and 230 after July 1932 – led to no practical results. The party could not influence events in Germany, and could not point to its achievements in central politics. In turn, the governing parties did their best to draw attention to the Nazis' impotence. The procedural rules of the Reichstag were altered in February 1931 to make it impossible to make spending proposals without a simultaneous measure to raise revenue – in other words to make parliamentary parties bear the dilemmas of government. In response, the Nazis and the German Nationalists withdrew from the Reichstag. The retreat only highlighted their dilemma. It was hard to avoid losing credibility as the party remained inactive, even after the big victory of July 1932. Again in August Hindenburg tried to bring Hitler into the government, but without giving him the Chancellorship or key ministries (Defence or the Interior). Hitler refused, but appeared powerless in consequence. The Nazi vote then began to collapse: in the November 1932 elections, the NSDAP lost 4.3 per cent, and 34 seats.

When Hitler did come to power in January 1933, he was able to make his own terms and above all to use the Prussian police force (after July 1932 under the control of the Reich) to crush potential opposition. The key appointment was Hermann Göring as Prussian Minister of the Interior. In January 1933, the old right, which had placed Hitler in office, may still have believed the 'discrediting through power' argument of the depression. 'No danger at all. We've hired him for our act', Franz von Papen, the Vice-Chancellor in the new government, remarked. Papen's associate, Alfred Hugenberg, was convinced that 'nothing much will happen ... We'll be boxing Hitler in.'[28]

Papen's and Hugenberg's boasts in retrospect of course appear staggeringly naive. But it is possible to see how they had come to this view. The NSDAP had relied on putting together a socially highly disparate and heterogeneous electoral constituency: peasants, artisans, in some cities in the Ruhr as well as in Berlin a substantial working class vote, and in other cities, such as Hamburg, a solidly upper middle class support[29]. Recent research has demonstrated conclusively that there is no typical social profile of the Nazi voter. Each of the different constituencies required separate sorts of appeal and varied propaganda: in consequence the movement could not clarify its aims without losing support, and could not participate in power until it could ensure that opposition outside but also within the party might be crushed by police terror. The Nazi government used repression to escape from its unfulfillable promises to the German population.

Until 1933, the German story is merely a variation on a European theme. The flight away from political responsibility occurred throughout Europe: after 1932, for instance, French governments ruled principally – as Brüning had done – through decree laws. Would be Strong Men, such as von Papen, Laval, Gömbös, Pilsudski, Salazar or Metaxas governed by ignoring parliaments.

German governments had had one advantage in dealing with this flight of political parties away from power: at least until 1932. They could claim that someone else – outside Germany – had caused the political and economic crisis, and that they were trying to remove the causes of disaster. The reparations settlement imposed by the Treaty of Versailles played a unique role in Weimar politics. Nationalist and far right campaigns generally took the Versailles settlement as their major target, and as a means of criticising the Republic. Yet in two important ways, reparations helped to stabilize German democracy.

The politics of depression relied on blaming other people for the crisis. Opposition parties of course blamed the government. Reparations on the other hand provided something outside Germany that might be held responsible. Pamphleteers and politicians had no difficulty in showing how the reparations settlement had impoverished Germany, and forced her to dump exports on the world, and provoked the rise of protectionism, and thus logically made it impossible for Germany to sell the goods needed to pay the reparations. Versailles had, they claimed, resulted in the world depression.

Secondly, the logical corollary was that the depression could not be cured until reparations had ended, and that revising reparations should therefore be the major goal of German politics. Attempts to improve Germany's position acted like a cement binding in the face of the centrifugal 'flight from responsibility'. Hermann Müller's highly incoherent coalition – it ranged from right wing liberals to socialists – held together while the government negotiated the Young reparations plan, which would bring substantial relief. It held through the Paris Experts' Conference of the spring of 1929, and through the two international conferences at The Hague. Only after the Reichstag had passed the necessary legislation to allow the Young Plan to go into effect did the coalition collapse (two weeks after the Reichstag vote).

In 1931 and 1932 Brüning realized that he needed this sort of political activism in order to survive politically and to maintain the precarious balance of German politics. The plan for an Austro-German customs union – which might have provided a unifying focus for German politics, particularly since the French opposed it so bitterly, failed. This scheme had offered a pleasant way of externalizing the German problem by blaming it on France. A new attempt to revise the reparations arrangement and alter the terms of the Young Plan began with the government's appeal on 5 June 1931, which accompanied an Emergency Decree imposing budget cuts. There is little doubt that this decree contributed to the economic catastrophe: partly because of the deflationary effect, but chiefly because of the loss of international confidence in Germany called forth by the prospect of new German-French clashes over reparations. On the other hand, the decree was necessary as a response to the emerging fiscal crisis of inevitably rising social expenditure and of falling revenues; and coupling the decree with a demarche on reparations offered a way out, perhaps the only way out, of the domestic German political morass.

Brüning held to this line consistently, putting the diplomacy of reparations revision at the forefront of his political agenda, until in May 1932 he was dismissed by President von Hindenburg and succeeded by von Papen. He claimed in the spring of 1932, and continued to boast afterwards (as well as in his memoirs) that he had only been 'one hundred metres from the goal' of abolishing reparations.

Revision had become the principal way of uniting German politics in the face of the centrifugal pressures exerted by the unpleasant nature of economic choices during the depression. Papen expected to achieve enormous popularity on his return from the Lausanne conference (June–July 1932) which effectively ended the payment of reparations. At the conference he had been astonishingly successful. He was disappointed and surprised by the indifference and then by the hostility of the reaction. What had in fact happened was that the unifying bracket that had clamped German politics together – the prospect of reparations revision – had been removed, while the explosive force of the wish to avoid responsibility for economic decisions remained. Papen found that demanding, preparing, and negotiating an end to reparations brought better political results than actually achieving it.

He could only count on the support of a handful of deputies in the Reichstag: in the no confidence motion of 12 September he had 42 positive votes, and 512 against (with 5 abstentions). His successor von Schleicher was unable to construct any substantial political basis of support during his short-lived ministry. After 30 January 1933, Adolf Hitler used police repression and intimidation to abolish other parties or force them to dissolve themselves. Since the summer of 1932, reparations had fallen away as a means of linking republican parties to a policy that accepted the basic premises of the international order, while trying to change them. Nazism solved the problem of political integration in a different way. Assertive nationalism could now be used to deal with the problem facing all German politicians of this era: how to rule during a depression. And in addition Hitler also benefited from the chance fact that the depression was coming to an end (the trough in fact had been in the summer of 1932).

Hitler came into power because of the electoral strength of his movement, and because of a miscalculation by conservatives (by von Papen and the circle around President von Hindenburg) about discrediting Hitler through association with depression government. The miscalculation belongs to the realm of historical chance and accident; on the other hand the argument that the conservatives made stemmed from a very characteristic standpoint, from the belief that it was possible to weaken mass movements by putting them in the position of having to reveal their cards and make political choices. Both this argument and the political position of the men who set it out came not through chance or accident but from the political logic imposed by economic failure: the avoidance of government and the political disintegration of the republican parties.

If this logic applied world wide, it should also be borne in mind that Germany's economic failure at the beginning of the 1930s was exceptionally severe. A stalemate economy had resulted in the politicization of wages and the budget, in a spiral of economic decline, and in a situation in which democratic politicians had no choices. But politics claims to be about choices: and a failure to elaborate visions and alternatives leads to a discrediting of the political system caught in such a dilemma. It was in this sense that German democracy fell as a victim to the depression.

Notes

1. *Wochenberichte des Instituts für Konjunkturforschung*, 5/41 (11 Jan. 1933), 6/30 (25 Oct. 1933); Ernst Wagemann, *Konjunkturstatistisches Jahrbuch 1936* (Berlin, 1935), pp. 52–3.
2. See Gerald D. Feldman, 'Economic and Social Problems of the German Demobilization 1918–19', *Journal of Modern History* 47 (1975) pp. 1–47. Also Gerald D. Feldman, *Army, Industry and Labor in Germany 1914–1919* (Princeton, 1966).
3. Walter G. Hoffmann, *Das Wachstum der deutschen Wirtschaft seit der*

Mitte des 19. Jahrhunderts (Berlin, Heidelberg, New York, 1965), p. 151.

4. Dietmar Petzina, 'The Extent and Causes of Unemployment in the Weimar Republic' in Peter Stachura (ed.), *Unemployment and the Great Depression in Weimar Germany* (London, 1986).

5. Hoffmann, *Wachstum*, p. 104, p.826.

6. Malcom Falkus, 'The German Business Cycle in the 1920s', *Economic History Review* 28 (1975), pp. 451–65; Carl T. Schmidt, *German Business Cycles 1924–1933* (New York, 1934); David S. Landes, *The Unbound Prometheus: Technological Change and Industrial Development in Western Europe from 1750 to the Present* (Cambridge, 1969), pp. 371–2.

7. 30 Aug. 1929, J. P. Morgan to T. W. Lamont, Baker Library (Harvard) 181–1.

8. 9 June 1932, L. Galantiere memorandum, Federal Reserve Bank of New York, German Govt. file.

9. The standard work is Robert Brady, *The Rationalization Movement in Germany: A Study in the Evolution of Economic Planning* (Berkeley, 1933); but see the criticisms in Harold James, *The German Slump: Politics and Economics 1924–1936* (Oxford, 1986), pp. 146–61.

10. Eugen Schmalenbach, *Finanzierungen*, 6th ed. (Leipzig, 1937), p. 309.

11. Enquête-Ausschuss, *Der Bankkredit* (Berlin, 1930), p. 168.

12. Carl-Ludwig Holtfrerich, 'Zu hohe Löhne in der Weimarer Republik? Bemerkungen zur Borchardt-These', *Geschichte und Gesellschaft* 10 (1984), pp. 130–1.

13. The 'Borchardt debate' began with two articles published in 1979 and 1980, both reprinted in: Knut Borchardt, *Handlungsspielräume der Wirtschaftspolitik* (Göttingen, 1982).

14. See Jürgen Kruedener, 'Die Überforderung der Weimarer Republik als Sozialstaat', *Geschichte und Gesellschaft* 11 (1985), pp. 358–76; and Theo Balderston, 'The Beginning of the Depression in Germany 1927–1930: Investment and the Capital Market', in *Economic History Review* 36 (1983), pp. 395–415, and 'The Origins of Economic Instability in Germany 1924–1930: Market Forces versus Economic Policy', in *Vierteljahrschrift für Sozial- und Wirtschaftsgeschichte* 69 (1983), pp. 488–512.

15. *Protokoll über die Verhandlungen des sozialdemokratischen Parteitages Heidelberg 1925* (Berlin, 1925), pp. 282–3. Also see *Deutsche Sozialpolitik: Erinnerungsschrift des Reichsarbeitsministeriums* (Berlin, 1929).

16. James, *German Slump*, p.52.

17. See Edward W. Bennett, *Germany and the Diplomacy of the Financial Crisis 1931* (Cambridge Mass. 1962).

18. 17 Jan. 1932, Schäffer diaries, Institut für Zeitgeschichte, Munich; 19 Mar. 1932 Schäffer to Brüning, in Eckhard Wandel, *Hans Schäffer: Steuermann in wirtschaftlichen und politischen Krisen* (Stuttgart, 1974), p. 226.

19. Especially at the 1927 Kiel Congress of the party: see James, *German Slump*, pp. 260, 266.

20. James, *German Slump*, p. 282.
21. Hans Mommsen, 'Die Stellung der Beamtenschaft in Reich, Ländern und Gemeinden in der Ära Brüning', *Vierteljahrshefte für Zeitgeschichte* 21 (1973), pp. 151–65.
22. John E. Farquharson, *The Plough and the Swastika: the NSDAP and Agriculture in Germany 1928–1945* (London, 1976).
23. See Larry E. Jones, 'The Dying Middle': Weimar Germany and the Fragmentation of Bourgeois Politics', in *Central European History* 5 (1969), pp. 23–54. Jones's work has now been brought together in a book: *German Liberalism and the Dissolution of the Weimar Party System 1918–1933* (Chapen Hill, 1988).
24. 2 Oct. 1931 Hilferding to Kautsky, Kautsky papers, International Institute for Social History, Amsterdam, IISG, KD XII 653; Wilhelm Keil, *Erlebnisse eines Sozialdemokraten* (Stuttgart, 1948), p. 407.
25. At the last SPD party congress in the Weimar Republic, at Leipzig in June 1931: Heinrich A. Winkler, *Der Weg in die Katastrophe: Arbeiter und Arbeiterbewegung in der Weimarer Republik 1930 bis 1933* (Berlin, Bonn, 1987).
26. On Silverberg, see Reinold Neebe, *Grossindustrie, Staat und NSDAP 1930–1933: Paul Silverberg und der Reichsverband der Deutschen Industrie in der Krise der Weimarer Republic* (Göttingen, 1981), pp. 159–68. On Hilferding and a possible Nazi-Centre coalition, see Schäffer's diary for 27 Aug. and 9 Nov. 1932.
27. Henry A. Turner, *German Big Business and the Rise of Hitler* (New York, 1985), p. 302.
28. Joachim Fest, *Hitler* (New York, 1975), pp. 362, 366.
29. Thomas Childers, *The Nazi Voter: The Social Foundations of Fascism in Germany 1919–1933*, (Chapel Hill 1983), Richard Hamilton, *Who Voted for Hitler?* Princeton 1982, and Jürgen Falter, 'The National-Socialist Mobilization of Votes', in Thomas Childers (ed.), *National Socialism and the Politics of Mass Mobilization 1919–1933*, (London 1987), summarizes the most comprehensive and revealing survey of German voting patterns: Jürgen Falter, Thomas Lindenberger, and Siegfried Schumann, *Wahlen und Abstimmungen in der Weimarer Republik: Materialien zum Wahlverhalten 1919–1933*, (Munich 1986).

Carl-Ludwig Holtfrerich

Economic Policy Options and the End of the Weimar Republic

Historians agree that the scale of the Great Depression in Germany played a prominent part in bringing about the rise of Hitler and his Nazi party to power. There also seems to be a consensus that Chancellor Brüning's policy of deflation contributed heavily to the deepening of the depression in Germany. To label this policy as Brüning's is especially appropriate since during his term of office from 30 March 1930 to 30 May 1932 most of the important laws were enacted by emergency decree instead of the normal parliamentary process.

The disagreement begins when it comes to a judgement on the room for manœuvre for the Brüning government to pursue policies other than the one that was actually followed. Before the fundamental reinterpretation posed in 1979 by the Munich economic historian Knut Borchardt,[1] Chancellor Heinrich Brüning's economic policy had been presented as *the* example of a wrong political choice with disastrous economic and political consequences: namely mass unemployment and increasing political radicalization which led into the final dissolution of the Weimar Republic. In his classic study on the Great Depression in Germany, based on the then dominant Keynesian thinking, Gerhard Kroll expressed a generally accepted view in concluding that the Great Depression in Germany was not 'an inevitable catastrophe, but the consequence of human weakness and error'.[2] As late as 1976 the German economist Gottfried Bombach wrote in a volume on employment theories and on proposals for employment policies during the depression in Germany: 'Brüning remains a puzzle. His arguments for a strict deflationary policy are widely known ... There is agreement that Brüning failed'.[3] These and the many other similar assessments are logically based on the assumption that Brüning had alternatives of economic policy at his disposal and that he picked the wrong option, namely the notorious combination of balancing the budget by cutting government expenditures and raising taxes and of lowering production costs by cutting wages, prices, and interest rates. While Brüning, throughout his term of office, relied on his policy of fiscal restraint and price and cost-cutting measures to overcome the depression, his successor, von Papen, finally gave up the policy of deflation and launched substantial employment programmes that were financed through budget deficits covered by money creation, the later classical Keynesian remedy for fighting depression and unemployment.[4]

In his widely noted article first published in 1979, Knut Borchardt posed the question why Chancellor Brüning pursued his deflationary policies for so long and did not turn to counter-cyclical fiscal policies. Borchardt asked 'whether it was really a lack of reasonable judgement and capability of those in Government that has to bear the main burden in explaining the dreadful outcome',[5] or whether the political room for manœuvre in economic policy actions was so narrow that Brüning had no policy options but the one he actually pursued. If the latter were true, Borchardt contends, Brüning could not be accused of failure and guilt for the dissolution of the Weimar Republic. In other words, the standard judgement of historians about Brüning's economic policy would lack a logical basis, because the course of deflation was inevitable. In Borchardt's staging of the drama of the Weimar Republic, Brüning was a hero. He fought bravely, but as in a classical tragedy he perished.

I shall discuss the issue raised by Borchardt in three stages. In section one I present a summary of Borchardt's argument.

In section two I provide a critical examination of the political setting for his inevitability thesis. In section three I review critically the economic setting of the Borchardt thesis.

1.   A Summary of Borchardt's Argument

The main questions Borchardt asks are the following:[6]

1. When should and could a countercyclical antidepression policy have been started?
2. Were proper tools of antidepression policy available? The second question is split up into three problem areas:
   a) Were such anticyclical policy measures technically available?
   b) Were they politically available, i.e. did domestic and foreign political circumstances leave any room for manœuvre to the German government for an early expansionary antidepression policy? And:
   c) What would have been the probable effects of suggested countercyclical policy measures?

In trying to answer the first question Borchardt seeks to take into account the level of experience, which contemporaries of the depression had with downswings of economic activity. He argues that we should not judge from hindsight. This would make it easy to accuse and condemn those who were responsible for policy making at the time because one cannot expect 'prophetic gifts of governments, especially not a knowledge which only the descendants can possibly have'.[7] Specifically, Borchardt points out that contemporaries' experience was shaped by the business downturn in 1920/21 in the world economy and in 1925/26 in Germany. In both cases the decline in production activity and in employment had been faster than after 1929, but had soon ended in a new upswing generated by the economy's inherent powers of recovery, that is without government interference in support of expansion. This had been the usual pattern to which also the depression after 1929 seemed to conform, especially when signs of recovery were visible all over the world in the first months of 1931. In mid-1931, however, the banking crisis broke out with the crash of the *Creditanstalt* in May

1931 in Austria, the crash of the DANAT Bank in Germany in July and the international run on the Bank of England's gold reserves which in September 1931 forced her into leaving the gold standard and into letting the pound exchange rate float and depreciate. Only after these events had aggravated the crisis and drastically depressed economic activity still further could politicians perceive that the usual pattern of slump and recovery would not work and that expansionary policies were necessary to counteract the depression. At this time expansionary anticyclical policy measures to stimulate the economy and to create jobs began to be proposed and discussed – government programmes which, compared to traditional emergency employment measures, were of a new character and of new dimensions. Thus, Borchardt argues, the answer to the first question is: summer 1931. At this time the German government could and should have started an active antidepression policy of the sort which later on was termed Keynesian. According to Borchardt, however, it was by then already too late for timely counter-measures to prevent the rise of unemployment in Germany to 6 million persons in the winter of 1931/32 because of the nowadays well-known time lags between business cycle policy measures and their effects. At best such measures could have succeeded in advancing the bottom of the depression, which was actually reached in the summer of 1932, and the ensuing economic recovery by some months.

As to the second complex of questions concerning the availability of antidepression policy measures, Borchardt argues along the following lines. In principle two sources could have been tapped for the deficit financing of government employment programmes: foreign credits, i.e. capital imports, or domestic credits by the Reichsbank. The second alternative would have clashed with the legal restrictions on the government's access to Reichsbank credit; it would have reflated the economy, but put strain on the balance of payments and the exchange rate. The first one would also have reflated the economy, but at the same time provided gold and foreign exchange reserves necessary to increase the money supply under existing cover requirements and to counteract the consequent strains on the balance of payments and the exchange rate. These alternatives played a role in the different expansionary programmes proposed to the government from the summer of 1931 onwards. But by then, Borchardt argues, both sources of credit were technically and/or politically unavailable to the Brüning government. Foreign credits, to which especially the Bank of France would have had the means, were technically available, but when needed in the summer of 1931 the French government had tied them to political conditions, – the renunciation of the project of a German-Austrian customs union, and restraint in armaments and in the German government's efforts to revise the Treaty of Versailles. The Brüning government was unable to meet these French demands, Borchardt argues, because in view of the growing right-wing opposition the Chancellor was eager to make himself known to the public as a stern defender of Germany's national interest. He was also under pressure from President Hindenburg who had threatened to resign should Brüning accept the French credits under those conditions. This would probably have brought about the end of the Weimar Republic a year and a half earlier than its actual demise.

As regards domestic credits from the Reichsbank, these were neither technically nor politically available. On the technical side, the Reichsbank's legal status was that of an institution independent of the government. By law the Reichsbank was restricted in extending its credit to the government and was tied to fixed rules to cover its bank note circulation in gold and foreign exchange. This was part of international treaties, the Dawes agreement of 1924 and the Young agreement of 1929/30. The latter in principle also excluded a devaluation of the German mark, one possible policy tool of reacting to the crisis, especially after Britain's devaluation in September 1931, and one way to free domestic credit and money creation from restrictions by currency cover regulations.

The political availability of Reichsbank credit for counter-cyclical employment programmes could not be exploited by the Brüning government for two reasons, reports Borchardt:

1. An earlier stimulation of economic activity through government measures – say, in the summer of 1931 – would have worked against the German government's foreign

policy objective to get rid of reparations by demonstrating Germany's economic and financial incapacity to pay.

2. Within Germany itself, public opinion resisted credit creation for financing budget deficits, because this had been at the origin of the great inflation during and after World War I. The horrors of the hyperinflation of 1922/23, above all, were mobilized by those who opposed public works programmes, while in fact, as we now know, they resisted a stabilization of the Weimar system and of the social compromise on which it was based. Deficit-financed public works programmes, Borchardt contends, were proposed only by political outsiders until the spring of 1932 (when the programme by the German Trades Union Federation was published in April), by intellectuals who lacked the support of a strong political force. 'For an alternative policy', argues Borchardt, 'there would have had to be a political force. No such force existed anywhere until mid-1932. Anyone expecting that under these circumstances Brüning could and should have pursued a different policy of stabilization ... is suggesting a control over the circumstances which he in fact did not possess.'[8]

With regard to his last question on the probable effects of suggested countercyclical policy measures, Borchardt arrives at the conclusion 'that none of those plans could have turned the economic tide significantly',[9] because the relative scale of the proposed government measures for stimulating economic activity was small in comparison to what, in the light of modern experience, would have been necessary to fill the gap between potential supply and actual demand.

In addition to the limitations on Brüning's room for manoeuvre in economic policy matters to which I have already referred, Borchardt emphasizes a further important factor which was more deep-rooted than the cyclical strains on the economy. This was the consequence of what is often claimed to be the structural weakness of the German economy in the 1920s already before the world economic crisis broke out in 1929. On the one hand, the state had continuously lived beyond its means in Weimar Germany. On the other hand, the Weimar period had been characterized by battles between social groups over the distribution of the national income and by politically determined wage increases. Early on, generous wage concessions had helped to ward off the threat of radical social upheaval during and after the Revolution of 1918/19. But during the period of Germany's postwar inflation, cost increases could easily be forwarded to consumers by raising prices. German trades unions kept pushing wages up even after the currency stabilization of 1923, when entrepreneurs found it more difficult to cover cost increases. The unions were able to do so because their position in German society and especially vis-à-vis entrepreneurs was strengthened as a result of the war economy and of the compulsory state mediating of collective bargains during the Weimar Republic. This, Borchardt continues to argue, caused the unusually high 'real wage position' of the wage-earning population and the extremely disadvantageous profit situation in the second half of the 1920s. The distortions show up when comparing those years with both the prewar *Kaiserreich* and the Federal Republic of Germany. The profit squeeze, in turn, caused the low propensity to invest, the relative stagnation of economic growth and the unusually high unemployment – variables that indicate, according to Borchardt, the 'sick' state of the Weimar economy even before the outbreak of the Great Depression. Many of those responsible for economic policy viewed the outbreak of the crisis as a chance to remedy the state of sickness – the traditional view that business crises were a means to rid the economy of its weak spots. An early counter-cyclical policy would not, therefore, have conformed to the intentions of political forces that expected the crisis to bring about a basic restructuring of economic, financial and social policies, on the one hand, and of wage policies, on the other. Many hoped for more than just a return to the pre-depression unemployment rate of 8.4 per cent in 1928; they hoped for a new constellation of economic data that would guarantee sustained economic growth. The cure to Weimar's structural economic problems actually resulted from the depression experience, according to Borchardt. He views with regret only the fact that Hitler became the heir of Brüning's success. He concludes: historians should not criticise Brüning's policy pretentiously, but instead study the tragedy which it was, that already before the outbreak of the depression there existed 'an economic system which in the long run would have been unviable surrounded by a political system which was hardly viable any longer'.[10] Borchardt thus acquits Brüning of the charge of historical guilt for 'the terror' of the depression, and thereby for the dissolution of the Weimar Republic.

2. The Political Availability of Countercyclical Policy Measures

While Borchardt contends that the political environment left Chancellor Brüning no choice but to pursue his deflationary policy course, Brüning himself viewed such matters less fatalistically. This is evidenced in the preface to his memoirs where he expressly points out that there are 'always different solutions to grave problems. Nothing is more dangerous than when political leaders or parties believe in the infallibility of a single definite solution.'[11]

Is Borchardt's judgement, nevertheless, tenable that Brüning did, in fact, face political constraints that left him no choice but his economic policy of deflation. In discussing the political constraints I shall concentrate only on the domestic political scene, since Germany's international commitments and obligations in connection with the reparation issue were also strongly reflected in the positions taken by the domestic political parties and social groups. It is, in fact, astounding how broadly Brüning's deflationary policies were not only encouraged and praised by the foreign reparation creditors, but were in principle accepted or tolerated by those domestic political parties or social groups that were not in fundamental opposition to the Weimar Republic. Support or toleration ranged, at least temporarily, from the trades unions and the SPD as representatives of the working class to the DVP, a party mainly backed by liberal industrial employers, i.e. predominantly export-oriented modern industries as opposed to home-market-oriented heavy industries.

Two of the four main emergency decrees by which Brüning executed his deflationary policies until December 1931, had already been enacted when the German banking crisis broke out in July 1931. It then became evident that the depression had left the course of a normal business-cycle downturn and it was then that all kinds of plans for expansionary economic policies were proposed – from outside government circles, but also from within. The opposition to Brüning's deflationary policy mounted, as he states in his memoirs.[12] Even within his cabinet and the government bureaucracy, some prominent members saw the need for reflationary measures and came up with different proposals.

My following brief account seeks to demonstrate that there was more than one economic policy option that might have been politically feasible after the summer of 1931 had it received the same energetic support from Brüning as his continued deflationary course. The authors or supporters of all these proposals advanced or advocated *re*flationary policies, but defended them against the charge of being *in*flationary, which was used in public discussions and by Brüning himself to discredit them and turn them down. Finance Minister Hermann Dietrich and his State Secretary Hans Schäffer, Economics Minister H. Warmbold, his State Secretary Ernst Trendelenburg and the young *Oberregierungsrat* Wilhelm Lautenbach, the President of the Government's Statistical Office Ernst Wagemann and Labour Minister Adam Stegerwald were known to be seriously contemplating or favouring expansionary monetary and/or fiscal policy measures in the second half of 1931 or in early 1932. Wilhelm Lautenbach of the Economics Ministry, who has been called the German Keynes with 'perhaps, the clearest overall view of the problem',[13] proposed in August/September 1931 a fully fledged programme of deficit spending for stimulating economic activity, albeit in combination with a policy of price and cost reductions and of defending the mark exchange rate even after the devaluation of the British pound.[14] State Secretary Ernst Trendelenburg, the '*eminence grise*' in the Economics Ministry, accepted parts of the Lautenbach argument and agreed that a credit expansion was needed.[15] H. Warmbold, Economics Minister in Brüning's second cabinet from October 1931 onwards and closely connected with the interests of the German chemical industries, emphatically demanded credit creation and even threatened to resign when Brüning came through with the fourth and last as well as most painful of the deflationary emergency decrees on 8 December 1931.[16] Brüning agreed with Warmbold's demand for expansionary policies in principle, but not in timing. He was politically determined to postpone such measures as well as a 20 per cent devaluation of the mark until after the end of reparations.[17]

Hans Schäffer, State Secretary and the most competent man in the Finance Ministry, produced a memorandum on 2 September 1931, summarizing his thoughts on policy measures to overcome the crisis which, as the source indicates, were inspired by meetings of representatives from various ministries.[18] His proposals were not aired in public at the time, but were certainly further discussed in government circles and among experts close to the government. Schäffer argued that the government could behave towards a deflationary economic crisis in three different ways: by simply letting it burn itself out; by accelerating the deflation in order to reach an early bottom of the crisis; or by intervening to check the deflation in order to keep the price level on a certain height.

The first variant, letting the deflation burn itself out, had been the attitude of the Reich's government in the great crisis of the 1870s and 1880s, so Schäffer contended. The second variant, the enforcement of the deflation, is the category to which Brüning's policy belonged. Schäffer expressed doubts, however, that it would be possible through this strategy to attain the policy objective, namely to reduce production costs. He argued that the share of wages, i.e. variable costs, which could perhaps be reduced by a deflation, had diminished in total production costs since the nineteenth century. As against that, the share of fixed production costs, like interest payments, depreciation etc., had increased. Consequently, when a deflation reduced production, the – by definition – unchanged fixed costs had to be carried by a smaller number of produced items. This accounted for an increase in fixed costs per unit, which, according to Schäffer, had become higher than the decrease in variable unit labour costs which could possibly result from the deflation. Schäffer drew the conclusion that a rise in production was better suited to reduce production costs than wage cuts produced by the deflation. He was thus led to favour an economic policy oriented towards the third variant, namely to check the deflation and to stop prices from falling. He envisaged a public works programme with a volume of 2.5 bn Marks, which the Reichsbank should finance. This, he argued, meant not 'inflation, but only the mitigation of a monstrous deflation'.[19]

In January 1932 Ernst Wagemann, President of the Reich Statistical Office and like his brother-in-law, the Economics Minister Warmbold, close to the liberal export oriented industrialists' camp centred on *IG Farben*, published a plan aimed at softening the cover regulations for bank note circulation and thus at providing the Reichsbank with additional room for credit and money expansion (totalling 3 bn Marks) in order to stimulate demand.[20] This plan aroused substantial public debate and strong opposition also from Brüning himself for its allegedly purely inflationary character.

On 3 March 1932 the Labour Minister in Brüning's cabinets, formerly chairman of the Christian trades unions, Adam Stegerwald, proposed to Brüning a work creation programme amounting to 1.2 bn Marks. Obviously because he knew Brüning's standard counter argument, namely 'inflation', too well, he tried to sell it to the Chancellor by a different approach than the one used by the authors of the above mentioned proposals. He acknowledged that it might in fact be inflationary, but pointed towards the even greater threat of increasing political radicalism: 'It seems to me that the dangers of the political situation are so great in this respect that one must perhaps not deter from measures of financing, which under different circumstances would appear to be dangerous.'[21]

Leading representatives of heavy industry turned against Brüning and his government when the economic crisis deepened in autumn 1931 and became receptive for the message of the demonstration of the antirepublican right-wing 'Harzburger Front' on 11 October 1931.[22] The German People's Party, which mainly represented the interest of industrialists, withdrew support for the Brüning government in the Reichstag session of 15 October 1931. The party's chairman, Dingeldey, reproached Brüning for not having attempted to form a coalition government of national concentration, after the deepening of the crisis by the bank failures in the summer had alienated more and more people from his unpopular policies of deflation and had driven them into the camp of the political right. He offered his party as the bridge to integrate the national right into government responsibilities. To this the Social Democrat Aufhäuser replied: 'Herr Dingeldey wants to construct the bridge to the Third Reich. I believe that Herr Dingeldey has already found the bridge; the bridge between Dingeldey and the National Socialists and the German Nationals is inflation.'[23] It should be pointed out that the term 'inflation' was at the time the standard label for expansionary monetary and/or fiscal policies to create employment and revive economic growth.

Since July 1931 representatives of German industry, prominent among them Paul Silverberg, had criticized the Reichsbank for its deflationary monetary policies and demanded credit creation.[24] In October/November 1931 Silverberg used his membership in the temporary Economic Advisory Council (*Wirtschaftsbeirat*) to demand expansionary credit creation up to a volume of two billion Reichsmark.[25]

The ADGB, the free trades union organization, had already at the end of 1931 asked experts (Woytinsky, Tarnow, and Baade) to outline a work creation programme, which was published on 26 January 1932 – almost at the same time as the Wagemann plan – and was accepted officially by the trades union congress on 13 April 1932. It provided for additional public spending in the range of 2 bn Marks, the financing of which would indirectly be provided for by the Reichsbank. This would not be inflationary, the authors argued, because the growth of production would compensate for the creation of additional purchasing power.[26]

On 21 December 1931, the German Employers Association also demanded the elaboration of a programme for expansionary economic policies by the central committee of the Provisional Reich Economic Council (*Vorläufiger Reichswirtschaftsrat*), an advisory body to the government in which they, the trades unions and other representatives of economic life were organized.[27] Published on 12 March 1932, the programme advocated credit creation for additional government spending to stimulate the economy. In its resolution the Council mentioned that all sections of the economy were calling for public work creation, that a constantly stronger shrinkage of the economy was imminent, and that private entrepreneurial initiative, which could reverse this process of shrinkage, largely lacked the necessary objective prerequisites and psychological predisposition. Therefore, the state should shoulder this task. The Reichsbank should keep its credit potential open for such purposes. The possible danger of inflation no longer seemed to be a problem. 'To act against the danger of a further shrinkage of the economy with all possible means', was considered the most urgent task.[28]

Since late 1931 almost every interest group seemed to agree on the need for expansionary employment measures by the government, and by March 1932 even the differences over methods of financing them had been bridged, when – by the way – German trades unions and SPD politicians were still quarrelling over this question.[29] But Brüning still stayed his course and continued denouncing any such plans as 'inflationary', and that right through the Reichstag debate on economic policies on 10 and 11 May 1932, less than three weeks before his dismissal.

My account has aimed to demonstrate that political pressure for a revision of deflationary policies increased within Brüning's own government and among powerful interest groups that had more or less supported it. Brüning himself stated in his memoirs from autumn 1931: 'On the domestic scene attacks on the government of the Reich founded on the notion of inflation gathered force.'[30] And he also remarked: 'If we had not pursued such a ruthless financial policy in the face of all the resistance, Germany would have been finished and would have had to capitulate along the whole range of foreign-policy issues. Inflation was tempting, almost the whole business community was pressing in this direction ...'[31] That there was less fear of inflation among the public than among the many politicians who expressed it when they opposed work creation programmes, is evidenced by the fact that about 21,000 different proposals concerning monetary policy were sent to the Reichsbank and to the *Berliner Handelshochschule* (Berlin business school) during those years of depression, which overwhelmingly advocated to cut the link between the Reichsmark and gold in order to mitigate the deflationary pressure.[32] This hardly supports the hypothesis that the domestic scene created constraints for Brüning's political room for manœuvre which left him with only the option of deflation.

These findings lead to the question why Brüning – in spite of the growing demand for expansionary monetary and fiscal measures even among his supporters – stubbornly pursued his deflationary policies until the end of his Chancellorship. It would be a theoretically possible, but incorrect, answer to say that Brüning did not see that the economic consequences of the crisis would be worsened by his policies. He actually *expected* mass unemployment, a lower living standard, which would remain below the level of 1927/8 for a number of years to come, and a 'steady recovery of the economy' only by 1935 at the earliest.[33] The answer to the question posed above rather lies in the political field, in the political aims which were pursued by Brüning himself as well as by the political forces which had supported his policies at least for some time. Brüning himself noted in his memoirs that the depression to him was 'not so unwelcome'.[34] He made use of the crisis to pursue both his domestic and foreign political aims.

In domestic politics he particularly intended to consolidate the public finances and especially in that connection, to reform the social welfare system – in other words, to reduce social expenditure. Brüning's reaction to the so-called Wagemann plan in January 1932 demonstrates how much he felt his reform efforts disturbed by public debate about expansionary policies to stimulate the economy. In a cabinet meeting Brüning expressed his opinion that the Wagemann plan created 'the wholly misleading notion that all of a sudden a credit of 1 to 2 billion was available and that all the reform measures were no longer necessary. He has had the greatest difficulty bargaining over social security reform since this Plan emerged. The whole line that he was holding intact was endangered.'[35]

Foreign policy considerations – above all the aim to bring a complete end to reparations – seem to have been even more important for Brüning's determination to stick to deflationary policies. The Chancellor declared in 1930 that Germany should reach a position where it could 'make use of the world crisis at any time, to put pressure on all the other powers'. A moratorium of two or three years for reparation payments was 'no solution, one would have to go the whole hog'. The role that the depression had to play in this political endeavour becomes apparent when Brüning remarks: 'We were able to turn our [economic] sickness into our weapon.'[36] It was for this reason that Brüning had postponed all expansionary measures to stimulate the economy until after a final agreement to end reparations had been reached. Brüning had expressly agreed secretly with Reichsbank President Luther that a 20 per cent devaluation of the Mark, which was considered economically necessary, should take place only after reparations had ended.[37]

But along the deflationary road Brüning lost political support, as did the liberal and bourgeois parties on whose backing he relied. It is true that they and the Social Democrats had in unison with Brüning denounced the Nazis' money and credit expansion idea (the so-called Feder-Geld) for stimulating economic activity and employment as inflationary and irresponsible, as they did, for example, in one of the few discussions in the Reichstag following the formation of Brüning's second cabinet on 10 October 1931. Even the Communist Party and the German National People's Party continued throughout the various election campaigns of 1932 to warn that a Nazi government would mean 'a new inflation'.[38]

But the electorate evidently became less fearful of 'inflationary' work-creation schemes than of the experience of prolonged depression. The public's fear of the inflation became less important than the politicians' 'fear of the inflation fear', a term coined in November 1931 by Gerhard Colm.[39] Identifying the Nazis with inflation became a weak argument in the competitive struggle of political parties for votes. The price that Brüning demanded from the German population for the end to reparations was judged by more and more citizens as being too high. The Nazis promised employment and economic growth as well as a radical abolition of the Versailles Treaty. However inconsistent this might have been in reality, the betterment of economic conditions became the electorate's primary concern, while Brüning and the parties supporting him still subordinated economic recovery measures to reparation politics.

After Hitler had been invited to speak at the Düsseldorf Industrial Club in January 1932, he became more acceptable as a political leader to some heavy industrialists in the Ruhr. Big business, in the red due to the record under-utilization of capacities, had become increasingly disenchanted with Brüning's hesitation to reflate the economy and to use the crisis for an all out attack on Weimar's social welfare. Small business and its employees, threatened by bankruptcy, flocked to the Nazis.[40]

Farmers, big and small, under tremendous financial pressure from the fall of agricultural prices and relatively high interest rates on their debts, contributed massively to the Nazi successes at the polls in state and federal elections in 1932.[41] The Nazis had promised autarky, i.e. the exclusion of foreign competition, and financial relief from what they dubbed 'interest slavery'. White-collar employees, civil servants and blue-collar workers in handicraft and small-scale manufacturing were embittered by Brüning's deflationary emergency decrees and voted strongly for Hitler and his party. As Thomas Childers has so ably demonstrated, the Nazis' electoral propaganda had capitalized on this anti-deflation mood. It promised a job to every German and an increase in government spending to stimulate the economy.[42]

There can be no doubt that in 1931/2 there was a strong popular demand for government action to stimulate the economy, which Brüning and – until the final agreement on reparations in June/July 1932 – practically all non-Nazi parties were loath to satisfy. Is this situation correctly described in Borchardt's terms as one which lacked room for manœuvre and 'a political force' as an alternative to Brüning's deflationary course? I would prefer to call it an avoidable failure in political leadership, defined as a situation in which democratic parties pursue goals of some political power elites, but disrespect the electorate's primary concerns. They thus drive voters into the arms of extremists who are clever enough to lure them by offering radical solutions to the public's most pressing needs.[43]

If the Nazis were able to mobilize such tremendous political support for their promises to revive the economy,[44] could Brüning and his political camp not have done better with actual measures in that direction? It seems to me that Brüning's situation is better described by *lack of determination* than by lack of options or of a political force to pursue expansionary economic policies after July 1931.

3.   A Critical View of the Economic Setting of the Borchardt Thesis

From the political let me now turn to the economic pillar of the inevitability argument. Borchardt has pictured the Weimar economy between the hyperinflation and the Great Depression as an economy in a 'sick' state that was in need of a deep crisis experience in order to remedy the situation. He especially pointed out that net investments in relation to the net social product, i.e. the investment ratio of the economy, was on average considerably lower between 1925 and 1929 than in the years 1910–13.[45] According to data compiled by Walther G. Hoffmann the ratio was 11.1 per cent as against 15.2 per cent in the earlier period. It is, however, illuminating to take a look at the yearly figures:[46]

1910	13.3%	1925	12.8%
1911	15.1%	1926	6.5%
1912	16.6%	1927	15.2%
1913	15.5%	1928	13.1%
		1929	7.3%

Clearly the low average for the period 1925–9 as a whole is mainly due to the ratios in the years 1926 and 1929, while the other years show more satisfactory results. In 1927 the investment ratio even equalled the average for 1910–13.

Contemporary observers not only regarded the German economic situation in 1928 and also its development since 1924 as quite satisfactory, but even expressed some enthusiasm about it. Reparation Agent S. Parker Gilbert wrote in his report of 22 December 1928, on the German economic situation:

German business conditions generally appear to have righted themselves on a relatively high level of activity. A year ago, it will be recalled, German business was in the midst of a process of expansion which threatened to result in over-production in certain of the principal industries .... As the year 1928 comes to a close, it appears that this over-expansion has been checked before it reached dangerous proportions, and that a condition of relative stability has now been attained .... Since 1924, when stabilization was achieved and the execution of the Experts' Plan began, Germany's reconstruction has at least kept pace with the reconstruction of Europe as a whole, and it has played an essential part in the general process of European reconstruction.[47]

Borchardt as well as other economic historians[48] (see also Harold James in this volume) have claimed that the relatively low investment activity, when viewed as the average of the years 1925–29, was due to excessive wage increases, i.e. wages exceeding the growth of labour productivity. I have pointed out elsewhere that Borchardt created a wrong impression of labour productivity growth by comparing data on productivity *per employed person* in the interwar period with those of the pre-World War I and post-World War II periods.[49] He did not take account of the fact that working hours were sharply reduced in post-World War I Germany and that therefore productivity *per man hour* was not only higher in the second half of the 1920s than before the First World War, but with an annual average rate of 5.6 per cent from 1925–29 also grew faster than during Germany's 'economic miracle' from 1950–59 (4.7 per cent p.a.) and much faster than in the period up to the First World War (1.8 per cent p.a. 1850–1913). It would have been contrary to economic reasoning, indeed, had the much discussed rationalization movement in Germany after the hyperinflation not led to significant gains in productivity.

Compared with 1913, labour productivity *per man hour* and real hourly gross earnings in industry (the only reliable wage data we have) had both risen in the second half of the 1920s. They rose more or less in tandem. The available statistics do not show that wage increases in industry clearly broke the limits drawn by labour productivity increases in the

Table 1   Indices of real hourly wages/earnings and of labour productivity per man hour in Germany 1913/14 (= 100) to 1932

	Real hourly wages as per collective agreements, in industry	Real gross hourly earnings in industry	Labour productivity per man hour in	
			industry and craft	the economy as a whole
1913/14	100	100	100*	100*
1924	82	86	—	—
1925	95	103	114.1	105.7
1926	103	109	118.2	105.5
1927	104	114	124.1	118.0
1928	111	125	118.1	121.0
1929	115	130	127.2	131.5
1930	122	131	133.8	136.6
1931	126	132	135.1	137.8
1932	119	125	139.7	137.8

* 1913.

For the method of calculation and sources, see Holtfrerich, 'Zu hohe Löhne', pp. 126–131.

economy as a whole (see *Table 1*). This is supported by evidence on a considerable wage drift, i.e. effective wages exceeding collectively negotiated wages; in other words, entrepreneurs voluntarily paid more than they were required by wage agreements with the trades unions.

A look at the figures on investment activity in different sectors of the German economy is also revealing. Again according to data from Walther G. Hoffman,[50] annual average investment outlays in constant prices fell short of their 1913 level in the sector 'home construction' (by almost 30 per cent) and in agriculture (by more than 60 per cent) in the second half of the 1920s. As against that, real annual average investment outlays in manufacturing industries and other private business *(Gewerbe)* in 1924–29 equalled the 1913 level in spite of the sharp cyclical downturns in 1926 and 1929.

Had wage developments been the principal cause for the lagging investment activity, the sharpest downturn of investment activity should *not* have shown up in agriculture, where self-employment weakened the importance of wages, but in manufacturing industries, where contracted labour played a much more prominent role. As is well-known, the agricultural crisis in the second half of the 1920s was a world-wide phenomenon and its causes have nothing to do with the development of wages in Germany. As to home construction, we know that it is highly dependent on the level of interest rates. Interest rates in the second half of the 1920s were about double what they had been in prewar Germany. This, together with rent control since World War I, is sufficient explanation of the investment downturn in this sector of the economy without recourse to wage pressure.[51]

As I and – on the basis of a different source – Juergen von Kruedener have pointed out,[52] the employers' contributions to social insurance as a percentage of wages were higher in Weimar Germany than in 1913. For industrial workers they had risen from roughly three per cent of their wages in 1913 to 5.5 per cent in 1925 and 7.5 per cent in 1929. Compared with 1913, this added 2.5 to 4.5 percentage points to wage costs in the 1920s. In certain years these additions to production costs might have violated the distributional margin provided by productivity developments. But from 1926 to 1929 they hardly changed and therefore became neutral in the distributional conflict.

Borchardt has also used long-term statistics on the cumulative real wage position of employed persons to demonstrate that wage pressure caused the 'sick' state of the Weimar economy. This, he tries to show, was remedied in the 1930s, thus preparing the ground for a relatively healthy development in the Federal Republic in the 1950s and 1960s.[53] The development of the cumulative real wage position of employed persons is by definition almost exactly a reflection of the development of labour's share in national income. Statistics on labour's share confirm that the pre-depression German economy in the second half of the 1920s was indeed 'off the rails'.[54] But Borchardt - in my view – errs when he interprets this high share as a result of wage pressure and when he sees the 'sick' state of the economy as being caused by the high share of labour income in national income. Hoffman's long-term data demonstrate clearly that labour's share in national income had varied cyclically in Germany's economic development since the middle of the nineteenth century and this variation had little to do with trades union power or wage pressure. It was always a *symptom* of business conditions, not its *cause*.[55] This is also evidenced by the fact that labour's share in national income reached an all-time maximum when the depression was deepest, i.e. in 1932 in Germany and a year later in the United States, where union power was extremely weak in the 1920s and early 1930s.

In Germany, business recovery under the Nazi government caused profits to grow and labour's share in national income to fall, though at the same time the sum of real wages and salaries in absolute terms increased in tandem with employment. Economic expansion, and *not* the demise of the welfare state nor even the destruction of the labour unions by the Nazis, proved to be the proper remedy for whatever 'sickness' had befallen the economy in the decade before. The depression experience certainly provided no cure at all. From this economic perspective, the policy of deflation was unnecessary, counter-productive and avoidable as well.

If the Weimar economy's high share of labour income in national income is accepted as a *symptom* of an unsatisfactory economic development, where do we have to look for the economic *causes*? A major theoretical argument against real wage pressure being the main cause of economic growth problems has been introduced into public discussions in the Federal Republic of Germany by Professor Ernst Helmstädter, a neo-classical, supply-side oriented economist and until 1988 a member of the German Council of Economic Advisers to the Government *(Sachverständigenrat)*. He opposes the view that insufficient profits and investments are caused and can be remedied by changes in the level of wages. According to him, trades unions and employers negotiate about *nominal* wages and do not have the power to determine the level of *real* wages. Real wages are the result of the complex interplay of market forces that finds expression in price developments. In his view, excessive real wages together with unemployment are not caused by union power, but by more objective circumstances, namely a flattening of aggregate supply curves and consequently a compression of differential rents or profits. According to Helmstädter, relatively low profits result from a lack of dynamic competition in the economy, of pioneering entrepreneurs, of new markets and new products with high rates of return.[56]

This situation is typical of encrusted markets. The increased government interference with market forces (= regulation, e.g. in the housing market) and the movement towards an intense industrial concentration in Weimar Germany certainly created such conditions. In 1927 J.A.Schumpeter wrote: 'The effective wage level in Germany allows for the assumption that the trades union policy in our country explains relatively little of the actual unemployment, in contrast to England and Northern Europe.' Instead, Schumpeter based his explanation of Weimar's pre-depression unemployment on the erosion of free competition and on the growing trust movement in Germany. 'When entrepreneurs ... proceed united instead of competing with each other, then they are not forced to increase production to such a point that the whole labour force is employed.'[57]

Other prominent economists at the time expressed similarly critical views of the role of cartels and syndicates for Germany's economic development, among them Adolph Löwe, Emil Lederer and Moritz Julius Bonn. Heinrich August Winkler has recently summarized a good deal of the contemporary discussion on the cartellization and concentration movement as a cause of the unemployment in Germany between hyperinflation and the Great Depression.[58] The Reich's Labour Minister Adam Stegerwald in June 1931 estimated the additional financial burden that the pricing policies of the cartels and syndicates placed on the German population at 5 bn Reichsmarks.[59]

There is one further point so far neglected in the discussion of the German labour market problems in the second half of the 1920s. S. Parker Gilbert, the Reparation Agent in Berlin, already noted in his December 1928 Report: 'The annual growth in the working population, which reflects the high birth-rate in Germany in the years immediately before the war, has been a complicating factor throughout the difficult period of adjustment since stabilization, and at times it has much intensified the problem of unemployment, already difficult enough on other accounts.'[60] The annual increase in the working population was estimated at about 400,000 until 1930 followed by a sharp drop to 100,000 in 1931 and annual decreases of about 100,000 in the years 1932–34. Labour market statistics for 1928 and 1929 confirm this assessment almost perfectly: between those years the number of employed persons *(Arbeitnehmer)* decreased by only 126,000, but the number of unemployed persons increased by roughly 540,000.[61]

In my view, however, the primary cause of the Weimar economy's partly unsatisfactory performance even before the Great Depression was the high price of capital, with interest rates double the level of prewar Germany.[62] The worldwide agricultural crisis and the notorious barriers to international trade after the First World War both added to Germany's economic problems, notably an acute dependence on world market conditions on account of the reparations obligations. In these crucial areas, namely the capital market, the market for agricultural production and access to world markets in general, conditions were different, i.e. more favourable to economic growth, during West Germany's economic development in the 1950s and 1960s. On the other hand, there was hardly less concentration of industry and cartellization in the Federal Republic than in Weimar Germany. And the supply pressures on the labour market were also comparable; while the working population grew rapidly in the 1920s due to high birth rates up to the First World War, it did so in the Federal Republic until the construction of the Berlin Wall in 1961 on account of the large influx of refugees from East Germany.

There may still appear to be a contradiction between my presentation of wage and labour productivity data in *Table 1* and the finding that labour's share in national income was considerably higher in the second half of the 1920s than before the First World War. A rising share of labour income in national income means by definition that average labour productivity lags behind average wage and salary increases. Since *Table 1* reveals that industrial real wages hardly exceeded productivity growth, how can we explain the divergence between the rates of growth of average productivity and of average labour income as reflected in the development of labour's share in national income?

The answer can be found in the statistics on the employment structure. This underwent a tremendous change in Germany mainly during the immediate postwar years, the period of economic reconstruction. To demonstrate this quantatively we have to rely on census data. The first census after the First World War was taken in 1925, the last before the War in 1907. The relation of salaried employees to wage earners had drastically shifted from 1:5.3 in 1907 to 1:2.8 in 1925.[63] As salaried employees earned more than blue-collar workers, labour's share in national income was bound, therefore, to rise, even when real wages, on the one hand, and real salaries, on the other, increased at the same rate as average labour productivity. The structural shift toward salaried employees, however, was caused neither by trades unions pressuring for wage increases nor by compulsory arbitration of wage agreements by the government, the two pet arguments that Borchardt shares with entrepreneurial interest groups of the Weimar Republic. Rather, it seems, the increase of labour's share in national income was caused by structural factors beyond the reach of collective bargaining.

For Schumpeter[64] and other contemporaneous economists,[65] domestic capital formation, not wage and social expenditure as such, was the main problem of the pre-depression Weimar economy. This corresponds to my view that the high price of capital – the level of German interest rates – constituted the core of the problem. How did it come about and what could have been done to prevent it?

Table 2 contains data on the distribution of the German national income in 1913 and in the years 1925–31. The most striking change between 1913 and the second half of the 1920s occurred in unearned income from financial assets. The share dropped by more than ten percentage points to 2.0 per cent in 1925 to recover only slightly during the following years. Many Germans who had lived on income from financial assets before the War were now faced with the need

Table 2   Distribution of the national income on the territory of the post-World War One German Reich, 1913 and 1925–31 in per cent

	1913	1925	1926	1927	1928	1929	1930	1931
Entrepreneurial Income								
Agriculture and Forestry	12.5	9.5	9.3	8.4	7.7	7.6	7.4	8.2
Commerce and Industry	20.1	18.2	17.3	17.0	16.2	15.5	14.2	13.2
Undistributed Corporate Income	2.6	1.5	1.4	1.9	1.7	1.2	0.6	–1.8
Government Entrepreneurial Income	2.4	2.4	3.3	3.4	3.3	3.2	3.3	1.7
Labour Income								
Wages and Salaries	45.3	56.3	55.5	54.9	56.5	56.6	56.4	57.9
Employers' Contributions to Social Insurance	1.1	2.1	2.6	2.7	3.0	3.2	3.4	3.9
Unearned Income								
Financial Assets	12.5	2.0	2.5	3.0	3.7	4.2	4.6	5.3
Real Estate	2.0	0.9	1.0	1.1	1.1	1.1	1.3	1.6
Pensions	3.0	9.2	11.4	10.5	11.2	12.0	14.3	17.6
Plus Government Revenue Not Contained in Private Income	0.2	4.3	4.2	4.9	4.0	4.7	5.7	6.6
Minus Double Entry Items Due to Government Transfer Payments	1.7	6.4	8.5	7.8	8.4	9.3	11.2	14.2
Total	100.0	100.0	100.0	100.0	100.0	100.0	100.0	100.0

Source: Statistisches Reichsamt, *Das deutsche Volkseinkommen vor und nach dem Kriege* (= Einzelschriften zur Statistik des Deutschen Reichs No. 24), Berlin: Hobbing 1932, p. 84.

to earn a living through employment. Together with the different age structure of the German population in the 1920s, compared with the prewar period, this explains why the labour-force participation rate in Germany had risen to 51.3 per cent in 1925 as against 45.5 per cent in 1907. At the same time it contributes to the explanation of the approximately ten percentage points increase in the share of wages and salaries in national income also displayed in *Table 2*.

The share of entrepreneurial income in agriculture and forestry was much lower in the interwar years than in 1913, which is a due reflection of the agricultural crisis. The entrepreneurial income share in commerce and industry was also lower in the 1920s than in 1913, but had fallen less than in the primary sector. It reflected mainly the relative and even absolute reduction of self-employed persons in Germany from the prewar period into the 1920s.[66] Only with the worsening of business conditions from 1928 onwards do the data reflect the real squeeze on entrepreneurial profits.

Many economists, economic historians, and contemporary observers have pointed out that the great German inflation from 1914 to 1923 destroyed capital.[67] Of course, this can be true only in a financial sense, as the reconstruction of physical capital, such as factories, iron works, railroads, commercial ships, was promoted rather than hindered by the inflation. As to finance capital, debtors gained what creditors lost. But the redistribution affected capital markets, because debtor groups typically disposed of their income in a different way than the traditional creditor groups. The average household and the different levels of government that found themselves relieved of debts as a result of the German hyperinflation, of course, tended to consume more and to save less than the typical former *rentier* who often belonged to the richest classes in prewar German society. The economic function of the *rentier* class had been to contribute to a high macroeconomic savings rate to allow for capital formation as a prerequisite for high investment, economic growth, and full employment. When the income share of the *rentier* class was eroded by the inflation, it was largely taken up by wage and salary recipients, as can be interpreted from the data in *Table 2*.

This change in the distribution of the German national income explains at the same time the relatively higher level of consumption, the reduced savings and investment rate, and the higher level of interest rates on the capital market in Weimar Germany during the second half of the 1920s.[68] One theoretically possible solution to the economic dilemma of the Weimar Republic in my view would have been to stimulate a process whereby the working class would not only have absorbed the national income shares from the financial wealth owners, but would have assumed the economic function of the *rentier* class as well, namely to save and to contribute to capital formation. This could have been promoted by government incentives to save, such as the policy implemented by the West German government after the Second World War, or by collective bargaining agreements providing for a compulsory investment of parts of wage income into capital formation funds owned by the workers or employees.

The German trades unions had a big stake in the democratic and social institutions of the Weimar Republic, as did the liberal industrial bourgeoisie. Instead of quarrelling over the level of wages and wage increases, the collective bargaining partners and the government should have addressed the issue of savings and capital formation. The extreme weakness of the Weimar economy in this respect was hidden behind the influx of foreign capital for some years (not dissimilar to the US economy in the 1980s). The German government and collective bargaining partners should have devoted their attention much more to the inflation-induced destruction of a most important traditional source of capital formation, namely *rentier* income, than to the allegedly excessive wages. In my view the economic system and the social compromise of the Weimar Republic could have been viable, had it included an arrangement for the promotion of capital formation from wage and salary income in order to meet the requirements of the economic system as it emerged from the hyperinflation.

Notes

I am grateful to Knut Borchardt and Ian Kershaw for comments and suggestions on the first draft of this paper.

1. Knut Borchardt, 'Zwangslagen und Handlungsspielräume in der großen Wirtschaftskrise der frühen dreißiger Jahre: Zur Revision des überlieferten Geschichtsbildes' (1979), reprinted in K. Borchardt, *Wachstum, Krisen, Handlungsspielräume der Wirtschaftspolitik. Studien zur Geschichte des 19. und 20. Jahrhunderts* (Göttingen, 1982), pp. 165–182.

2. Gerhard Kroll, *Von der Weltwirtschaftskrise zur Staatskonjunktur* (Berlin, 1959), p. 710. Throughout my paper the quotations in English from German sources are my translation.

3. Gottfried Bombach, 'Einleitung', in G. Bombach et al. (eds.), *Der Keynesianismus II: Die beschäftigungspolitische Diskussion vor Keynes in Deutschland. Dokumente und Kommentare* (Berlin, 1976), p. 6.

4. Wilhelm Grotkopp, *Die große Krise. Lehren aus der Überwindung der Wirtschaftskrise 1929/32* (Düsseldorf, 1954), pp. 74–77.

5. Borchardt, 'Zwangslagen', p. 166.

6. See also Carl-Ludwig Holtfrerich, 'Alternativen zu Brünings Wirtschaftspolitik in der Weltwirtschaftskrise?' in *Historische Zeitschrift*, 235 (1982), pp. 605–631.

7. Borchardt, 'Zwangslagen', p. 170.

8. Borchardt, 'Zwangslagen', p. 173.

9. Borchardt, 'Zwangslagen', p. 174.

10. Borchardt, 'Zwangslagen', p. 182.

11. Heinrich Brüning, *Memoiren 1918–1934* (Stuttgart, 1970), p. 13.

12. Brüning, *Memoiren*, pp. 370, 408. How the opposition in all layers of society against the seemingly helpless Brüning government grew, especially after the banking crisis in July 1931, and how Brüning's mistrust even of friends and loyal collaborators (like Hans Schäffer) contributed to his growing isolation, is the central thesis of the article by Werner Jochmann, 'Brünings Deflationspolitik und der Untergang der Weimarer Republik', in Dirk Stegmann et al. (eds.), *Industrielle Gesellschaft und politisches System. Beiträge zur politischen Sozialgeschichte* (Bonn, 1978), pp. 97–112.

13. George Garvy, 'Keynes and the Economic Activists of Pre-Hitler Germany', in *Journal of Political Economy*, 83 (1975), p. 398.

14. Wilhelm Lautenbach, *Zins, Kredit und Produktion*, ed. by Wolfgang Stützel (Tübingen, 1952), pp. 137–155. Knut Borchardt, 'Zur Aufarbeitung der Vor- und Frühgeschichte des Keynesianismus in Deutschland. Zugleich ein Beitrag zur Position von W. Lautenbach', in *Jahrbücher für Nationalökonomie und Statistik*, 197 (1982), pp. 366–369.

15. Harold James, *The Reichsbank and Public Finance in Germany 1924–33* (Frankfurt/M., 1985), p. 145.

16. Brüning, *Memoiren*, p. 479. Henry Turner found that Brüning's fourth emergency decree 'offended even some of his most loyal supporters in big business.' For the first time such a decree reduced cartel prices (by ten per cent) and interest rates on mortgages and other long-term loans (by 25 per cent). That step 'seemed nothing less than a staggering blow to the sanctity of contracts, the very foundation of the capitalist system.' Henry A. Turner, Jr., *German Big Business and the Rise of Hitler* (New York, 1985), p. 204.

17. Brüning, *Memoiren*, pp. 221, 367, 503.

18. For the text of the memorandum see Gerhard Schulz et al. (eds.), *Politik und Wirtschaft in der Krise 1930–1932. Quellen zur Ära Brüning* (Düsseldorf, 1980), pp. 933–935. Eckhard Wandel, *Hans Schäffer. Steuermann in wirtschaftlichen und politischen Krisen* (Stuttgart, 1974), pp. 307–315.

19. There is no evidence that Schäffer insisted on the implementation of his anti-deflation scheme before reparations were ended. Rather he seems loyally to have supported Brüning's orthodox stance in fiscal policy. The following evidence contributes to an understanding of Schäffer's seemingly contradictory positions.

Moritz J. Bonn, a professor at Berlin's business school and a financial adviser to the government several times during the Weimar Republic, corresponded with Schäffer extensively about the proposal. He rejected the idea of domestic credit creation for work-creation measures on the grounds that Germany's international credit-worthiness would suffer even more than it already had. He clearly rejected Schäffer's expansionary programme. It is, however, noteworthy that Bonn in his letter to Schäffer on 10 September 1931 refers to 'the many inflationary plans that circulate in Germany', and to 'the inflationary proposals that surface everywhere', contemporary statements that corroborate Brüning's similar contentions in his memoirs (see below). Bonn sent a second extensive comment on Schäffer's memorandum on 20 October 1931, where he again pleaded for the 'let-it-burn-out' alternative. Schäffer responded in a letter of 26 October 1931, which mirrors his frustration at the opposition to his expansionary proposal not only by Bonn, but by others also. He refuted the charge that his programme would be inflationary, but conceded that danger was imminent when a majority of people regarded it as such. 'The very fact that you, *sehr gerehrter Herr Professor*, and, as I am willing to concede, not you alone regard the plan as inflationary, definitely excludes its execution. Therefore you need no longer be afraid of an imprudence on my part.' Schäffer also reveals the psychological stress caused by the opposition to his proposal by Bonn and others: 'You must believe me that for someone in a position of responsibility it is psychologically hard to bear to let the crisis 'burn itself out', when he observes daily what else burns out with it. Perhaps there is no other way, but it is bitter to digest this insight.' Bundesarchiv Koblenz, Nachlass M.J. Bonn 52. Schäffer's abortive attempts to change Reichsbank President Luther's and the Brüning cabinet's priorities in favour of a work-creation policy are mentioned in Helmut Marcon, *Arbeitsbeschaffungs-politik der Regierungen Papen und Schleicher. Grundsteinlegung für die Beschäftigungspolitik im Dritten Reich* (Bern, 1974), p. 123.

But in executing the policy of fiscal balance Schäffer expected that the cancellation of reparations would take place in January 1932, the date originally planned for the Lausanne conference. He disagreed with Brüning over the postponement of the conference, as he saw the urgent need for the end of reparations in order to balance the budget, to avoid another financial panic in Germany and, on this basis, to revive the private economy and secure a propaganda success in the battle against unemployment for the Brüning government. Schäffer asked for his resignation in March 1932 after a series of conflicts within the government over budgetary matters. He actually resigned on 15 May 1932. See James, *Reichsbank*, pp. 156–7. Harold James, 'Gab es eine Alternative zur Wirtschaftspolitik Brünings?' in *Viertel-jahrschrift für Sozial- und Wirtschaftsgeschichte*, 70 (1983), pp. 533–534. Knut Borchardt, 'Noch einmal: Alternativen zu Brünings Wirt-schaftspolitik?' in *Historische Zeitschrift*, 237 (1983), pp. 79–81. Hans Staudinger, *Wirtschaftspolitik im Weimarer Staat. Lebenserin-nerungen eines politischen Beamten im Reich und in Preussen 1889 bis 1934*, ed. by Hagen Schulze (Bonn, 1982) pp. 92–94. On the growing alienation and differences between Schäffer and Brüning see Eckhard Wandel, *Hans Schäffer. Steuermann in wirtschaftlichen und politischen Krisen* (Stuttgart, 1974), pp. 221–223, esp. p. 227.

20. Rudolf Regul, 'Der Wagemann-Plan', in Gottfried Bombach et al. (eds.), *Der Keynesianismus III: Die geld- und beschäftigungs-theoretische Diskussion in Deutschland zur Zeit von Keynes. Doku-mente und Analysen* (Berlin, 1981), pp. 421–447. Borchardt objects that the plan was aimed at the long-term restructuring of the German monetary and banking system, not at an immediate stimulation of the business cycle. See Borchardt 'Noch einmal', p. 78. However, the rapid controversy which the plan caused in government and private circles proves that its short-term business cycles implications rather than its long-term structural effects mattered in the debate.

21. Schulz et al., *Politik und Wirtschaft*, p. 1316.

22. Reinhard Neebe, *Grossindustrie, Staat und NSDAP 1930–1933* (Göt-tingen, 1981), pp. 99–116. Turner, *German Big Business*, pp. 168–171.

23. *Verhandlungen des Reichstags, V. Wahlperiode 1930*, vol. 446 (Ber-lin, 1932), p. 2160.

24. Neebe, *Grossindustrie*, pp. 112, 248. Harold James, *The German Slump. Politics and Economics 1924–36* (Oxford, 1986), p. 315. James, 'Gab es eine Alternative', pp. 535–536.

25. Neebe, *Grossindustrie*, p. 114. *Akten der Reichskanzlei. Weimarer Republik. Die Kabinette Brüning I und II*, ed. Tilman Koops, vol. 1 (Boppard am Rhein, 1982), p. LXXXVIII.

26. Michael Schneider, *Das Arbeitsbeschaffungsprogramm des ADGB. Zur gewerkschaftlichen Politik in der Endphase der Weimarer Repu-blik* (Bonn-Bad Godesberg, 1975), pp. 231–6. The latest research on

this plan has concentrated on the differences within the trades union camp and between the SPD and the unions over the feasibility of this plan. See Wolfgang Zollitsch, 'Einzelgewerkschaften und Arbeits-beschaffung: Zum Handlungsspielraum der Arbeiterbewegung in der Spätphase der Weimarer Republik', in *Geschichte und Gesellschaft*, 8 (1982), pp. 87–115. Heinrich A. Winkler, *Der Weg in die Kata-strophe. Arbeiter und Arbeiterbewegung in der Weimarer Republik 1930 bis 1933* (Berlin, 1987), pp. 497–505.

27. *Der Vorläufige Reichswirtschaftsrat 1927-1932*, ed. by the Büro des vorläufigen Reichswirtschaftsrats (Berlin, 1933), p. 245.
28. Schulz et al., *Politik und Wirtschaft*, pp. 1324–29.
29. Winkler, *Der Weg in die Katastrophe*, pp. 499–500.
30. Brüning, *Memoiren*, p. 370.
31. Brüning, *Memoiren*, p. 408.
32. Jürgen Schiemann, *Die deutsche Währung in der Weltwirtschaftskrise 1929–1933. Währungspolitik und Abwertungskontroverse unter den Bedingungen der Reparationen* (Bern, 1980), p. 225. Borchardt questions the truth of contemporary second-hand – albeit official (by Reichsbank President Luther) – reports on these proposals and beyond that denies that they could have been representative of the public's attitude towards 'inflation'. Knut Borchardt, 'Das Gewicht der Infla-tionsangst in den wirtschaftspolitischen Entscheidungsprozessen wäh-rend der Weltwirtschaftskrise', in Gerald D. Feldman (ed.), *Die Nachwirkungen der Inflation auf die deutsche Geschichte 1924–33* (München, 1985), pp. 256–257. Borchardt writes on the devaluation problem in general in his 'Zur Frage der währungspolitischen Optionen Deutschlands in der Weltwirtschaftskrise', in Borchardt, *Wachstum*, pp. 206–224, and in his 'Could and Should Germany Have Followed Great Britain in Leaving the Gold Standard?' In *Journal of European Economic History*, 13 (1984), pp. 471–497.
33. Brüning, *Memoiren*. p. 192.
34. Brüning, *Memoiren*, p. 286. That the Brüning government 'instrumen-talized' the depression and the public's latent fears of another hyper-inflation to pursue the domestic political aim of an anti-welfare and anti-parliamentary *Reichsreform* and/or the foreign policy aim of free-ing Germany from her reparation obligations once and for all has been argued among others by Horst Sanmann, 'Daten und Alternativen der deutschen Wirtschafts- und Finanzpolitik in der Ära Brüning', in *Hamburger Jahrbuch für Wirtschafts- und Gesellschaftspolitik*, 10 (1965), pp. 109–140. Hans Mommsen, 'Heinrich Brünings Politik als Reichskanzler: Das Scheitern eines politischen Alleinganges', in Karl Holl (ed.), *Wirtschaftskrise und liberale Demokratie* (Göttingen, 1978), pp. 16–45. Werner Jochmann, 'Brünings Deflationspolitik', pp. 97–112. Gerhard Schulz, 'Inflationstrauma, Finanzpolitik und Krisenbekämpfung in den Jahren der Wirtschaftskrise, 1930–33', in Feldman, *Nachwirkungen*, pp. 261-96. Peter-Christian Witt, 'Finanzpolitik als Verfassungs- und Gesellschaftspolitik', in *Geschichte und Gesellschaft*, 8 (1982), pp. 386–414. P.-C. Witt, 'Die Auswirk-

ungen der Inflation auf die Finanzpolitik des Deutschen Reiches 1924–35', in Feldman, *Nachwirkungen*, pp. 43–95. The instrumentalization of deflation by employers in order to break the power of the trades unions is argued by Bernd Weisbrod, 'Die Befreiung von den "Tariffesseln". Deflationspolitik als Krisenstrategie der Unternehmer in der Ära Brüning', in *Geschichte und Gesellschaft*, 11 (1985), pp. 295–325.

35. Schulz et al., *Politik und Wirtschaft*, p. 1241.

36. Brüning, *Memoiren*, pp. 193 and 309 respectively.

37. Brüning, *Memoiren*, pp. 221, 367.

38. Thomas Childers, *The Nazi Voter. The Social Foundation of Fascism in Germany, 1919–1933* (Chapel Hill, 1983), pp. 226, 250.

39. Quoted in Winkler, *Der Weg in die Katastrophe*, pp. 500, 541.

40. Neebe, *Grossindustrie*, p. 116. Childers, *The Nazi Voter*, p. 201. Reinhard Neebe, 'Konflikt und Kooperation 1930–1933: Anmerkungen zum Verhältnis von Kapital und Arbeit in der Weltwirtschaftskrise', in Werner Abelshauser (ed.), *Die Weimarer Republik als Wohlfahrtsstaat. Zum Verhältnis von Wirtschafts- und Sozialpolitik in der Industriegesellschaft* (Wiesbaden, 1987), pp. 226–237, esp. p. 234. Turner, *German Big Business*, pp. 191–203, points out that the Nazis mustered a lot of support from businessmen at the helm of small and medium-sized firms in the course of 1931. He even speaks of 'a breakthrough' in 1931 (p. 203). Some data on the comparatively modest support of big industry for the Nazis, even after it had lost confidence in the Brüning government in autumn 1931, are reported in Thomas Trumpp, 'Zur Finanzierung der NSDAP durch die deutsche Grossindustrie. Versuch einer Bilanz', in *Geschichte in Wissenschaft und Unterricht*, 32 (1981), pp. 228–233.

41. Childers, *The Nazi Voter*, pp. 216–219.

42. Childers, *The Nazi Voter*, esp. p. 246.

43. On the divergence between the Brüning government's and the public's priorities see Udo Wengst, 'Heinrich Brüning und die 'konservative Alternative'. 'Kritische Anmerkungen zu neuen Thesen über die Endphase der Weimarer Republik', in *Aus Politik und Zeitgeschichte*, vol. B 50/80 (13 Dec. 1980), p. 24.

44. Turner, *German Big Business*, pp. 185–187, reports on a series of speeches by Nazi leaders (Funk, Feder, Wagener, and Strasser) in the Ruhr district from October to December 1931 on the party's view of economic issues. They were all very unspecific, but work creation and credit expansion were part of their message.

45. Knut Borchardt, 'Wirtschaftliche Ursachen des Scheiterns der Weimarer Republik', in K. Borchardt, *Wachstum*, p. 196. Borchardt, 'Zwangslagen', p. 176, note 67.

46. Walter G. Hoffman et al., *Das Wachstum der deutschen Wirtschaft, seit der Mitte des 19. Jahrhunderts* (Berlin, 1965), pp. 104, 826.

47. Allied Powers. Agent General for Reparation Payments, *Report of December 22, 1928* (Berlin, 1928), pp. 4–5. See also James W. Angell, *The Recovery of Germany* (New Haven, 1929).

48. Theo Balderston, 'The Origins of Economic Instability in Germany 1924–1930. Market Forces versus Economic Policy', in *Vierteljahrschrift für Sozial- und Wirtschaftsgeschichte*, 69 (1982), pp. 488–514, esp. p. 501. Jürgen von Kruedener, 'Die Überforderung der Weimarer Republik als Sozialstaat', in *Geschichte und Gesellschaft*, 11 (1985), pp. 358–376.

49. Holtfrerich, 'Zu hohe Löhne', pp. 122–141.

50. Hoffman et al., *Das Wachstum*, p. 258.

51. This corresponds to Balderston's finding that gross fixed investment in railways, public utilities and housebuilding which is highly sensitive to the state of the bond market 'fell as or more severely than gross fixed investment in industry'. Theo Balderston, 'Links between Inflation and Depression: German Capital and Labour Markets, 1924–31', in Feldman, *Nachwirkungen*, p. 165. For interest rate data see *Bevölkerung und Wirtschaft 1872–1972*, ed. by the Statistisches Bundesamt (Wiesbaden, 1972), p. 214.

52. Holtfrerich, 'Zu hohe Löhne', p. 131. Kruedener, 'Die Überforderung', p. 367.

53. See his diagrams 2 and 3 in Borchardt, 'Zwangslagen', pp. 175, 177.

54. Hoffman et al., *Das Wachstum*, pp. 87–88. Reiner Skiba, *Das westdeutsche Lohnniveau zwischen den beiden Weltkriegen und nach der Währungsreform* (Cologne, 1974), p. 186.

55. Borchardt, 'Zwangslagen', p. 179, note 76, saw the possibility for this kind of an alternative interpretation of the facts, but mentioned this important aspect only in a footnote, without further use of it.

56. Ernst Helmstädter, 'Die wirtschaftliche Lage am Jahresbeginn 1984 im Urteil des Sachverständigenrats', in H. Hanusch, K.W. Roskamp and J. Wiseman (eds.), *Public Sector and Political Economy Today. Essays in Honor of Horst Claus Recktenwald* (Stuttgart/New York, 1985), pp. 120–121.

57. Joseph A. Schumpeter, *Aufsätze zur Wirtschaftspolitik*, ed. by Wolfgang F. Stolper and Christian Seidl (Tübingen, 1985), p. 156.

58. Winkler, *Der Weg in die Katastrophe*, pp. 34–41, 730–731.

59. Akten der Reichskanzlei. Weimarer Republik, *Die Kabinette Brüning*, p. 1241.

60. Allied Powers. Agent General for Reparation Payments, *Report of December 22, 1928*, p. 161.

61. *Konjunkturstatistisches Handbuch 1933*, ed. by the Institut für Konjunkturforschung (Berlin, 1933), pp. 13, 15.

62. See the contemporary studies of the phenomenon in Karl Diehl (ed.), *Wirkungen und Ursachen des hohen Zinsfusses in Deutschland* (Jena, 1932). The greater importance of the high capital costs than labour costs is also emphasized by Richard Tilly, 'Bemerkungen zur Kontroverse über die Wirtschaftskrise der Weimarer Republik', in Hansjoachim Henning et al. (eds.), *Wirtschafts- und sozialgeschichtliche Forschungen und Probleme. Karl Erich Born zur Vollendung des 65. Lebensjahres* (St. Katharinen, 1987), pp. 347–374.

63. *Bevölkerung und Wirtschaft*, p. 142.

64. Schumpeter, *Aufsätze*, pp. 40, 45.
65. Cf. Harald Hagemann, 'Lohnsenkungen als Mittel der Krisenbekämpfung? *ü*berlegungen zum Beitrag der "Kieler Schule" in der beschäftigungspolitischen Diskussion am Ende der Weimarer Republik', in Harald Hagemann and H.D. Kurz (eds.), *Beschäftigung, Verteilung und Konjunktur. Zur politischen Ökonomik der modernen Gesellschaft. Festschrift für Adolph Lowe* (Bremen, 1984), pp. 97–129.
66. *Bevölkerung und Wirtschaft*, p. 142.
67. See Carl-Ludwig Holtfrerich, *The German Inflation 1914–1923. Causes and Effects in International Perspective* (Berlin, New York, 1986).
68. See also Tilly, *'Bemerkungen'*, pp. 348–357.

Dick Geary

Employers, Workers, and the Collapse of the Weimar Republic

Introduction

Traditional accounts of the Weimar Republic and its many problems begin with what might be described as a list of 'inherited' difficulties and structural weaknesses from its very inception: the stigma of Versailles and defeat, the burden of reparations, the survival of anti-republican elites in the army, bureaucracy and judiciary. Such problems were then compounded by the horrors of the inflation and hyperinflation, which led to declining living standards and obliterated the small savings of many Germans, who thus came to resent the new political order. Against the background of economic chaos and political upheaval it is scarcely surprising that there were a series of left-wing and communist insurrections between 1919 and 1923, as well as the Kapp (1920) and Beer Hall (1923) Putsches on the right, and the growth of separatist sentiments in parts of the Rhineland and Bavaria.

Yet the Weimar Republic survived these early crises, when the problems of defeat and reparations were at their most urgent. In fact, coalition governments held together in the mid-twenties in Germany when it came to dealing with the problems associated with the Treaty of Versailles. It was a very different issue which sabotaged coalition government once and for all in 1930, namely the issue of the level of unemployment benefits and how one was to fund them. Furthermore, the Republic collapsed in a *deflationary* crisis characterized by falling prices and mass unemployment, not in the period of inflation or hyperinflation. This suggests that at least part of an answer to the riddle of Weimar's demise is related to the differing experiences of inflation in the early twenties and depression in the early thirties. What is certainly true is that employer attitudes to both labour and the political structure of Weimar differed in the two quite distinct periods; whilst labour, which possessed a degree of industrial muscle and political strength in the early 1920s and was thus able to defend the Republic against the Kapp Putsch in 1920 through means of an almost total work stoppage throughout the Reich, was infinitely weaker and more seriously divided in the depression.

This is not to argue that either industry's increasingly hostile attitude to the political settlement or labour's impotence is the key to the overthrow of the Weimar Republic. It has been convincingly argued that the military and agrarian lobbies were much more influential in determining the trajectories of government between 1930 and 1933, when Hitler assumed the Chancellor's mantle.[1] It is also the case that it was the rural areas of Protestant Germany, not the industrial conurbations, which provided the Nazis with their greatest electoral triumphs (in percentage terms).[2] Moreover, even had German labour been united and even had it fought the Nazi takeover, it is doubtful that such resistance would have proved successful, as the tragic events of 1934 in Austria make clear: there a united and numerically powerful labour movement was destroyed by the combined forces of police, army, clerical conservatism and Austrian fascism. This said, however, the stability of political systems cannot be reduced to set formulae or mathematical calculations of some supposed balance of supporters and opponents of the regime. The alienation of some social groups creates a *climate* of crisis and instability, which may radicalize their social enemies. Thus the army of the unemployed did not itself turn to the Nazis; but its presence and the problems of its upkeep were instrumental in generating middle-class anxieties. Equally, the ability of the Weimar Republic to survive the immediate post-war crisis rested to some extent on the willingness of employers to tolerate the new state and a degree of admittedly transitory cooperation between capital and labour. What follows, therefore, is an attempt to identify the attitudes of workers and their employers towards the Weimar Republic and ask why sections of both groups were prepared to countenance its destruction.

Employers

That there exists some connection between the interests of big business, the collapse of the Weimar Republic and the rise of Hitler has been an article of faith for many. After all, the industrial magnate Fritz Thyssen was prepared to admit that 'I paid Hitler';[3] and many giant firms such as Krupp and I G Farben were the beneficiaries of Nazi government after 1933. Although East German historians are prepared to concede that it is dangerous to generalize about big business as a whole and are prepared to recognize that some sections of industry were more closely connected to the Nazi movement than others, they nonetheless continue to argue that there did exist an intimate relationship between the rise of Nazism and the machinations of the business community. Above all they see declining heavy industry, experiencing a crisis of profitability, as more likely to listen to Hitler and his cronies than the dynamic, export-oriented sectors, such as electricals and chemicals.[4]

Both the idea that industry played a major role in financing the National Socialist German Workers' Party (NSDAP) and the contention that the differing behaviour of industrialists can be derived from simple differences of economic interest have come under sustained attack in the West, especially from the American historian Henry Ashby Turner.[5] Firstly, Turner has demonstrated that the Nazi Party was capable of funding itself from a wide-range of agitational activities and services. It did not *need* the financial support of big business. Secondly, the number of industrialists who actually joined the Nazi movement was small and the *temporary* membership of lead-

ing figures such as Emil Kirdorf was no more typical than
the more systematic support of Fritz Thyssen. Where firms
did give money to the Nazis, as in the case of the Flick concern,
they did so not because they were committed to the cause
but as a form of political insurance; for such firms tended
to distribute funds to all the bourgeois political parties, and
in fact more of such funds found their way to the German
People's Party (DVP) or the German National People's Party
(DNVP) than to the Nazis. Big business was less influential
in the removal of Brüning in 1932 or of von Papen as Chancellor in the same year than other actors; and the decision to
appoint Hitler as Chancellor was, according to Turner,
Papen's own and not one dictated by industry. Finally, no
clear-cut correlation existed between support for Hitler and
sectoral interests, not least because the high degree of both
vertical and horizontal cartelization of German industry ren-
ders nonsensical attempts to distinguish between different sectors. In any case there were heavy industrialists who retained
their distance to Nazism, whilst some leading figures in the
supposedly more liberal electrical and chemical industries *can*
be found distributing funds to at least some figures in the
NSDAP.

Most Western historians would agree with many of the
above points. But they do not tell the whole story. Although
industrial contributions to Nazi funds may have been made
with reservations, they were contributions nonetheless and
scarcely demonstrate a faith in the democratic order. Secondly,
it is possible to list a not inconsiderable number of
businessmen who did establish contact with various National-
Socialist organizations or individuals. In any case, there is
no obvious answer to the question: what constituted *typical*
behaviour on the part of industrialists? As the West German
historian Dirk Stegmann has pointed out,[6] it is simply not
possible to argue from the behaviour of some *individual*
employers that the conduct of different sectors of industry
is amenable to no general or structural arguments. *In general*,
there is evidence to suggest that the chemical and electrical
industries, together with some firms in processing and finishing in engineering, were more willing to collaborate with organized labour and work within the constraints of the Weimar

political system than certain other branches of industry. For example, the German Democratic Party (DDP), which emerged after the 1918 revolution as *the* bourgeois party committed to the survival of the Republic, received early funding from the Siemens electrical firm. Carl Duisberg of the chemical giant IG Farben was a firm supporter of democratic values and advocated compromise between capital and labour, as did Hermann Bücher of AEG. In 1926, when Paul Silverberg, head of the national industrial pressure group, the *Reichsverband der deutschen Industrie* (RDI), advocated the necessity of collaboration with Social Democrats, his speech was denounced by many industrialists but supported by leading figures in chemicals, electricals and engineering, by men such as Duisberg, Hans von Raumer, and Siemens. These same groups attempted to revive that collaboration which had existed between capital and labour in the early years of Weimar in the shape of the *Zentralarbeitsgemeinschaft* (ZAG) in 1930, an attempt sabotaged by the opposition of heavy industrial interests. In general the dynamic chemical, electrical and finishing industries remained more loyal to Heinrich Brüning, Chancellor from 1930 to mid-1932, than did heavy industry. Committed to international reconciliation to protect their exports and low prices for basic materials these sectors were less willing to cooperate with the agrarian lobby and bitterly opposed to agricultural protection.

The *relative* tolerance and openness of the branches of industry described above is fairly easy to explain. They remained quite prosperous when the rest of the Weimar economy was experiencing serious difficulties. The machine industry, but especially chemicals and electricals, were remarkably buoyant, in the latter case even until 1931. Their stance on international collaboration and hostility to protectionism obviously reflected their dependence on export markets; whilst the high level of profitability of these firms enabled them to be conciliatory in wage negotiations. Furthermore, labour costs were of less concern to chemical and electrical employers than to those in coal, iron and steel. Whereas labour costs in the chemical industry constituted a mere 15 per cent of total costs in 1927, the comparable figure for coal-mining was over 50 per cent. Hence the greater freedom of manœuvre of business in the former sector. The situation of heavy industry was much more dire; and to this we will return below.

If some differences of behaviour can be detected between the various branches of industry, it is also the case that industry's attitude(s) towards the institutions of the Weimar Republic changed over time. What follows, therefore, is an attempt to examine the evolution of those attitudes; and here the central concern will not be 'which or how many industrialists supported the Nazis?', but, to my mind, the more significant question, 'what was the relationship between industry and *the Weimar Republic?*'; for even if most businessmen did not welcome Hitler as Chancellor, many were prepared to tolerate a coalition-government which included him. Above all, many industrialists had come to the conclusion in the early 1930s that the institutions of Weimar had to be eradicated if German business was to see a return of profitability and success.

In the early years of the Weimar Republic German industry did reveal a certain degree of willingness to go along with the new institutional relationships and engage in some degree of cooperation with organized labour. At this stage it would certainly be incorrect to assume that businessmen rejected Weimar on ideological grounds; and it is probably true, as Turner has argued, that they were indifferent to specific constitutional arrangements. During the Kapp Putsch of 1920, for example, industry did not side with the counter-revolutionaries, though it did display a marked degree of apathy on the question of the Republic's survival. Between 1918 and 1922 there was an unprecedented degree of cooperation between trade-union leaders and representatives of the business community, which was all the more remarkable given the authoritarian attitudes of employers in the days of the Second Reich. In 1918 during the revolutionary upheavals Carl Legien, leader of the Free (social-democratic) Trade Unions, and the industrial tycoon Hugo Stinnes, spokesman of business interests, drew up an agreement which involved recognition of the unions, a shorter working-day, and an undertaking on the part of employers to disband the so-called 'yellow' (i.e. company) unions. This cooperation was further cemented in the *Zentralarbeitsgemeinschaft*, a forum of trade-union and employer discussion to try and agree common objectives. It is on the basis of such developments that the controversial American historian David Abraham has argued that the stability of Weimar to the late 1920s was predicated on an alliance between organized labour and the more conciliatory branches (dynamic, export-oriented, capital-intensive) of industry.[7] This alliance, he believes, remained characteristic of the mid- as well as the early- 1920s; and there is some evidence that more progressive elements of industry played an important role in the representation of business interests between 1925 and 1930. Duisberg became head of the RDI in 1925, whose leadership also included Hermann Bücher of the electrical industry. In the wake of these developments the more reactionary heavy industrialists of the Ruhr believed that the organization had been hijacked by 'Berlin political types'. It is also true that the *Reichsverband der deutschen Industrie* launched no full-scale attack upon the welfare and social policies of Weimar politicians before 1930. But this somewhat rosy view of industry's role requires serious qualification.

Firstly, the apparent collaboration between capital and labour in the immediate post-war years did not appeal to large numbers of workers, who, as we will see, deserted Social Democracy and moderate unionism for the Communist Party (KPD), left-communism or anarcho-syndicalism long before the onset of depression in 1929. The largest German trade union, that of the metalworkers (DMV) had deserted the *Zentralarbeitsgemeinschaft* by 1920. Equally, the Stinnes-Legien agreement and the willingness of industry to engage in negotiation with labour in the same years was predicated upon a set of very particular circumstances. Business in these years enjoyed a quite spectacular profitability, generated by the inflation, which effectively reduced labour costs and enabled debts from previous investment to be written off very rapidly. The international devaluation of the mark made German goods cheap on foreign markets and foreign goods dear within the Reich. Thus, to return to a point made in the introduction, the years of inflation were no disaster for many German industrialists, some of whom, such as Stinnes, actually encouraged the Reichsbank in its inflationary increase in the issue of money and credits. In such a conjuncture employers could afford some degree of latitude in their dealings with trade unions and wage negotiations. Furthermore collaboration between capital and labour in the early years of the Weimar Republic was facilitated by industry's fear that something far more disastrous than welfare reform, namely outright revolution, might confront it in the absence of compromise. Thus the Stinnes-Legien agreement and the construction of the ZAG were not necessarily a reflection of a genuine desertion of anti-labour values on the part of German industry, but rather a matter of pressing expediency. Thus Stinnes himself described the role of cooperation as creating a 'breathing-space'; whilst Jakob Wilhelm Reichert, director of the Association of German Iron and Steel Industrialists, declared that the issue confronting his members was 'How can we save industry?'.[8] That industrial cooperation with the Weimar Republic and the new influence it bestowed upon both trade unions and the German Social Democratic Party (SPD) was conditional at best and invariably fragile is further indicated in a programme drawn up as early as 1922 by the RDI: for this looked forward to a reduction in taxation, social security provision and wages, embodied in the Weimar settlement, and above all the destruction of the statutory eight-hour working day. Even if Weimar industrialists were prepared to accept equal 'political' rights for all, they continued to believe that the running of the economy should be left to 'die Wirtschaft', i.e. themselves; and as soon as the threat of revolution and the inflationary boom of 1919 to 1922 were past, some sections of the business community were already concerned to eradicate the gains of labour.

By 1924 industrialists had driven a massive hole through the eight-hour day legislation. The so-called stabilization crisis of 1923/4 saw employers exploit the onset of large-scale unemployment to dismiss communists from their plants. In the mid-1920s the yellow (company) unions were resurrected by some of the larger employers in defiance of earlier agreements; and Abraham's contention that a 'progressive' fraction of capital was in the ascendant until the late 1920s is more than a little misleading. As the German historian Bernd Weisbrod has argued,[9] even when men such as Duisberg played a leading role in the *Reichsverband*, the coal, iron and steel interests of the Ruhr exercised something resembling a 'power of veto' over industrial policy. Thus the high cartelized prices of German coal and steel producers were protected in a number of trade agreements, to the detriment of processing and finishing industries. Thus Silverberg's advocacy of reconciliation with the SPD in 1926 encountered widespread resistance, not only from heavy industry in the shape of the *Langnamverein* (the 'Association for Furthering the Joint Economic Interests of the Rhineland and Westphalia'), but also from industrial organizations in Saxony, Hannover and Bavaria. And attempts to revive the *Zentralarbeitsgemeinschaft* in 1930 were also sabotaged by opposition from the same lobby.

Even if German industrialists were relatively indifferent to details of the political constitution, there were certain aspects of the Weimar Republic which confronted them with a challenge utterly different to anything they had witnessed before 1914, when they largely refused to recognize trade unions and when the state adopted an essentially hostile stance towards the organizations of labour. Genuinely democratic government at national and local level meant that Social Democrats now had an influence on the determination of policy; and a consequence of this was that the Weimar Republic became a welfare as well as a democratic state. Pensions, illness and accident benefits were increased, as was the range of potential beneficiaries. A new system of unemployment insurance benefits came into existence. Local authorities built parks, stadiums, swimming pools and, most important of all, council houses for the benefit of the less privileged sections of the community. There were also radical alterations in the labour law, which restricted the length of the working day, forced firms to take on invalids and demobilized soldiers, decreed that workers could not be dismissed on the grounds of sex, religion or politics, and made the dismissal of over 50 workers at any one time subject to official approval. Dismissals also had to be negotiated with a 'factory council', an institution established by law in all large firms in 1920 which gave employees some say on working conditions within their individual factories. In addition a system of legally binding collective wage agreements, trade union recognition, and state arbitration in industrial disputes, which at least until 1928 seems to have benefitted labour, or at least its less-skilled sections, robbed employers of their previous dominance in the labour market.

It was these aspects of Weimar, rather than political principle or innate conservatism, which so infuriated many German industrialists and which the RDI's plan of 1922 already sought to remove. For welfare legislation meant welfare *taxation* and taxation on wealth that had remained more or less untouched before the First World War. Employers believed that state arbitration led to artificially high 'political wages', that management should be left free to manage, and that what was being imposed on them was nothing less than a 'trade-union state' *(Gewerkschaftsstaat)*. Whether rightly or wrongly, therefore, problems of profitability and competitiveness were blamed on labour and in particular on the political structure which conferred such influence upon trade unions and Social Democrats. The extent of industrial hostility to these arrangements varied from time to time. As we have already seen, threatened by revolution and buoyed by an inflationary boom, industry could tolerate a degree of welfare reform in the early 1920s. Thereafter the situation changed; and it changed above all for heavy industry.

We have noted earlier that heavy industry disapproved of Silverberg's call for collaboration with Social Democrats in 1926 and undermined attempts to revive the ZAG in 1930. In 1925 Jakob Reichert of the iron and steel industry, supported by Ernst von Borsig, locomotive manufacturer and head of the uncompromising Employers' Association, and Fritz Thyssen, subsequently head of the giant United Steelworks concern, called for rule by Presidential decree rather than parliamentary majority. In 1928 the iron and steel industrialists of the Ruhr became involved in an industrial dispute, the *Ruhreisenstreit*, in which they locked out about 250,000 workers. Their intention in this struggle was not simply to win a particular battle over wages but to challenge the whole Weimar system of state arbitration and collective wage agreements, as several of them were not loathe to confess. The collapse of coalition government in 1930 on the issue of unemployment benefits was not simply a consequence of the pressure of trade unions and radical Social Democrats on the leadership of the SPD but also of the pressure that the heavy industrial lobby exercised within the DVP. It was also heavy industry, together with smaller concerns in Saxony, that believed Chancellor Brüning too hesitant in dismantling welfare taxation and labour legislation in 1932, and who were horrified by General Schleicher's schemes for reflationary collaboration with the unions in the later part of the same year.

The less tolerant and uncooperative stance of at least some, though by no means all, representatives of heavy industry in the Weimar Republic is not difficult to understand. As explained above, coal, iron and steel were especially sensitive to labour costs; and by the mid-1920s they were already experiencing a crisis of profitability. The territorial losses imposed by the peace settlement of 1919, in particular the loss of Alsace-Lorraine, meant a decreased base of raw materials, which now had to be purchased abroad and at much greater cost. As a result these industries sought salvation in protection, cartelization and high prices. Hence their disinterest in international collaboration and their hostility to trade treaties. The loss of international markets, economic rationalization – amalgamation, concentration, the use of new technology in the mid-1920s – and a consequent sharp rise in productivity proved to be a fatal combination; for it meant that these sectors worked well below their capacity. German steel works produced at just 60 per cent of their capacity in 1925, 77 per cent in the peak year of 1927 and 55 per cent in 1930. Such overcapacity became a disaster in the years of depression. Thus coal, iron, and steel could not afford to buy industrial peace and claimed – whether correctly or incorrectly is a subject of debate in the earlier part of this volume – that high wages and welfare taxation were ruining them. Hence the temptation to blame the Weimar system of labour relations rather than their price-inflexibility and raw material costs for their difficulties; and hence their desire from 1930 at the latest to see the labour law and welfare legislation of the Republic swept aside. Of course, to grant Turner's point, not all of those associated with 'heavy industry' were radically anti-Republican. Krupp, who controlled a huge vertical empire which embraced locomotive and sewing-machine manufacture as well as the production of coal, iron and steel, was not happy about confrontation with the arbitration authorities in the 1928 lock-out; Otto Wolff, with interests in coal and steel, advocated cooperation with the trade unions; and Paul Silverberg, whose objective appears to have been the generation of mass support for industrial policies (via the SPD in 1926, and via the Chancellor Schleicher and the Nazi Gregor Strasser in 1932), also admonished his colleagues to cooperation with labour organization in his controversial 1926 speech. Significantly Silverberg had interests not only in coal and lignite production but also large scale electricity generation; and he often acted as mediator between the heavy and the finishing industries. So not all of heavy industry was unwilling to compromise; whilst some other branches of industry were at least until the 1930s willing to tolerate the Weimar settlement, as we have seen. But as time passed and the economic situation became ever more desperate it was the less progressive groups of capital which came into the ascendancy. In 1930 a series of organisational changes in the *Reichsverband der deutschen Industrie* increased the representation of heavy industrial interests and in the following year the headship of that organization passed from Duisberg to Krupp. In the depression, industry in general became more critical of the Weimar Republic. Even Duisberg declared in January 1930 that 'capital is being destroyed through the unproductive use of public funds ... Only a radical reversal in state policies can help ...';[10] and although the electrical and chemical industries were not opposed to some degree of reflation in 1932, they were more than a little disturbed by Schleicher's courting of the 'left' Nazis, such as Strasser, and the Free Trade Unions.

From 1928 one can detect a radicalization of the industrial critique of Weimar. In that year the attempt to settle the reparations question through the Young Plan, the electoral success of the SPD, which again entered government, a series of arbitration settlements viewed as favourable to labour, and the fact that the state had supported locked-out steel workers during the *Ruhreisenstreit*, all seemed to confirm Weimar as a 'tool' of trade-union interests. The call for an end to 'cold socialization', of the exclusion of Marxists – by which Social

Democrats and trade-unionists rather than Communists was meant – from government and influence increased in intensity. A few industrialists such as Thyssen joined the NSDAP. Others – Paul Reusch, managing director of the *Gutehoff-nungshütte*, Fritz Springorum of Hoesch iron and steel, Albert Voegler and Ernst Poensgen, a representative of steel interests, deserted to the ultra-nationalist Harzburg Front. More commonly industrialists desired some 'bourgeois bloc' to govern, initially without the Nazis, whose economic policies were viewed with more than a little suspicion. Yet the fragmentation of the innumerable bourgeois parties and the electoral triumphs of the Nazis between 1930 and 1932 made the hope of an anti-socialist bloc *without the NSDAP* sheer fantasy. Thus in March 1932 Springorum argued that a 'rightist government is possible only with the cooperation of the NSDAP'.[11] By this time Hitler and Göring were making serious attempts to woo the industrial lobby through the good offices of Thyssen, Hjalmar Schacht, the banker, and Wilhelm Keppler, a key liaison figure between the Nazi Party and big business. In 1932 the more liberal factions of industry continued to support the Chancellor Heinrich Brüning, although Saxon and Ruhr industrial interests were less pleased with his record, as the mechanisms of state arbitration and some degree of welfare reform still remained on the statute book. The more aggressive anti-labour stand of Brüning's successor Franz von Papen, reflected in severe wage reductions and a cut-back in welfare expenditure, also generated some degree of satisfaction in industrial circles. On the other hand von Papen's fall, primarily dictated by agrarian interests, brought into the Chancellor's office General von Schleicher, who embarked upon a strategy which most of industry saw as a threat: cooperation with the Free Trade Unions and 'left' Nazis, an ambitious reflationary programme of job-creation and the intent to reintroduce some of the labour legislation abolished by his predecessor. These policies regenerated industrial support for von Papen; but von Papen was unable to form a parliamentary majority without the Nazis. A point had been reached whereby a bourgeois bloc including the Nazis could be envisaged as the road by which the hated welfare legislation and constraining labour law could be removed. Such a coalition may not have been the first preference of most industrialists. Many believed Hitler would prove malleable, especially after the Nazis lost two million votes in the second (November) Reichstag elections of 1932 and when an internal crisis began to grip the NSDAP. Yet the important point is that by 1933 industry wanted rid of the Weimar Republic.

As stated in my introduction, industrial interests were less prominent than others in the removal of Brüning from office. The same applies to von Papen's fall later in 1932. It is also clear that big business was far less enamoured of the Nazis than were smaller employers, who often combined virulent anti-socialism with a marked hostility to competition from their larger rivals. Yet industrial interests did play a role in undermining coalition government through the DVP in 1930; whilst the more general hostility of business to an integral part of the Weimar system, namely the labour law and welfare legislation, was one amongst many factors that deprived the Republic of legitimacy. Had capital and labour united in support of the political order, it would certainly have been in a better position to survive.

Workers

In 1920 the German working class downed tools virtually to a man to defend the new Republic against the Kapp Putsch. Throughout its brief history the Weimar Republic found its most loyal support from the Social Democratic Party, which recruited primarily from the ranks of workers, and the labour wing of the Catholic Centre Party, especially the Christian Trade Unions, which played a major role in the introduction of the welfare legislation described above. This is scarcely surprising, given the new role that democratic government conferred upon the SPD, previously excluded from power, and the fact that industrial workers were the main beneficiaries of changes in the labour law. Furthermore the evidence that industrial workers turned to the Nazis far less readily than middle-class or rural Germans is overwhelming.

Contemporary commentators often believed that a significant section of the German working class, especially the

younger unemployed, flocked into the ranks of Nazi supporters. There is certainly a crude correlation between the
rise in the Nazi vote and the onset of mass unemployment
in the depression. Some of the greatest electoral successes
of the Nazis in urban Germany were in areas of high working-
class unemployment, such as the textile and engineering centre
of Chemnitz-Zwickau in Saxony and the shoe-making town
of Pirmasens in the Palatinate. Certainly the organization of
Nazi stormtroopers, the *Sturmabteilung*, recruited significantly from the unemployed, as both contemporary accounts
and recent research have demonstrated. These points need
to be noted, but they also need to be treated with caution;
for an analysis of various indices of working-class allegiance
suggests a very different picture.

Elections to factory council elections and trade-union membership figures suggest that Nazi penetration of the industrial
working class was none too great. The overall results of factory council (*Betriebsrat*) elections held throughout Germany
in 1931 produced 115,671 Free (socialist) Trade Union
representatives, 10,956 representatives from the Christian
(mainly Catholic) Unions, and 4,664 from the Communist
opposition. Only 710 representatives of the Nazi factory cell
organization (NSBO) secured election. In the Ruhr the NSBO
mobilized under four per cent of the factory-council electorate
and did especially badly in coal-mining and metalwork. Only
amongst rural labourers did Nazi success achieve anything
resembling respectability. Significantly the NSBO performed
better in elections to the white-collar *Angestelltenräte* than
in those to the blue-collar *Arbeiterräte*. NSBO membership
was also puny in comparison to that of the socialist and Catholic unions. In January 1933 the Nazi factory cell organization
had some 300,000 members, many of whom were white-
collar employees. In comparison the communist *Revolution-
äire Gewerkschafts opposition* (RGO) had 250,000 members; but we know that most KPD supporters remained in
the Free Trade Unions. These latter unions could count no
fewer than 4,000,000 members, whilst the Christian Trade
Unions had a membership of around 1,000,000.

Analysis of party membership confirms that the 'typical'
Nazi was not an industrial worker. Whereas approximately

90 per cent of Communist Party membership and over 60 per cent of SPD membership were recruited from manual workers, the equivalent figure for the NSDAP in January 1933 was approximately 30 per cent, of whom most came from rural or small-town crafts, rather than the industrial centres, and few of whom were unemployed. (Here there seems to be a clear difference between the more 'proletarian' and radical SA and the Nazi Party.) Even these figures need to be treated with caution, however. Many of these workers came from families higher up the social scale; for the depression was characterized by high levels of *downward* social mobility. Some of the youngsters sheltering in the SA hostels (*Jugendheime*) in Frankfurt had come into the towns from the countryside; whilst many Nazi apprentices came from non-proletarian backgrounds. Nor are Nazi accounts of their support to be trusted. A non-party source commented in 1930 that of the supposed 48 per cent working-class NSDAP membership in Düsseldorf, 34 per cent of total membership were in fact artisans and only 14 per cent were industrial workers.[12] Clearly industrial workers were underrepresented in Nazi Party membership, something less true of white-collar workers: only four per cent of KPD members and 10 per cent of SPD members came from the white-collar group, whereas the figure for the Nazi Party rises to 24 per cent.

Factory-council elections, trade-union membership, and party membership all point in a similar direction, therefore: the Nazis had only limited success amongst the industrial working class. What of electoral support? It is well known that the highest levels of electoral support secured by the NSDAP came from the rural areas of Protestant Germany. In Catholic areas and in the industrial conurbations the Nazis performed far less well. The more industrial the town, the less impressive the result. In the first (July) elections of 1932, for example, the Nazi vote peaked at 37.4 per cent of all votes cast in the Reich, but reached only some ten percentage points lower in the Ruhr. The more working-class the neighbourhood, the lower the working-class Nazi vote, which reached some 25 per cent in such neighbourhoods in the elections of July 1932, again well below the national average.

That 25 per cent does of course represent a not insignificant number of voters; but it would be wrong to conclude that those voters were 'workers' just because they lived in 'working-class' districts. For in such neighbourhoods were to be found shopkeepers, small businessmen, small masters of the metal industry, caterers, landlords. Thus it has been calculated that in one supposedly working-class and 'red' district of Altona, no fewer than 40 per cent of the residents could be classified as 'lower-middle-class'.

None of this is meant to say that the Nazis made no headway in recruiting working class support; but they were more likely to do it in areas of artisan or domestic production (Pirmasens in the Palatinate and Plauen in Saxony) rather than heavy industry (the Ruhr) or engineering (Berlin, parts of Saxony). They were more successful in rural areas and small provincial towns than the big cities; and had a marked degree of success with rural labourers, one of the few groups which seemed to have switched support from the KPD to the NSDAP and *vice versa*. A significant percentage of the female electorate also gave its support to the Nazis by 1932. These groups had one thing in common: they had no strong traditions of prior trade-union or socialist mobilization. In a sense, therefore, the Nazis could enter a political vacuum, which was not to be found in the largest cities – the centres of trade-union, social-democratic and communist organization.

It is important to realize that workers in craft and domestic industry were far from marginal to the German labour force of the early 1930s. Something like a third of the industrial labour force was self-employed or worked in firms of five employees or fewer. Cottage production remained common in parts of the textile trade (especially in Saxony), leather goods, instrument and toy manufacture, and the Pirmasens shoe-making industry. Furthermore, over 50 per cent of all registered as 'workers' in the occupational census of 1925 lived in small towns or villages of under 10,000 inhabitants. Here then there existed real potential for Nazi action; and this explains why the Nazis could mobilize a fair degree of working-class support without denting the combined socialist and communist vote in the big cities. In fact throughout the Reich that combined vote remained more or less constant at around 30 per cent of the electorate, thus suggesting that Nazi support came from elsewhere. As the recent statistical studies of Jürgen Falter have revealed, some Social Democrats (more often than Communist voters) do seem to have deserted to the Nazis;[13] but most who left the SPD turned to the KPD, as did those Catholic industrial workers who abandoned the Centre Party.

A further factor made the expansion of Nazi support possible in working-class areas without denting that of the traditional parties of labour. In some districts of Essen and Berlin that produced a relatively high working-class Nazi vote there lived workers who had voted National Liberal before the First World War and Nationalist (DNVP) immediately thereafter. This German equivalent of the 'working-class Tory' was likely to be resident in company housing, belong to a 'yellow' union, and work for a firm, such as Krupp, with a strong paternalistic tradition. Such workers had usually been beyond the reach of socialists and could convert to Nazism with relatively little difficulty.

A final comment on the electoral statistics: recent research has shown the contention that the unemployed, or at least the manual unemployed, rallied to the Nazi banner to be utterly mythical. Unemployment was overwhelmingly concentrated in the large cities of over 100,000 inhabitants, i.e. precisely where the Nazis did least well. Those places where the NSDAP gained working-class support, as in provincial towns and rural areas, experienced low levels of unemployment. My own work on the Ruhr towns of Bochum and Herne, and above all the research of Falter indicates that the manual unemployed were the least likely group in German society (with the exception of Catholics) to vote for Hitler. What the manual unemployed did was to turn to the Communist Party, whose vote climbed to almost six million in the November election of 1932.

When Hitler became Chancellor in late January 1933 he thus confronted an essentially hostile working class, something that can be understood in terms of the lack of appeal of certain aspects of Nazi propaganda: support for agricultural protection and thus higher food prices, together with support for wage reductions and welfare cuts, already practised in the states of Thuringia and Brunswick, where the Nazis exercized local power before the 'seizure of power', scarcely appealed to urban consumers. Within the ranks of organized labour Nazis were often seen as, and indeed sometimes were used as, strike-breakers. In theory therefore the working class which had defended the Republic against the Kapp Putsch in 1920 might have been expected to present something of a thorn in the new Chancellor's side. After all, the combined SPD/KPD vote in the Reichstag elections of November 1932 had been higher than that achieved by the NSDAP. At the same time the *Reichsbanner*, a republican paramilitary organization recruiting primarily though not exclusively Social Democrats, outnumbered the SA by a fair margin. We also know that there was considerable pressure from the rank and file of that organization to resist the so-called Papen coup of mid-1932, when the Chancellor ousted the coalition SPD-Centre Party government of Prussia. This raises, therefore, a somewhat hackneyed though still important question: why was the numerically powerful and densely organized German labour movement to prove so impotent when its greatest enemy came to power?

A standard and legitimate response to the question identifies the division between Communists and Social Democrats as a crucial factor in weakening the working-class response to fascism. The two parties seemed to spend as much time feuding with one another as fighting the Nazi menace; and above all the German Communist Party adopted a policy that was frankly suicidal. After Ernst Thälmann became leader of the KPD in 1925 the party underwent a process of Stalinization which resulted in the disillusionment or expulsion of many comrades. Increasingly the organization lost its independence and became subject to direction from Moscow. Internal party debate was thus stifled, rendering the KPD less capable of reflection and sensitivity to specifically German problems. In particular the KPD received instructions in 1927/8 to abandon collaboration with Social Democrats; and for most of the next five years the party was to display an open hostility to the major party of the German working-class, now dubbed 'social-fascist'. In 1927 the Chinese Communist Party, which had previously collaborated with the Kuomintang on Stalin's instruction, was destroyed by its former ally, giving cause for concern about 'united front' tactics. At the same time as a radicalization of Russian domestic policy associated with party purges, the abandonment of the New Economic Policy, and the drive against the kulaks, the Comintern adopted an equally radical stance on the international scene, declaring that the temporary period of capitalist stabilisation was now at an end and that the collapse of capitalism was imminent. Under these conditions of the so-called 'third period', revolution reappeared on the agenda; and both fascism and social democracy were decried as agents of the bourgeoisie in a last-ditch attempt to defend the existing capitalist order. According to this analysis capitalism was about to collapse and fascism could not save it. Thus the fascist threat was not to be exaggerated, as Thälmann was still saying in 1931. Only the work of moderate socialists in misleading workers away from the socialist revolution might stave off the glorious dawn of proletarian dictatorship. Thus Social Democrats became 'social-fascists', props of the system, and the first task of the Communist Party was to be the unmasking of SPD policies. The KPD was to conquer the German working class *against* the SPD and the old trade-union organization. Then one could deal with fascism.

It is painfully obvious that such a strategy woefully underestimated the threat of Nazism, helped to divide the labour movement and undermined support for the Weimar Republic within the German working class. There were even cases where Communists and Nazis collaborated, as in a referendum to remove the SPD government in Prussia and the infamous Berlin transport workers strike of autumn 1932. This last event, however, has all too often been misunderstood by commentators: the original strike committee included Social Democrats as well as Communists, and Nazi transport workers only agreed to join the action very late in the day. It is moreover the case that the KPD became to some extent obsessed with maintaining its own constituency rather than extending its appeal to new groups and became enmeshed in a *Lagermentalität*. The above, however, is only part of the story. In the first place it was Communists who bore the brunt of the street-fighting against the Nazis, and this with a great deal of success before the Papen coup of 1932, after which police intervened more regularly to aid the Nazis. Secondly it is all too easy to exaggerate the bureaucratic inflexibility of the KPD, which did develop new strategies based on women, youth and the unemployed in the neighbourhoods. In 1932 the Communist Party became somewhat less committed to the 'social-fascist' line; and there were some places where young Communists and Social Democrats cooperated in anti-fascist actions on a local level. Most important of all, one has to realise that unlike the case in Britain or France, where the denunciation of fellow Socialists appears to have worked against the Communist parties, the KPD was at its most popular precisely when at its most radical. The 'social-fascist' argument therefore was not simply a foreign import but struck chords amongst at least some sections of German working class; and it might even be argued that had German Communism been less critical of Weimar more workers might have deserted to the Nazis. Significantly the 'social-fascist' line made headway inside the Reich not immediately after it was propounded in Moscow but after the events of May Day 1929 in Berlin. On that day a communist demonstration which had been forbidden by the social-democratic police chief Karl Zörgiebel nonetheless assembled and was attacked by the police, leading to four days of fighting in some 'red' districts of Berlin and a number of deaths. This was far from the only time when representatives of the SPD sent police, troops or *Freikorps* against left-wing demonstrations; for they had done such on several occasions when in national government between 1918 and 1923. In Prussia Communists were dismissed from public office by SPD ministers; whilst the Free Trade Unions also mounted an anti-communist campaign during the depression. It was thus *mutual* hostility which split the German labour movement. The fact that the SPD 'tolerated' the deflationary economic policies of Brüning, refused to adopt a reflationary package of job-creation proposed by the unions in 1932, and had condoned economic rationalization in the mid-1920s, even sending a delegation to the USA to marvel at the wonders of Fordism, further fuelled the KPD's claim that the SPD was indeed a prop of the prevailing system.

Also worthy of note is the fact that the KPD was not alone in underestimating the staying-power of Hitler and his henchmen: the Free Trade Unions, the Catholic labour movement and the SPD were all to some extent guilty of the same mistaken judgement. Thus the newspaper of both the national party and of the Berlin branch of Social Democracy (*Vorwärts*) on 1 January 1933 wished its readers a 'Happy New Year', and with an eye on Nazi electoral losses in November 1932, declared that the fascist threat was on the wane. Thirty days later Hitler became Chancellor! To a certain extent the Social Democratic Party fell victim to its own fatalistic optimism, which declared that ultimately victory would come to it. Thus the reaction of the SPD leadership to the Papen coup of 1932 was to advocate no immediate action. Rather the membership was to wait for the next parliamentary elections to rectify the situation. The Party was further constrained by its commitment to constitutionalism (unlike Kapp, Hitler did not seize power in an unconstitutional coup); by its 'organizational fetishism' which put the preservation of the party above all else; and by the fact that the Free Trade Unions could not be expected to back any kind of adventurism. If anything the trade-union leaders were even more fetishistic about organizational survival: in January 1933 Theodor Leipart, Legien's successor as the chairman of the Confederation of Free Trade Unions, declared that 'organization, not demonstration, is the word of the hour'.[14] It is also clear that leading Social Democrats shared a humanitarian philosophy which feared the shedding of blood and also the prospect of a civil war which would probably end in disastrous defeat. Thus neither wing of the German labour movement was prepared for the blow which struck it after January 1933.

The paralysis and division which enveloped the organized working class in Germany in the early 1930s was not, however, simply a consequence of competing political ideologies and organizations. Indeed those latter divisions and the general demobilization of the German working class were equally a function of the most profound disaster of all, namely the depression. The Kapp Putsch's defeat of 1920 at the hands of a working-class general strike was made possible by the fact of full employment in the inflationary boom. The strikes and aggressiveness of labour organization were based upon a position of strength in the labour market and new-found political representation. Admittedly the massive upheavals of late 1923 were related to the onset of mass unemployment, hyperinflation and the Ruhr occupation. But the workers involved were acting at the end of over three years of more or less continuous employment. They came, moreover, from many sections of the working class: skilled and unskilled, employed and unemployed. At this point in time boundaries between the many working-class political groups were fluid and not related too closely to economic and social cleavages. By the early 1930s the situation was quite different: strikes were few and far between, the demonstrations of the unemployed smaller and less dangerous. This emerges quite clearly from a systematic study of police reports on the unemployed in the Ruhr in 1923 on the one hand and the depression on the other.[15] Tens of thousands stormed town halls day in day out in 1923 and the police chiefs despaired of the survival of the social order. In the early 1930s the mood of police officials was quite different, for they believed the unemployed were difficult to get out onto the streets and that they (the police) had the situation in hand. The demonstrations of 1929 were smaller and less frequent than those of 1923, those of 1931 and 1932 smaller still. The key to this lies in the depression. The depression robbed labour of its industrial muscle; it compounded the division between Social Democrats and Communists, which increasingly became a social as well as a political divide; it set worker against worker, the employed against the unemployed; and it demoralized many of those without work.

In order to understand the impact of the economic crisis of 1929 to 1933 it is above all necessary to realize just how catastrophic the depression was. The number of officially registered unemployed reached over 6 million, i.e. approximately one third of the total labour force, in April 1932, the nadir of the German slump. According to the trade unions the real figure was at least seven million; and some recent research suggests that by the time the young, women, casual and seasonal workers are included, the number of unemployed may have hit nine million! In some traditional centres of union and political militancy levels of unemployment were even higher in the winter of 1931/2: 60 per cent in metalwork and a gruesome 90 per cent in the building trade. A further 25 per cent of trade-unionists were working short-time in the same period. The consequences of such distress are obvious: those without jobs lost the ability to take industrial action. That is why the KPD, over 80 per cent of whose membership was unemployed in 1932, had to develop a new strategy in the neighbourhood, however much it might still talk of strike action. Those in work, on the other hand, could be terrified into submission by the threat of dismissal. There are examples from the pits of the Ruhr of workers signing away their holiday entitlement and refusing to sign off sick in the depression for fear of being sacked. Even in centres of communist electoral strength strike calls were rarely heeded; and there are even reports of KPD activists refusing to obey such calls.[16]

A second consequence of mass and long-term unemployment was a hardening of the division between the respective constituencies of the SPD and the KPD. The latter became a party overwhelmingly of the unemployed, whilst around 70 per cent of Social Democrats remained in jobs. The SPD was a party still of skilled workers, whereas the KPD's composition became less skilled after 1927. Social Democrats were older, Communists younger. The former came from the 'respectable' working class, the latter recruited increasingly from the inner-city slums and areas with high levels of criminality and illegitimacy. Thus a process of social (and in some cities residential) segregation took place within the Weimar working class at its very base. What once had been fluid and relatively obscure political differences were now granted a social reality that derived above all from the experience of unemployment.

Thirdly, the depression set worker against worker not simply in the political arena but in everyday life. One community would fight with another to save *its* pit, even at the expense of other communities and other pits. Worker competed with worker for a job. Elder married men argued that the young and single should be sacked first. Unemployed pickets fought with still-employed miners desperate to keep their jobs. And for the unemployed themselves the experience of joblessness might awaken bitterness and political radicalism, as evidenced by the increase in support for the KPD. In some cases it did produce the communist street-fighters. But it also led many into apathy, resignation, and despair, as several commentators, including the policemen mentioned above, noticed.[17] The beneficiary of this fragmentation and privatization of grief was, of course, Adolf Hitler, not only before but also after 1933.

Conclusion

None of the above is intended to suggest that organized labour played a key role in the collapse of the Republic. That discredit redounds much more clearly on the heads of rural and middle-class Germany, where liberalism had never been too strongly established. Nor is it implied that a working class united behind the Republic could have saved it. Not only must one bear in mind the tragic lesson of labour's failure in the First Austrian Republic in 1934. It is also necessary to realize that the industrial working class of Weimar Germany was nothing like as numerous as is often imagined. At its largest – and calculations vary – it constituted 40 per cent of the total labour force and began to decline numerically thereafter, especially in the depression. On the other hand, white-collar workers, many of whom did turn to the Nazis and who by the early 1930s were better organized than manual employees, grew rapidly in number. Between the occupational censuses of 1907 and 1925 the number of 'workers' grew by a mere 29 per cent, whereas the number of *Angestellte* (white-collar workers in the private sector) rose by 129 per cent. By late Weimar white-collar workers in the public and private sectors constituted not much less than 30 per cent of the labour force, another quarter or so of which worked in agriculture. Even within 'industry' many 'workers' were engaged in artisanal and cottage production, as we have already seen, and stood outside the ranks of organized labour. Independent artisans, small shopkeepers and their helpers made up something like

14 per cent of the Weimar work force. Under these circumstances it was asking too much of labour to expect it to save the Republic *single-handedly*. That, of course, indicates the crucial problem: the political isolation of the German working class.

This does not mean, however, that labour played no role in the collapse of the Weimar Republic. The fact that a large section of the German working class either expected more of the 1918 Revolution than just democratic and welfare reform, whilst others became increasingly alienated by the experience of unemployment, produced a mass communist movement which saw the destruction of the Republic as a means of realising its revolutionary goal. Thus anti-Republican sentiments found a broader audience than that of the traditional élites or a desperate lower middle class. The anti-system majority in the Reichstag in 1932 was composed of both Communists and Nazis. It was this which paralysed the prospect of coalition government. Furthermore the existence of radical parties on both political extremes made it that much more difficult for the SPD or the bourgeois parties of the centre to compromise for fear of losing their membership in the increasingly dire consequences of depression. The very fact that the German political parties were so closely allied with particular economic interests made compromise all the more difficult when a pitiably small economic cake had to be shared out.

There was another way in which organized labour contributed to the demise of Weimar: not by its own behaviour so much as by the resentment of the rest of German society at its gains. Before 1914 the representatives of organized labour had been excluded from the political process. Thus the agrarian lobby was protected at the expense of urban consumer, employers defended against employees, landed property and the wealthy scarcely touched by direct taxation. After 1918 industrialists had to *compete* with unions in the political as well as industrial arena; agricultural protection was at least partially dismantled; taxes hit peasants, large landowners and business to support the sick, ill, unemployed, and other welfare initiatives. Labour law restricted the former dominance of employers. It was not a romantic, mystical conservatism, some supposed 'fear of freedom', which alienated large sections of German society but the *consequences* of freedom, of democratic government, which gave a voice to the masses, including the urban working class. Relatively the groups which had previously been privileged in the Empire lost out to organized labour. This was resented from the start, but became insupportable as German agriculture plunged into a crisis of indebtedness and industry saw its profits squeezed, in some cases actually destroyed, in the depression of 1929 to 1933. This is not to agree with those who claim that labour priced the Weimar Republic out of existence. (In international comparison Germany was a relatively low-wage economy and some of industry's problems were of its own making.) Other societies have been able to tolerate much higher levels of public expenditure, welfare taxation and wages without collapse. The marked polarization of German society even before 1914, however, and the loss of previous privileges of the economic elites in the Weimar Republic meant that the non-proletarian sections of the community were not so tolerant; and the crisis of a welfare state in depression led to its destruction.

Notes

1. Henry Ashby Turner Jr., *German Big Business and the Rise of Hitler* (Oxford, 1985), especially ch. 6.
2. See the works cited on 'Nazis, Workers and Voters'. Below, p. 217.
3. Fritz Thyssen, *I Paid Hitler* (New York, 1941).
4. Eberhard Czichon, *Wer verhalf Hitler zur Macht?* (Cologne, 1967); Kurt Gossweiler, *Grossbanken, Industriemonopole, Staat* (East Berlin, 1971); G.W.F. Hallgarten, *Hitler, Reichswehr und Industrie* (Frankfurt, 1962); Jürgen Kuczynski, *Klassen und Klassenkämpfe im imperialistischen Deutschland und in der BRD* (Frankfurt, 1972), pp. 418–74; Wilhelm Treue, 'Die Einstellung einiger deutscher Grossindustrieller zu Hitlers Aussenpolitik' in *Geschichte in Wissenschaft und Unterricht* (1966), p. 496.
5. Turner, Op. Cit.
6. Dirk Stegmann, 'Zum Verhältnis von Grossindustrie und Nationalsozialismus' in *Archiv für Sozialgeschichte* 13 (1973), pp. 399–482; 'Kapitalismus und Faschismus in Deutschland' in *Gesellschaft* 6 (1976), pp 19–91; 'Antiquierte Personalisierung oder sozialökonomische Faschismusanalyse' in *Archiv für Sozialgeschichte* 17 (1977), pp. 275–96.

7. David Abraham, *The Collapse of the Weimar Republic* (2nd edn., New York/London, 1986), pp. 74–105.

8. Quoted in Michael Schneider, *Unternehmer und Demokratie* (Bonn, 1975), p. 37f.

9. Bernd Weisbrod, *Schwerindustrie in der Krise* (Wuppertal, 1978).

10. Quoted in Abraham, p. 254.

11. Quoted in ibid, p. 311.

12. Wilfried Böhnke, *Die NSDAP im Ruhrgebiet* (Bonn, 1974), p. 199.

13. Jürgen Falter, 'Wer verhalf der NSDAP zum Sieg?' in *Aus Politik und Zeitgeschichte*, 14 July 1971, pp. 3–21; 'Wählerbewegungen zur NSDAP' in Otto Büsch (ed), *Wählerbewegungen in der europäischen Geschichte* (Berlin, 1980), pp. 159–202; and above all (with Dirk Hänisch), 'Die Anfälligkeit von Arbeitern gegenüber der NSDAP' in *Archiv für Sozialgeschichte* 26 (1986), pp. 179–216.

14. Quoted in Frank Deppe et al., *Geschichte der deutschen Gewerkschaftsbewegung* (Cologne, 1977), p. 212.

15. See police reports on both the Communist Party and on the unemployed in Hauptstaatsarchiv Düsseldorf (A 16839, 16841, 16844, 16848, 16910, 17146).

16. Bergbauarchiv Bochum 32/4290.

17. See note 15 above. Also comments in *Herner Anzeiger* 5 August 1932.

Richard Bessel

Why Did the Weimar Republic Collapse?

I

The history of the Weimar Republic stands under a dark shadow – the shadow of its collapse and Germany's subsequent descent into the 'Third Reich'. That history is, of course, not without positive aspects which have fascinated subsequent generations. But when these aspects are discussed, their contours are delineated against the looming backdrop of Weimar's failure. The understandable desire to examine the positive aspects of Germany's first 'experiment' in democracy – the promise of the socialist aspirations of 1918 and 1919, a democratic constitution containing admirable commitments to individual rights and social justice, the world's most developed system of social welfare during the 1920s, the exciting expressions of 'Weimar culture' – inevitably leaves the historian with the task of explaining how the promise was sabotaged. The history of Weimar thus becomes the history of an 'experiment' undermined, and the main question becomes one of exposing who or what did Weimar in. If only, it has been argued, people had not 'allowed the Weimar experiment to fail' by thinking mistaken thoughts and engaging in mis-

taken actions,[1] or if only the Left had not been divided and
had been determined truly to transform economic structures,[2]
then perhaps the brave experiment could have survived and
prospered.

Recently, however, Gerald Feldman has suggested that the
'experiment' metaphor may be far too positive in its implications and thus misplaced. Instead of regarding the Weimar
Republic as a brave experiment gone wrong, more appropriate might be 'to consider Weimar as a gamble which stood
virtually no chance of success'; according to Feldman, 'Weimar had to try its luck in a house which never provided its
customers with an even chance'.[3] Economic constraints in
particular, both domestic and international, greatly limited
the possibilities for positive political action – regardless of
whether or not the actors involved had correct thoughts. This
is not to throw the idea of human agency out the window
when discussing why democratic politics collapsed in Weimar
Germany, but it is to put the actions of those involved into
perspective. One is tempted to cite Marx's famous dictum
from the *18th Brumaire*: 'Men make their own history, but
not of their own free will; not under circumstances they themselves have chosen but under the given and inherited circumstances with which they are directly confronted.'[4] There are
few better descriptions of the dilemmas facing Germans
between 1918 and 1933.

Before attempting to offer some reasons for the collapse
of Weimar democracy, a few preliminary remarks are in order.
First, it is necessary to be clear about what is being investi-
gated. The question about the collapse of the Weimar Republic concerns the viability of democratic politics. By politics
we mean essentially the setting of priorities for the exercise
of power and the distribution of resources. For the first time
in modern German history, the German people became active
participants in these processes: questions of how power would
be exercised (and against whom) and how resources would
be allocated were subject to democratic constitutional structures; a popular basis was needed for policies within a democratic framework. As is only too well known, this basis
crumbled depressingly quickly in Weimar Germany. The pressures, particularly with regard to distributional conflicts,

appear to have been too great to be accommodated within a democratic framework. Thus democratic politics in this wider sense broke down, leaving only democratic politics in a narrow sense: the politics of propaganda – the demagogic politics of appealing to an electorate unable or unwilling to make the painful choices dictated by 'the given and inherited circumstances with which they are directly confronted'. Democratic politics thus was reduced to form without content: to an irresponsible playing to the gallery, to propaganda. Once that had happened, it was hardly surprising that the best and most successful practitioner of this empty democratic politics proved to be the Nazi Party – which always had regarded the practice of democratic politics as a matter of propaganda.

The second point which needs to be stressed is that the answers to questions about the viability or otherwise of Weimar democracy and the reasons for its collapse appear different depending upon where one chooses to look. For example, those who look to the Left to have provided a possible alternative to the ultimately disastrous history of Weimar Germany – suggesting that the revolution should have been carried beyond the adoption of a democratic constitution and fundamental transformations made in economic structures and the ownership of the means of production, or that a united Left might have warded off the erection of a Nazi dictatorship – tend to focus their attentions upon the urban working class. Things look rather different, for example, when one is examining the options available to the Reich Office of Economic Demobilization or the Reich Treasury immediately after the First World War, or when one concentrates attention upon those groups (comprising the majority of the population) for whom 'Socialism' remained anathema. Similarly, the possibilities for action and the political power that the German working class might have exercised during the Weimar period appear in a different light when viewed from the proletarian neighbourhoods of Berlin or the Ruhr industrial region than when viewed from the rural backwoods of Pomerania or Mecklenburg. It is of more than passing significance that the most significant economic compromises of 1918 – the employers' recognition of the trade unions and the agreement on the eight-hour day – came under successful attack first in the Pomeranian countryside,[5] and that in the early 1930s the Nazis registered stunning successes in the Protestant rural districts of northern and eastern Germany.[6] We should remember that rural Pomerania was no less a part of Weimar Germany than Berlin, and that no single region or set of regions alone could have provided the social and economic supports to political democracy.

II

The Weimar Republic was burdened with enormous handicaps, which in large measure provide the parameters of its history. Perhaps the most important, but often overlooked, was the enormous cost – economic, political and social – of a lost world war. Instead of being able, as Germany's wartime leaders had hoped, to present the bill for the war to the Allies, the vanquished Germans themselves were confronted with not only huge war debts (having financed the war effort in large measure by recourse to the printing press) but also the burden of reparations. Germany's external trading links were disrupted and her currency weakened. Both industrial and agricultural production after the War were only a fraction of what they had been in 1913: in 1919 German industrial production stood at roughly 42 per cent of the 1913 figure and German grain production at roughly 48 per cent.[7] Even after allowance is made for the losses of population, territory and resources which followed defeat, these were huge reductions which could not help but be reflected in lower standards of living. It was not until 1927 that German industrial production exceeded the 1913 figure; and German grain production during the 1920s never exceeded three-quarters of the 1913 figure – even though Germany's population in the late 1920s was only slightly less than that living within the boundaries of the Empire before the War.[8]

The costs of the War and the subsequent readjustment to a peacetime economy cast a shadow over German government finance for the whole of the Weimar period. The problem of the huge debts and reparations bill arising from the War was one aspect of this; the costs of the demobilization, in particular the determination of the Reich Government to ease the transition to peacetime production and provide work for the millions of returning soldiers, formed another – making it necessary for state and national government to continue their dependence upon massive deficit spending into the post-war period.[9] Considering the position in which they found themselves, it is hardly surprising that postwar governments opted for inflationary fiscal policies rather than measures which would contract economic activity, increase unemployment and raise taxation sufficiently to stabilize the currency in the aftermath of the War. According to Heinz Haller, the amount of taxation required to meet the costs of reparations, social-welfare programmes and the normal running of government without inflationary consequences would have involved trebling the prewar tax levels relative to national income – at a time when living standards were considerably below those of 1913; to accomplish this, it would have been necessary to have 'a strong government that had the entire population behind it and was thus in a position to demand great sacrifices'.[10]

However, after the First World War, and indeed for the whole of the Weimar period, 'a strong government that had the entire population behind it' was precisely what was absent from German politics. Weimar governments lacked the basis of support, and popular legitimacy, to push through unpleasant but necessary measures on a basis of democratic politics; and the failure to push through these policies – a failure which led to the hyperinflation of 1922–3 – then further undermined the legitimacy of Weimar governments. It is hardly coincidental that the painful measures taken by the Stresemann cabinets in late 1923 to halt passive resistance in the Ruhr (which had made impossible any stabilization of German finances, currency or foreign relations) and to introduce a stable currency rested on emergency measures which bypassed the Reichstag. It should be remembered that the famous Article 48 of the Weimar Constitution was used not just by the Republic's enemies during the early 1930s but also provided a necessary tool of its defenders – Ebert and Stresemann – during 1923. There was, it appeared, an insufficient democratic basis for democratic politics.

The financial problems left behind by the War did not disappear with the stabilization of 1923–4. Reparations still had to be paid; and their payment involved a complex network of international loans to Germany, which helped the Germans generate the surpluses necessary to pay the reparations bill but which made Germany particularly dependent upon a continuing inflow of foreign (essentially American) capital.[11] More than that, the German government was faced with enormous, continuing financial obligations to the war victims – the hundreds of thousands of invalids, widows and orphans who had become dependent upon state benefits. It has been estimated that roughly 2.7 million German soldiers returned from the First World War with some sort of permanent disability, and in 1923 the Reich Labour Ministry estimated the number of war widows in Germany at 533,000 and of war orphans at 1,192,000.[12] In 1926, for example, permanent war-related pensions were being paid to 792,143 disabled veterans, 361,024 widows, 849,087 fatherless children, and 62,070 children with no living parent; the scale of the problem may be judged from the fact that during the mid-1920s nearly one third of the funds at the disposal of the Reich government (that is, after subtracting the amounts transferred back to the *Länder* or committed to reparation payments) were swallowed up by pension costs.[13]

Thus the First World War left Germany a much poorer place than it had been in 1913, and the social and economic costs of the War formed one of the heaviest burdens of the past which confronted the new democratic political system. The problem, however, was not just that the German economy had suffered a body blow, but that few Germans fully appreciated how much poorer their country had become. Paradoxically, part of the difficulty may have been that the seemingly overwhelming problems of the demobilization and the immediate postwar transition were overcome with too much apparent ease, and that as a result Germans still measured their situation during the 1920s against (a largely mythical image of) conditions in 1913. The thrust of the demobilization efforts was in large measure to return to 'peacetime' conditions, i.e. conditions as people perceived them to have been before the War. Indeed, it was common during the War and even in late 1918 for economic projections to be made on the assumption that the end of the conflict would be followed by a return to 'peacetime' prices.[14] The extent to which '1913' was regarded during the 1920s as somehow 'normal' (and, by implication, conditions during the Weimar period as 'abnormal' and therefore blameworthy and illegitimate) is striking. Economic statistics during the 1920s and early 1930s invariably measured things against figures from 1913; and the disorder of Weimar could be juxtaposed with a rosy picture of the 'good old days' before the War. It is revealing in more ways than one that the success of the currency stabilization rested partly on the psychological benefits of pegging the value of the new currency at the level of the old, prewar gold Mark.[15]

All this reinforced two dangerous illusions in Weimar Germany: that it was possible to return to prewar conditions, and that the War had not really circumscribed the possibilities for German power politics or economic development. This may sound surprising, especially when considered against the chorus of protest about the allegedly harsh terms of the 'Diktat' of Versailles, the 'intolerable' levels of 'unjust' reparations payments, the dwelling on the sacrifice made by Germany's soldiers during the War and the legacy of the 'front spirit' for German politics. But that was precisely the problem. The idea of a 'front generation' was at least partly a myth.[16] The incessant din about the injustices heaped upon a defeated Germany, allegedly undefeated on the field and stabbed in the back at home, in effect served to re-enforce an idea that things would be normal if only the external burdens, imposed by the Allies, could be lifted. That is to say, the constant – indeed ritual – complaints about Versailles in effect served to disguise the extent to which the War really had impoverished Germany, that Germany was a poorer place not just because she had lost the War but because she had fought it.

These illusions were dangerous not least because they helped fix the political agenda of the Weimar Republic so as to favour certain parties and disadvantage others. In order to function, a democratic political system needs a certain responsible consensus recognizing the parameters of policy making. That is to say, if politics is the 'art of the possible', successful democratic politics must be based upon a clear recognition of what in fact is possible. As long as the truth about the War, its causes and consequences, remained excluded from mainstream public political discussion, it was impossible fully to face harsh economic and political realities. The popular rejection of the peace settlement did provide a basis for consensus, but the anti-Versailles consensus was essentially negative, serving to undermine policies which took account of these realities. Responsible politics remained a hostage to myths about the First World War, and Weimar democracy eventually had to pay the price. This was recognized, prophetically, by the great Social Democratic revisionist Eduard Bernstein, who engaged in a courageous but unsuccessful campaign to commit the SPD to tell the truth about the War. Speaking at the first postwar congress of the SPD, in Weimar in June 1919, he urged that the Party break free of the shackles it imposed on itself when it voted for war credits in 1914: 'Let us get out of this bind, become free at last, in this matter, too ... Let us be done with bourgeois notions of honour. Only the truth, the whole truth, can help us.'[17]

Bernstein received little support from his comrades, and it is revealing that among the delegates most bitter in their condemnation of his views (especially the suggestion that nine tenths of the Allies' demands were 'unavoidable necessities') were two Social Democrats who later were most prominent in the governing of Weimar Germany: the long-serving Prime Minister of Prussia, Otto Braun, and the last SPD Reich Chancellor, Hermann Müller. Only one delegate sided with Bernstein in the debate, Gustav Hoch, who warned that 'we have to face the great danger that a nationalist tide will overwhelm us, which would mean an unspeakable disaster precisely for the working class and for the socialist republic'.[18] Hoch was more prophetic than he possibly could have imagined at the time. As long as blame for the War, and blame for the sacrifices and difficulties which necessarily came in its wake, was not placed squarely on the representatives of the old political system, it was impossible for those identifying with Weimar democracy to deal completely honestly with the problems facing them and maintain the popular support necessary for successful democratic politics. As long as the public language of politics was based on misunderstandings and lies, responsible politicians remained at a severe disadvantage. Those who profited was politicians uninterested in responsible democratic politics, those who purveyed the politics of propaganda and demagogy – ultimately the Nazis.

III

The question needs to be posed: what, if anything, could the Left – or the bourgeois centre – have done in these circumstances? Were there possibilities and political opportunities which, had they been grasped, might have enabled democracy to survive or at least led to an outcome less catastrophic than what came about in 1933? A great deal of time and intellectual effort has been devoted to the search for an untapped or suppressed democratic potential in the unrest of 1918 and 1919, a potential which might have provided the basis for a genuine socialist revolution and the destruction of the reactionary, anti-democratic forces which eventually destroyed Weimar. To be sure, the new government headed by Friedrich Ebert, with his trusty 'bloodhound' Gustav Noske, did all it could to suppress left-wing radicalism, and thus bears more than a fair share of responsibility for the bitterness and divisions left in the wake of the transformations of 1918 and 1919. Yet it would be too easy simply to blame the failure of Weimar democracy on an alleged betrayal by the Majority Social Democrats of their working-class supporters and their unwillingness to carry through fundamental social and economic reforms. For one thing, as outlined above, those who had to pick up the pieces left behind when the old order abdicated government and responsibility in the autumn of 1918 faced a difficult if not impossible task. Was it really advisable to embark on a programme of fundamental social and economic transformation when millions of soldiers had to be demobilized and reintegrated into civil society in a matter of weeks, when the economy was in a terrible state and industrial and agricultural production at extremely low levels, when the

Allies were maintaining their blockade and formulating harsh peace terms, when a large proportion of the population remained hostile to Social Democracy and socialism, when insurgents were threatening the territorial integrity of the Reich from the Rhineland to West Prussia and Upper Silesia, when there was a severe coal shortage and the transport system was in chaos, and when the threat of starvation hung over a sizeable proportion of Germany's urban population?

The intention here is not to offer a defence of Friedrich Ebert, but to stress that it would have required a lot more than good intentions and a diffuse democratic potential among the working class to effect a thorough transformation of German society and economy in the aftermath of the First World War. Wolfgang Mommsen is therefore quite right to assert that the argument that the 'democratic potential' of the workers' and soldiers' councils could have provided the basis for a fundamental democratization of German society 'has an unmistakably utopian ring about it'.[19] The Left, in the form of the Majority Social Democrats, did not come to power in November 1918 because they had a clear-cut programme of action or a clear plan for a transformation of German society. They came to power because the mess left behind by the old order was dumped in their laps, and in November 1918 there simply was no one else in a position to accept responsibility for Germany's future. True, they also came to power on the basis of some quite exaggerated and unfounded hopes for a better future on the part of their working-class supporters; but this was to prove a giant millstone around the necks of both German Social Democracy and the Weimar Republic. In essence, the Left was given a brief opportunity to direct the German government machine because Germany's aristocratic and bourgeois political elites temporarily were paralysed. Seen in this way, the creation of the Weimar Republic was perhaps less the consequence of a triumph of the Left than of a colossal failure of elite politics in Germany.

The dilemma facing the Majority Social Democrats also was reflected in the activities of Joseph Koeth and of his short-lived super-ministry directing the economic demobilization after the First World War. As Gerald Feldman has stressed in his seminal article on the economic demobilization after the First World War, Koeth's work 'long outlasted the brief tenure of the Demobilization Office', as it 'predetermined so many of the basic patterns of economic and social life in the Weimar Republic'.[20] Koeth regarded the economic demobilization over which he had been put in charge as a two-stage process: first, overcoming the emergency created by the sudden return of the soldiers in the wake of the Armistice; and second, attempting to sort out the structural problems involved in the transition from war to peace (including the coal shortage, the serious threats to agricultural production, and the need to channel labour towards those areas where it was most needed). Tampering with the basic structure of the German economy – bringing large portions of German productive capacity into public ownership and putting into practice a genuinely socialist plan for restructuring the German economy – would have to wait. The pressing economic problems of late 1918 and early 1919 dictated rejection of ambitious structural plans and acceptance of a policy of 'muddling through' in order to achieve 'the preservation of the economy'. According to Koeth: 'Preservation of the economy meant simultaneously the preservation of the existing economic system' – not, he claimed, due to fundamental objections to a socialist economic system, 'but solely due to the conviction that in such a crisis any change, regardless of whatever the new system might be, would necessarily hasten the collapse of the economy'.[21] No doubt his politics during 1918/19 were rather less innocent than Koeth implied when describing his activities at the Demobilization Office in 1921. However, the question needs to be posed: Why did this pragmatic approach determine German economic policy during the crucial months after the November Revolution, and why were the more ambitious plans of Reich Economics Minister Rudolf Wissel, for an extension of socialist economic organization, put on the back burner and then removed altogether?

The answer lies in large measure in the overwhelming and threatening character of the difficulties facing the governments which replaced the Imperial system. They had no 'socialist' answer to the enormous and immediate problems confronting them; nor, for that matter, did their critics on the left. All they could offer was the desperate but rather feeble attempt to supply order, in the social and economic spheres, which the old regime finally had so blatantly failed to maintain. It is hardly surprising that in such inauspicious circumstances they too failed, and that in such circumstances they felt compelled to pursue pragmatic policies to deal with the pressing problems of the moment and in effect consigned plans involving fundamental structural change to oblivion.

Before condemning the Majority Social Democrats for their failure in 1918/19 to carry through a 'genuine' socialist revolution – whatever that may have meant – it should be recognized that to have done so not only might have led to the 'economic collapse' which Koeth (and not only he) feared; a socialist transformation also probably would have been opposed by a majority of the German population. Even in the heady atmosphere of January 1919 the socialist Left proved unable to gain a majority of the popular vote in the elections for the National Assembly. And not even the DDP, the left-liberal coalition partners of the Majority Social Democrats, were prepared to support socialist attempts to abolish the private ownership of property or to jettison the market economy and institute socialist economic planning. Order may have broken down in many German cities in late 1918 and 1919, and in early 1919 Berlin may have presented a picture not unlike modern Beirut, with armed groups battling it out in the absence of a strong central government; however, in most of the country, and especially in the countryside, order had not broken down completely and the state structure had not collapsed. In such a situation it probably would have been mistaken to believe that a determined socialist policy, which perhaps might have satisfied the more radical elements amongst the urban industrial proletariat, could command widespread support in the country at large. Quite the contrary! Such a policy carried with it the serious possibility of open civil war. The potential for such violence was shown graphically enough by the rapid growth of the *Freikorps* and the brutality with which they suppressed the radical Left at the behest of Gustav Noske, by the discontent within the armed forces which surfaced in March 1920 with the failed Kapp Putsch, and with the right-wing terrorism which claimed the lives of Kurt Eisner, Rosa Luxemburg, Karl Liebknecht, Hugo Haase, Matthias Erzberger, and Walther Rathenau. No less important was the fact that against this backdrop of potential and actual violence – of a latent civil war – most Germans simply wanted to put their own lives in order after the upheavals of war, revolution, and inflation.

The dilemma of Germany's first experiment in democracy was that it took place in a country too advanced for either a continuation of the old autocratic system or a genuine popular socialist transformation, too divided to allow the smooth working of liberal democracy, and too impoverished to patch up the social cracks created by not only capitalist development but also the specific problems of the War and its immediate aftermath. The political collapse of 1918 was a striking failure of elite politics. However, it was not the complete collapse of German elite politics: there was no German parallel to the situation in the Russian countryside from the summer of 1917, where peasant communities 'destroyed the official rural power structure and rejected the authority of virtually all institutions that were not rooted in the villages'.[22] In Germany in 1918 and 1919 most civil servants stayed at their posts and continued to carry out their tasks (successfully marginalizing the council movement), factory owners continued to run their factories, and large landowners continued to run their estates – even though they had to swallow the bitter pill of recognizing the collective bargaining rights of their employees. What occurred in Germany was a temporary abdication of responsibility and a partial abdication of power by the country's traditional elites. This was to prove a heavy burden for the new political order. Not only did it characterize the crises which gave birth to the Weimar Republic; it also characterized, in a rather different constellation, the crises which surrounded its death.

IV

The disintegration of the Weimar Republic and the advance of the Nazi movement both point to a deep crisis of German elite politics. The nature of this crisis was rather different from, but related to, the crisis of elite politics which ushered in the Republic. The collapse of the Weimar Republic can be seen in large measure as the consequence of a failure of German political elites to accept, effectively to adapt to, and successfully to legitimate the democratic political system – a failure which took different forms in the different 'eras' of the Republic. At the time of the Republic's birth, Germany's political elites had been put onto the defensive by the collapse of the Imperial system, and in effect temporarily abdicated political responsibility. During the mid-1920s, when the Republic appeared relatively stable and the chances seemed good for its success, there was a conspicuous failure of both conservative and 'middle' political parties effectively to integrate their supporters (and themselves) into the Weimar system;[23] and during the terminal years of the Republic the total collapse of the bourgeois 'middle', the paralysis of parliamentary government, and, especially, the rise of the Nazis testify to the bankruptcy of traditional elite politics. It is hardly coincidental that the successful Nazi message was directed so stridently against Germany's political elites or that so many of the leading lights of the NSDAP, both at local and national level, were 'outsiders' to the traditional political game and to traditional interest organizations.[24]

In 1918 the failure of the old regime either to win the War or to manage German society had allowed the Left temporarily to occupy positions of power and paved the way for the establishment of a democratic political system. This set the scene for a number of compromises which ushered in the democratic, pluralist political system of the Weimar Republic: in particular, the compromises embodied in the Weimar constitution (for example, over the question of social ownership and over the relationship of church and state) and in agreements between employers and trade unions.[25] But the foundation upon which this 'system of political and social compromises' was constructed proved neither solid nor permanent; when the revolutionary wave ebbed the settlement of 1918/19 quickly came under attack. The successful assault on the eight-hour day, one of the major achievements of 1918, was an important indicator of the changed climate of politics in Germany which came about already during the early

1920s.[26] The nature of the stabilization in 1923/24, when the currency was stabilized within the framework of a radically deflationary economic policy, also revealed the fragility of the compromises of 1918. It involved strict controls over government expenditure, a reduction by roughly a quarter in the number of Reich employees, a rapid rise in unemployment generally, and considerable increases in the real costs of many important items of expenditure, (particularly rents, which had sunk to ridiculously low levels during the inflation as a consequence of rent controls). Necessary and inevitable though it may have been, the stabilization thus caused considerable hardship and its costs were borne largely by the working population.

To be sure, Weimar's period of 'relative stabilization' – the 'golden' years of the mid-1920s – witnessed a substantial economic recovery from the dark days of 1923 and early 1924, as well as impressive advances in the development of the social-welfare system. Economic production roughly recovered its prewar levels by 1928, and there were striking increases in the state's role in the provision of social welfare. As noted above, vastly expensive pensions programmes were put into place (after much delay and debate) after the First World War; the German state became actively involved in the construction of housing (with 81 per cent of the 2.8 million dwellings built between 1919 and 1932 being financed to some extent by the state);[27] and legislation was enacted in 1927 which provided statutory unemployment insurance for more than 17 million workers and employees – more than were covered by any comparable scheme in any other country. But these advances were far from secure and may have carried the seeds of their own destruction. Rather than helping to generate popular support for the Weimar system, they may well have contributed to its undoing. The advances of the 1920s raised expectations, led to increased levels of taxation and increased social-insurance contributions,[28] multiplied the potential points of conflict between the German state and its citizens, and proved extremely vulnerable to economic pressures which undermined the tax base. Total public expenditure in 1928/29 was roughly twice as great as before the War,[29] and it is worth considering the extent to which this burden undermined not just Germany's economic prospects (as Knut Borchardt has argued),[30] but also its political prospects. Indeed, one can analyse the troubled history of Weimar Germany profitably within the conceptual framework of a general crisis of the modern industrial state – a 'motivation crisis', as described by Jürgen Habermas, in which demands were generated which the state could not meet.[31] The vast increase in the numbers of people financially dependent upon the German state (for unemployment benefit, for war-invalid pensions, for housing or whatever) proved a tremendous burden for the Weimar Republic when the Depression struck and undermined the impressive edifice of the Weimar welfare state. Rather than a boon for Weimar democracy, the social welfare system proved a time bomb with a rather short fuse.

Thus even during its 'golden' years, the Weimar system failed to build a sufficient base of popular legitimation. That this occurred during a period largely of 'bourgeois' rule – between 1924 and 1928 the Reich government consisted of coalitions involving the Catholic Centre Party (and its Bavarian cousin, the BVP), the left and right liberals (DDP and DVP respectively), and the conservatives (the DNVP) – is significant. After the stabilization of German politics in the mid-1920s government was in the hands of the established political elites. However, this 'stabilization' proved rather short-lived and remarkably unstable. All the parties which participated in government coalitions during this period attracted a smaller proportion of the vote in May 1928 than they had in either Reichstag election in 1924; the DNVP ended up riven with divisions and eventually was hijacked by the intransigent and anti-parliamentary right-wing politics of media magnate Alfred Hugenberg; and when the Depression struck, traditional bourgeois (elite) politics already were dangerously fragmented.

The degree to which democratic politics lacked the necessary foundation became painfully apparent in the late 1920s. Three developments deserve mention in this regard: the Ruhr lock-out of 1928, the collapse of the unemployment insurance scheme, and the dissolution of the 'Grand Coalition' put together after the May 1928 elections under the leadership of Hermann Müller. All three illustrate how fragile was the democratic framework of the Weimar Republic.

The bitter Ruhr lock-out of November 1928 marked an important turning point in the political history of the Weimar Republic, in industrial relations and in the relations between German big business and the government. The leaders of Ruhr heavy industry refused to accept a state arbitrator's decision for a small wage increase – a decision which the Reich Labour Ministry made legally binding – and locked out nearly a quarter of a million workers. In essence, by attacking the system of state arbitration of industrial disputes, the heavy industrialists of the Ruhr were issuing a direct challenge to state intervention (especially by the Social Democratic Reich Labour Minister Rudolf Wissell) in industrial affairs on behalf of organized labour.[32] Although the outcome was a compromise, in that the employers secured a more modest wage increase but failed to demolish the system of state arbitration, the conflict demonstrated the lengths to which heavy industry was prepared to go in defence of what regarded as its vital interests. At stake was not simply a wage increase of between 2 and 4 per cent; at stake was the degree to which a democratic state, in which the interests of organized labour were represented, should be involved in shaping industrial relations in heavy industry. Although they did not win this round, the industrialists of the Ruhr in effect had given notice that they no longer wanted to play the democratic game.

The 'Act on Labour Exchanges and Unemployment Insurance' of 1927 had stipulated the provision of statutory unemployment insurance for more than 17 million German workers, to be paid for out of equal contributions by employer and employee and a state reserve fund to allow the scheme to cope with cyclical downturns in the economy.[33] However, the finances of the scheme were predicated on an average unemployment level of 800,000, which was lower than that reported at any point from 1928 to 1933, and the financial limits of the scheme were reached within a year. During the Depression, the programme collapsed almost completely under the weight of mass unemployment. Very quickly it became apparent that, in a democratic political framework, the Weimar welfare system could not be sustained.

It was the issue of raising employees' contributions to the Unemployment Insurance Fund which led to the collapse of the last Weimar coalition government with a parliamentary majority – the SPD-led government of Hermann Müller – in early 1930. The issue was the same as that which broke the British Labour Government in 1931. In the German case, Social Democrats were loathe to see employee contributions raised (or, better, to be a party to the inevitable raising of employee contributions), whereas British Labour politicians were loathe to see benefits cut. Business interests, which had asserted themselves in the DVP after the death of Gustav Stresemann in October 1929, pressed for cuts and helped to provoke the crisis which brought down the Müller government.[34] Neither the Social Democratic trade union leaders, who were unwilling to compromise over this issue (although the cuts brought in by Brüning after the SPD left government – and which were tolerated by the SPD in the Reichstag – were far greater than those which the Social Democrats had rejected in March 1930), nor the industrial interests, would give way sufficiently to allow a compromise solution to be found within a democratic framework.

V

The effective suspension of parliamentary government from 1930 onwards and the increasing reliance upon emergency legislation passed with Reich President von Hindenburg's signature revealed the bankruptcy of democratic politics in Weimar Germany. The tensions which had re-surfaced during the late 1920s increased to such an extent that they undermined democratic parliamentary government. This process had two components, as both major potential sources of support for democratic politics – Social Democracy and the bourgeois middle – proved unable or unwilling to shoulder the necessary responsibility. On the left, the SPD was pushed onto the defensive by a terrible combination of factors: economic pressures which undermined almost all the social-welfare advances for which the SPD had fought and with which the SPD was identified, and which hamstrung the social-democratic trade-union movement; a stagnant and aging membership and an inability to attract the younger generation; a political leadership which placed its faith in the existing legal and administrative framework at a time when these were increasingly fragile and under threat; and the challenge of the KPD, whose radical propaganda – aimed in large measure against the more compromising politics of the SPD – was successful in attracting increasing numbers of increasingly desperate supporters. Unlike in the early years of the Weimar Republic, when the Social Democratic labour movement was able to muster the support to defeat the Kapp Putsch, in the early 1930s the Left was effectively paralysed.

In and of itself, the paralysis of the Left perhaps was not sufficient to doom democracy to destruction. However, bourgeois political elites were unable to offer a constructive alternative either. In what remained of the middle ground, less and less support could be found for democratic politics. The left-liberal DDP saw its support wither away and sought revival in an ill-fated marriage with the *Jungdeutscher Orden* to form the *Deutsche Staatspartei*. But not even banishing the word 'democratic' from its name could provide the hoped-for basis for a new integrative party of the middle. The activities of the right-liberal DVP proved more instrumental to the collapse of parliamentary democracy but no more successful in retaining popular support for the middle ground of Weimar politics. Within the context of deepening economic troubles, increasingly bitter distributional struggles, and declining public support for democratic politics, party-political support for parliamentary government withered away.

But the problem was greater than that, for Germany's business interests found it increasingly difficult to work effectively within the Weimar political system at all. According to Harold James, after the collapse of the Müller government, 'it proved almost impossible either for the DVP industrialists to control their party effectively, or for them to succeed in their attempt to build up a coherent right-wing bloc that could carry pro-business policies'.[35] As Bernd Weisbrod has pointed out, during the Depression German heavy industrialists were determined that 'there should be no way back to the favourable conditions for the working-class organizations in the system of collective bargaining and in parliamentary democracy'.[36]

The problem was that they could not map out a way forward either. Germany's industrial elites were powerful enough to sabotage democratic politics, but they were not powerful enough to put anything constructive in its place.[37] It is revealing that the government probably most in tune with the desires of heavy industry, the 'Cabinet of Barons' headed by the renegade Centre Party politician Franz von Papen, served mightily to undermine democracy but, almost completely lacking popular support, was incapable of putting any stable political solution in its place. It also is revealing that business support for the Nazis came primarily from 'the middle reaches of industry, commerce and finance'.[38] The chiefs no longer were able to mobilize or control the Indians.

Similar arguments may be put forward with regard to agricultural interests. The position of Germany's agricultural elites, in particular of the Prussian Junkers, during the Weimar period was framed by the fundamental dilemma of having to defend their interests within a democratic framework at a time when their position vis-a-vis industry had weakened and the problems posed by world economic conditions became progressively more difficult.[39] This, however, they did with some success. Agricultural interests played a role in Weimar politics quite out of proportion to the importance of agriculture in the German economy. Particularly impressive was their success in channelling state subsidies into their own pockets through a succession of agrarian relief packages during the 1920s and early 1930s. However, successful though these relief programmes were in helping large landowners get their snouts into the trough of state subsidy, they proved disastrous in other respects. The aid programmes proved quite inadequate to rescue either German agriculture generally or the large estates, which were the main beneficiaries of state generosity, from the ravages of the downturn in agricultural prices during the 1920s and early 1930s. But they did make a substantial contribution to undermining the political base of Germany's agricultural elites. This was due partly to the scandal which surrounded the aid programmes, partly to the fact that large sections of German agriculture – especially in the western parts of the Reich, but also small family farmers in the eastern regions – received little or no relief, and partly to the fact that the economic problems posed by inefficient, overly indebted German agricultural producers in a world of falling prices probably were too great to be solved through any set of aid measures which the German government could afford.

Against this background, there was a huge upsurge in agrarian radicalism in Germany during the late 1920s and early 1930s, of which the militant and violent farmers' protests of 1928 and 1929 in Schleswig-Holstein were only the opening shots.[40] This agrarian radicalism was expressed in a hostility to the established political parties and political elites. The DNVP, the traditional mouthpiece of landed interests, suffered considerably at the polls in 1928 and 1930, despite the turn to the right under Hugenberg; after all, this was the party of the large landowners who profited from state subsidies while smaller farmers faced bankruptcy in increasing numbers. By the early 1930s the clear beneficiary of this wave of hostility towards established political groupings and the state which they controlled was the Nazi Party. Not only did the Nazi Party achieve its most impressive electoral results in Protestant rural districts where farmers had faced the greatest economic pressure – for example, East Prussia, Pomerania, and Schleswig-Holstein, where rural protest had developed into a terrorist bombing campaign in 1929; it also managed to oust the old elites from their positions of dominance in various agricultural associations. Particularly revealing were the successes of the Nazis in making inroads into the leadership circles of the *Reichslandbund* and the spectacular victories of the NSDAP across northern Germany in the elections of the Prussian agricultural chambers (*Landwirtschaftskammer*) in late 1931.[41] The Nazis had successfully assaulted the strongholds of Germany's agricultural elites, and their infantry in this assault were masses of angry and increasingly desperate small family farmers. It was indeed a telling sign of the times when, at the end of 1932, the *Landwirtschaftskammer* of the 'Border Province of Posen and West Prussia' announced the election of its new chairman, an independent farmer and leader of the SA in the region, Arno Manthey.[42] The advance of the NSDAP brutally demonstrated that in many a rural community the political hegemony of the large landowners was over. Agrarian elite politics had disintegrated, and the failure of Germany's agrarian elites to maintain their hegemony allowed the NSDAP to attract massive support in the Protestant countryside.

The dilemma facing Germany's military elites also presents parallels. By the beginning of 1933, probably only the Reichswehr could have imposed a solution excluding the Nazis from government. But its concerns lay elsewhere: in securing the resources regarded as necessary for its own development and the 'social underpinning' necessary to its plans for military expansion. Here, as Michael Geyer has demonstrated, the issue at stake was not whether there should be some restoration of the politics of the Empire; rather, it was how to secure the resources regarded by Reichswehr planners as essential for the development of a modern army.[43] Faced with the perceived necessity of securing ever larger resources for armaments during a period of economic contraction, it became increasingly difficult for Reichswehr planners to reconcile their needs with democratic politics in which other interests might be more successful in mobilizing support. At the same time, Germany's military elites were loathe to intervene to impose order on a deeply divided society and to risk a possible civil war. Those tasks, ultimately, were performed by the Nazis.

During the terminal phase of Weimar democracy, Germany's political and economic elites could destroy, but they could not build. Their failure to adapt successfully to democratic politics or to defend Weimar democracy was in large measure a failure to accept responsibility. Businessmen wanted to get on with their businesses; agricultural producers wanted protection and a return to profitability; military planners wanted to rearm. There was little concern for the wider political implications or who would bear the costs. The fundamental requirements of democratic politics – the willingness to set priorities and distribute resources within a pluralist democratic framework and the ability to secure a popular basis for such politics – were lacking. Thus when a peculiar combination of peculiarly severe economic and social challenges confronted the Weimar system, it collapsed under the strain. More than thirty years ago Karl Dietrich Bracher analysed the emergence of a power vacuum at the centre of German politics during the dying phase of the Weimar Republic.[44] This key to the tragedy of the early 1930s was an expression of the fundamental political failure of Germany's elites, who still were powerful enough effectively to veto democratic politics but were too weak to create or impose a viable alternative of their own. The role of the Nazis ultimately was to fill the vacuum, to pick up the pieces left behind after the Weimar Republic disintegrated, and to fashion them into a particularly destructive and murderous machine.

VI

In this discussion relatively little attention has been given thus far to organized labour and the Left. Although this most crushing defeat for the labour movement prompted intense debate about the tactics, and mistakes, of Germany's Communists and Social Democrats when confronted with the growing Nazi movement, there seems in fact little the Left could have done to turn the tide. Of course the Communist Party's denunciation of the Social Democrats as 'social fascists' was not exactly designed to promote unity in the face of the Nazi threat. And of course Social Democratic hostility towards the KPD was hardly conducive to building a united front in the hour of crisis. But to suggest that such policies were irrational and that some (never quite defined) form of 'unity' on the Left should have been top priority is to highlight options which never really existed and to substitute propaganda for analysis. Whatever the propaganda rhetoric, either at the time or subsequently, about the need to join forces in a 'united front', the fact was that the SPD and KPD were rivals and that their rivalry had deep roots. For one thing, as Wolfgang Mommsen has pointed out, the 'apparent stabilization of the Weimar system' in 1919 – when the SPD 'bloodhound' Noske unleashed the *Freikorps* to crush left-wing unrest in an orgy of violence – and 1920 – with the suppression of the Ruhr uprising – 'was achieved at the cost of a long-term polarization in German society, not least within the working class itself'.[45] For another, the identification of the SPD with the 'Weimar system' – and not least its control for much of the Weimar period of the Prussian police, whose attention often was directed against the urban proletarian slum milieu in which the Communists found their greatest support – gave the political divisions a real cutting edge.[46] Furthermore, the SPD and the KPD were competitors for working-class votes. Much of the KPD's success in attracting support during the early 1930s came at the expense of the Social Democrats. Although the divisions between Communist and Social Democrat often paralleled already existing divisions between the rough and respectable sides of working-class culture – between the old proletarian slum and the new working-class housing estate, between the unskilled and skilled, between the unemployed and the employed, between the young and the middle-aged – the two left-wing parties were rivals, not partners, in the struggle for electoral support.

What is more, it remains doubtful that a united Left, determined to stand and fight, would have been much more successful in preventing the slide into right-wing dictatorship than was a divided Left unwilling or unable to force a confrontation. What had worked in 1920, when a General Strike led to the collapse of the Kapp Putsch, was hardly an option in 1932 or 1933. Whereas in March 1920 the Republic still held promise and the disasters of the old order were fresh in popular memory, by 1932 German democracy had largely been discredited and dismantled under the pressure of economic crisis and loss of political legitimacy. And, perhaps most importantly for the Left, unemployment, which in early 1920 had been quite low (with 1.9 per cent of trade unionists unemployed in March 1920), reached absolutely crippling levels by 1932 (with 43.9 per cent of trade unionists unemployed in July).[47] Although the Social Democrats have been criticized for passively watching the slide into disaster – in July 1932, when the Reich government under von Papen removed the SPD-led Prussian government and thus destroyed at a stroke what had appeared the strongest bulwark of democracy, and again in January 1933 – it is doubtful that militant action would have met with success either. Ranged against the forces at the disposal of the German state, as well as the Nazis with their hundreds of thousands of young men marching around in brown uniform, with many of their supporters out of work and the rest fearful of losing their jobs, and without the support of a majority of the German people, the prospects for the success of active left-wing resistance – whether united or not – were slim indeed in the early 1930s.

This indeed is the ultimate tragedy of the Left during the terminal phase of the Weimar Republic, that it was largely irrelevant to the political machinations which led to the destruction of German democracy. Real political decision-making was going on elsewhere. The Left had been pushed out of power politics, and the success of the Nazis in mobilizing mass popular support effectively blocked that path for a return by the Left to centre stage. All that remained for the Left was either the politics of propaganda (which the Communists pursued with some considerable, if illusory, success) or the politics of resignation (which the Social Democrats pursued with rather little success). For the Social Democrats, tolerating the lesser evil (or, more concretely, tolerating the Brüning government in order to stave off something even worse) helped to undermine support for Social Democracy and failed to prevent the further dismantling of Weimar democracy. Support from the SPD, however grudging and ambivalent, ultimately proved a liability for a Chancellor Brüning dependent upon the goodwill of Reich President von Hindenburg for the passing of emergency legislation. For the Communists, in a paradoxical sense success meant failure. During the early 1930s the vote for the KPD grew impressively (or, as the majority of Germans no doubt regarded it, frighteningly), from 3.26 million in 1928 to 4.49 million in 1930 and 5.98 million in November 1932. But the Communists were largely the party of the unemployed, and the growth of the Communist vote, however much it may have been cheered in the pages of *Die Rote Fahne*, was a measure not of the strength of a militant working class but of its weakness. The Communists could organize hunger marches effectively; they could muster support in unemployment benefit offices; but they could not hope to organize workers at the point of production, much less organize a successful general strike.

Looking back over the tortured history of the Left in Weimar Germany, it is difficult to discern many instances where different policies would have made a substantial difference to the outcome. Perhaps the only major tactical mistake which did fall into this category was the fateful decision of the KPD to field its own candidate in the presidential elections of 1925, thus allowing the election of Paul von Hindenburg, who eventually handed over the keys of the Reich Chancellory to Adolf Hitler. But by the time the Depression hit, there is little the Left could have done to turn the tide.

The Left in Weimar Germany was crippled by the juxtaposition of a deep economic depression, attacking particularly severely a country whose political system lacked a firm basis of legitimacy, and longer-term and structural developments. Among these longer-term trends was the fact that the industrial working class, the traditional source of support for Marxist working-class politics, was no longer growing relative to other sectors of the population as it had been before the First World War. Weimar Germany was no longer a rapidly industrializing society; it had become a mature industrial society. Those sectors of the population which were growing fastest (service industries, women's employment, white-collar work, public-sector employment in education and health) were not the sources of support for traditional left-wing politics. Left-wing politics in Weimar Germany remained based upon a social and economic structure which was receding into the past.

In particular the fast growth of white-collar work posed a challenge to socialists, who had to come to grips with a rather different development of society and politics than that predicted by Marx. During the Weimar period there were growing numbers of white-collar workers, most of whom were ill-disposed to being placed on the same level as workers on the shop floor; although the socialist 'Afa-Bund' grew impressively immediately after the 1918 revolution, by the early 1920s the membership of the nationalist *Deutschnationaler Handlungsgehilfen-Verband* again outnumbered that of its socialist rival. According to Hans Speier, 'the politically decisive feature of white-collar trade union activity in the Weimar Republic was its animating purpose; to preserve the status and esteem of salaried employees vis-a-vis blue-collar workers'.[48] The framework of the Weimar state, which anchored the trade unions in the social and economic constitution of Germany, aroused fears that employees' privileges would be eroded; and when the economic crisis of the early 1930s struck, the added insecurities made many white-collar workers hostile to suggestions that they unite with workers on the shop floor and susceptible to nationalist, and ultimately National Socialist, politics.

The dilemma facing the Left in Weimar Germany was not just a matter of longer-term structural *economic* trends which were working against Marxist class politics. There were important cultural aspects to this as well. During the Weimar period we can discern the growth of a new consumerist culture, which began to cut across the older, more class-based working-class cultures within which Social Democracy had grown before the First World War. Increasingly, German workers and their families, and particularly the younger generation, were exposed to cultural (and, through these, to political) influences beyond the bounds of the working-class neighbourhood and socialist subculture. It often has been argued that before the War the Social Democratic movement in particular offered to workers 'a way of life which was significantly different from that of other groups';[49] with its array of clubs, societies, newspapers, and even retail outlets, a Social Democratic subculture had developed which to some extent insulated those within it from the dominant bourgeois political culture. Although the extent to which this picture was true even for Imperial Germany may be debated, it appears clear that the cultural hegemony of the working-class movement over sections of the working class in Weimar Germany faced new and powerful challenges. The shortening of the working day and the growth of leisure, the spread of department stores offering low-cost goods to working-class customers, and especially the tremendous growth of the cinema,[50] meant that the German working classes were exposed to cultural influences from outside their own working-class milieu.

Of course one should not overestimate the impact of this upon people who suffered from mass unemployment and for whom economic survival, and not the latest Charlie Chaplin film, was of paramount concern. Yet the majority of workers did have work; at least during the mid-1920s incomes were rising; and for the relatively affluent working-class family – the sort which formed the backbone of support for Social Democracy – 'consumerism' was an option. As James Wickham and Günter Berghaus have suggested, in rather different contexts, the advent of a consumerist culture during the Weimar period was a deep ideological challenge to the cultural hegemony of the working-class movement within the proletarian milieu.[51] Whereas most of the leisure-time pursuits of working people once took place within the proletarian milieu and could be organized by the Social Democratic movement, during the 1920s working-class women and youth especially were being exposed (or were exposing themselves) to 'bourgeois' influence and 'consumerist ideologies'. Instead of the collectivist culture of the socialist organizations, working-class youth came into increasing contact with an individualist consumer culture. As the working class was exposed to more and more cultural influences outside the working-class ghetto this tended to marginalize socialist-sponsored 'working-class' culture. What is more, these developments were most advanced in Germany's urban areas – that is, in the areas where the left-wing parties had their greatest reservoirs of support.

This line of argument is rather speculative, but it does suggest some deeper reasons for the political impotence of the Left in general, and of Social Democracy in particular, during the Weimar period. The inability of the Left to prevent the demise of German democracy and the success of National Socialism was not due simply to mistaken, divisive policies of the SPD and KPD. The basis of working-class politics as practised in Germany was being challenged and fragmented. Indeed, it could be argued that this impotence may in part have been a reflection of the beginning of the disintegration of class politics in modern Germany, a process which continued through the Nazi period and was given additional impetus after 1945.[52] Class still formed a powerful focus for political mobilization in Weimar Germany. The success of the Communists in attracting nearly six million votes in November 1932 on a militantly class-based platform certainly testified to this. But the success of the Nazi Party, which was able to profit from the fragmentation of Weimar politics to grow into an enormous 'catchall party of protest' and which managed to attract votes of millions of working people by the early 1930s, points in another direction. Although the urban proletarian slums remained bastions of Communist support and although the membership of Social Democratic trade unions remained surprisingly stable during the early 1930s, the Nazis succeeded because an increasingly large proportion of the electorate did not feel tied by the bonds of class politics.

VII

The collapse of Weimar democracy was due to a peculiar combination of long-term and short-term pressures. These pressures, many of which are found in other industrial societies, came together with particular force in Weimar Germany. Other societies have had to face deep political and social divisions, extreme conflict between employers and workers, mass unemployment, the burdens of a lost war, the need to legitimate a new political system, the contradictions inherent in an expansion of a modern social-welfare system, new and disturbing cultural challenges, and a willingness on the part of some elites to jettison democratic politics. None of these problems or pressures was unique to Weimar Germany. Nor was Germany the only country in which a democratic political system disintegrated during the interwar period; indeed, except in the Anglo-Saxon democracies and Scandinavia, stable democratic systems were the exception in Europe rather than the rule. Perhaps the remarkable thing about the Weimar Republic is not that it collapsed but that it lasted as long as it did. What was unique to Germany was the force with which all these pressures came together, in particularly concentrated form: Weimar Germany had the *most* democratic constitution; it developed the *most advanced* social-welfare system; it suffered the *worst* inflation; it had lost and had to pay for the *most* destructive war fought up to that time; due to its peculiar economic structure and position in the world economy it was *most* savagely affected by the Depression.

As Detlev Peukert has pointed out, the Weimar political system may well have been able to cope individually with each of the various destructive processes facing it.[53] But when these combined in the hothouse atmosphere of Weimar Germany, the Republic was doomed. It is this peculiar conjuncture which explains not simply the collapse of Weimar democracy, but why such destructive forces were unleashed to take its place. For the tragedy of the collapse of the Weimar democracy was not just that the Republic was destroyed, but that, in the final analysis, so were all the other alternatives short of a murderous Nazi dictatorship.

Notes

1. Hagen Schulze, *Weimar. Deutschland 1917–1933* (Berlin, 1982), p. 425.
2. Wolfgang Ruge, in the standard GDR textbook on the period, *Deutschland 1917–1933* (Berlin, 1974), p. 473.
3. Gerald D. Feldman, 'Weimar from Inflation to Depression: Experiment or Gamble?', in Gerald D. Feldman (ed.), *Die Nachwirkungen der Inflation auf die deutsche Geschichte 1924-1933* (Munich, 1985), quotes from pp. 385 and 401.
4. Karl Marx, 'The Eighteenth Brumaire of Louis Bonaparte', in Karl Marx, *Surveys from Exile, Political Writings*, Volume 2 (Harmondsworth, 1973), p. 146.
5. See, for example, the description of the tactics of agricultural employers in early 1923 in Staatsarchiv Greifswald, Rep. 65c, Nr. 944, ff. 179–81: The Landrat to the Oberpräsident in Stettin, Franzburg, 21 Mar. 1923.
6. See Alfred Milatz, *Wähler und Wahlen in der Weimarer Republik* (Bonn, 1965), p. 112; Thomas Childers, *The Nazi Voter. The Social Foundations of Fascism in Germany, 1919–1933* (Chapel Hill and London, 1983), pp. 215–19; Jürgen Falter, Thomas Lindenberger and Siegfried Schumann, *Wahlen und Abstimmungen in der Weimarer Republik. Materialien zum Wahlverhalten* (Munich, 1986), pp. 71–5.
7. From tables reproduced in Carl-Ludwig Holtfrerich, *The German Inflation 1914–1923. Causes and Effects in International Perspective* (Berlin and New York, 1986), p. 182.
8. Industrial and grain production figures in Holtfrerich, *The German Inflation*, p. 182; population figures in Statistisches Reichsamt (ed.), *Statistisches Jahrbuch für das Deutsche Reich 1932* (Berlin, 1932), p. 7.
9. Gerald D. Feldman, 'Economic and Social Problems of the German Demobilisation, 1918–19', *Journal of Modern History*, 47 (1975);

Holtfrerich, *The German Inflation*, p. 129; Harold James, *The German Slump. Politics and Economics 1924–1936* (Oxford, 1986), pp. 41–2.

10. Heinz Haller, 'Die Rolle der Staatsfinanzen für den Inflationsprozess', in Deutsche Bundesbank (ed.), *Währung und Wirtschaft in Deutschland 1876–1975* (Frankfurt/Main, 1976), pp. 140–1. Quoted in Holtfrerich, *The German Inflation*, p. 137.

11. Dietmar Petzina, *Die deutsche Wirtschaft in der Zwischenkriegszeit* (Wiesbaden, 1977), pp. 95–6.

12. See Robert Weldon Whalen, *Bitter Wounds. German Victims of the Great War, 1914-1939* (Ithica and London, 1984), p. 95.

13. Whalen, *Bitter Wounds*, pp. 156–7.

14. See Holtfrerich, *The German Inflation*, pp. 124–5.

15. See Holtfrerich, *The German Inflation*, p. 317.

16. See the, still rather tentative, discussion in Richard Bessel and David Englander, 'Up from the Trenches: Some Recent Writing on the Soldiers of the Great War', *European Studies Review*, 11 (1981), pp. 387–95.

17. *Protokoll über die Verhandlungen des Parteitages der Sozialdemokratischen Partei Deutschlands. Abgehalten in Weimar vom 10. bis 15. Juni 1919*, (Berlin, 1919), pp. 242–7. Quoted in Heinrich August Winkler, *Von der Revolution zur Stabilisierung. Arbeiter und Arbeiterbewegung in der Weimarer Republik 1918 bis 1924* (Berlin and Bonn, 1984), p. 213.

18. *Protokoll*, pp. 253–281, quoted in Winkler, *Von der Revolution zur Stabilisierung*, p. 213.

19. Wolfgang J. Mommsen, 'The German Revolution 1918-1920: Political Revolution and Social Protest Movement', in Richard Bessel and E.J. Feuchtwanger (eds.), *Social Change and Political Development in Weimar Germany* (London, 1981), p. 26.

20. Feldman, 'Economic and Social Problems of the German Demobilisation', p. 7.

21. Joseph Koeth, 'Die wirtschaftliche Demobilmachung. Ihre Aufgabe und ihre Organe', in *Handbuch der Politik. Vol. IV: Der wirtschaftliche Wiederaufbau* (Berlin and Leipzig, 1921), pp. 163–8.

22. Graeme J. Gill, *Peasants and Government in the Russian Revolution* (London, 1979), pp. 105–87. Quote from p. 131.

23. See Larry Eugene Jones, *German Liberalism and the Dissolution of the Weimar Party System 1918–1933* (Chapel Hill and London, 1988), pp. 225–391.

24. See Richard Bessel, 'Violence as Propaganda: The Role of the Storm Troopers in the Rise of National Socialism', in Thomas Childers (ed.), *The Formation of the Nazi Constituency 1919–1933* (London, 1986), pp. 142–3.

25. Eberhard Kolb, *The Weimar Republic* (London, 1988), pp. 13–19.

26. See Gerald D. Feldman and Irmgard Steinisch, 'Die Weimarer Republik zwischen Sozial und Wirtschaftsstaat. Die Entscheidung gegen den Achtstundentag', in *Archiv für Sozialgeschichte*, 18 (1978), pp. 353–439.

27. Kolb, *The Weimar Republic*, p. 90.
28. It was social contributions, rather than income tax, which formed the main component of the increased deductions from the pay of most working people in Weimar Germany. See Harold James, *The German Slump. Politics and Economics 1924–1936* (Oxford, 1986), p. 203.
29. Table in Peter-Christian Witt, 'Die Auswirkungen der Inflation auf die Finanzpolitik des Deutschen Reiches 1924–1935', in Gerald D. Feldman (ed.), *Die Nachwirkungen der Inflation auf die deutsche Geschichte 1924–1933* (Munich, 1985), p. 93.
30. Knut Borchardt, 'Wirtschaftliche Ursachen des Scheiterns der Weimarer Republik', in Hagen Schulze (ed.), *Weimar. Selbstpreisgabe einer Demokratie. Eine Bilanz Heute* (Düsseldorf, 1980), pp. 211–49, esp. p. 226.
31. Habermas defines a 'motivation crisis' as 'when the socio-cultural system changes in such a way that its output becomes dysfunctional for the state and for the system of social labour'. See Jürgen Habermas, *Legitimation Crisis* (London, 1976), p. 75.
32. Bernd Weisbrod, 'Economic Power and Political Stability Reconsidered: Heavy Industry in Weimar Germany', in *Social History*, 4 (1979), pp. 258–60.
33. See Bernd Weisbrod, 'The Crisis of German Unemployment Insurance in 1928/29 and its Political Repercussions', in W.J. Mommsen (ed.), *The Emergence of the Welfare State in Britain and Germany 1850–1950* (London, 1981), pp. 188–204.
34. See James, *The German Slump*, pp. 178–9; Jones, *German Liberalism*, pp. 355–8.
35. James, *The German Slump*, p. 179.
36. Weisbrod, 'Economic Power and Political Stability Reconsidered', p. 261.
37. This theme underlines much of the discussion in Henry Ashby Turner, *German Big Business and the Rise of Hitler* (New York and Oxford, 1985).
38. Turner, *German Big Business and the Rise of Hitler*, p. 191.
39. See Dieter Gessner, 'The Dilemma of German Agriculture during the Weimar Republic', in Richard Bessel and E.J. Feuchtwanger (eds.), *Social Change and Political Development in Weimar Germany* (London, 1981), pp. 134–54.
40. Gerhard Stoltenberg, *Politische Strömungen im schleswig-holsteinischen Landvolk 1918–1933. Ein Beitrag zur politischen Meinungsbildung in der Weimarer Republik* (Düsseldorf, 1962), pp. 111–13.
41. Dieter Gessner, *Agrarverbände in der Weimarer Republik. Wirtschaftliche und soziale Voraussetzungen agrarkonservativer Politik vor 1933* (Düsseldorf, 1976), pp. 248–51.
42. Archiwum Panstwowe w Poznanie, Oberpräsidium Schneidemühl, Nr. 368, f. 498: Landwirtschaftskammer für die Grenzmark Posen-Westpreußen to the Oberpräsident, Schneidemühl, 3 December 1932.
43. See Michael Geyer, 'Professionals and Junkers: German Rearmament and Politics in the Weimar Republic', in Richard Bessel and E.J.

Feuchtwanger (eds.), *Social Change and Political Development in Weimar Germany* (London, 1981), pp. 77–133; Michael Geyer, *Deutsche Rüstungspolitik 1860–1980* (Frankfurt/Main, 1984), pp. 118–39; Michael Geyer, 'Etudes in Political History: Reichswehr, NSDAP, and the Seizure of Power', in Peter D. Stachura (ed.), *The Nazi Machteroreifung* (London, 1983), pp. 101–23.

44. Karl Dietrich Bracher, *Die Auflösung der Weimarer Republik. Eine Studie zum Problem des Machtverfalls in der Demokratie* (5th edn., Düsseldorf, 1984). The first edition was published in 1955.

45. Mommsen, 'The German Revolution 1918–1920', p. 48.

46. See Eve Rosenhaft. 'Working-Class Life and Working-Class Politics: Communists, Nazis and the State in the Battle for the Streets, Berlin 1928–1932', in Richard Bessel and E.J. Feuchtwanger, *Social Change and Political Development in Weimar Germany* (London, 1981), esp. pp. 223–9.

47. *Statistisches Jahrbuch für das Deutsche Reich 1924/25*, p. 296; Statistisches Reichsamt (ed.), *Statistisches Jahrbuch für das Deutsche Reich 1933* (Berlin, 1933), p. 307.

48. Hans Speier, *German White-Collar Workers and the Rise of Hitler* (New Haven and London, 1986), p. 140.

49. Günther Roth, *The Social Democrats in Imperial Germany. A Study in Working-Class Isolation and National Integration* (Totowa, 1963), p. 159.

50. Between 1918 and 1930 the number of cinemas in Germany more than doubled, from 2300 to more than 5000 – more than in any other European country; in the mid-1920s an estimated two million Germans visited the cinema daily; and in the late Weimar period more films were produced in German studios than in the whole of the rest of Europe. See Kolb, *The Weimar Republic*, pp. 92–3.

51. James Wickham, 'Working-Class Movement and Working-Class Life: Frankfurt am Main during the Weimar Republic', in *Social History*, 8 (1983), pp. 315–43; Günter Berghaus, '"Girlkultur" – Feminism, Americanism and Popular Entertainment in Weimar Germany', in *Journal of Design History*, 1 (1988), pp. 193–219.

52. For some suggestive remarks about this continuity from the Nazi period to the history of post-1945 Germany, see Detlev J.K. Peukert, *Inside Nazi Germany. Conformity, Opposition and Racism in Everyday Life* (London, 1987), pp. 241–2.

53. See Detlev J.K. Peukert, *Die Weimarer Republik. Krisenjahre der klassischen Moderne* (Frankfurt/Main, 1987), esp. pp. 266–71.

DEBATE
AND
DISCUSSION

Comment on Harold James' Paper

Carl-Ludwig Holtfrerich

The function of a critical commentator is to pour water into the wine. Let me state at the outset that Harold James is offering a fine selection of wine, which would taste better without water than with it. So you might want to stop reading here.

I agree with James and others that democracy in the inter-war period collapsed in many countries under pressure from economic depression. But in Germany, it seems to me, parliamentary democracy was more than just a 'fair weather system'. Until its dissolution in the great depression it had proven its capacity to survive the stormiest weather conditions several times: civil-war-like conditions in 1919–20, the Kapp Putsch in March 1920, the Hitler-Ludendorff-Putsch in November 1923, the hyperinflation of 1922–3 as well as the harsh stabilization measures and crisis afterwards, the war-guilt clause of the Versailles Treaty, the early unreasonable reparations demands including the London ultimatum of May 1921, the Ruhr occupation by French and Belgian troops in January 1923, right-wing attacks on the social and political foundation of the Weimar Republic, the populist agitation and referendum against the Young Plan and a good part of the great depression.

Therefore I don't see that the label 'fair weather system' suits the Weimar Republic and that it 'required only a relatively small push to bring down the whole structure'. It is true that the first German Republic was constantly endangered and under attack. But in my view, democracy in Weimar Germany demonstrated an astonishing power of resistance. I think that James himself was aware of this when he wrote elsewhere that even in Britain to whose political system he attributes more than just a fair-weather status in the present paper, democracy 'would have found a price decline of German proportions an intolerable political burden'.[1]

On top of all the other problems it took the greatest depression ever in the history of the industrial world to bring Weimar democracy down. As yet, the Federal Republic of Germany has not been put to the test of such stormy weather. Even after 40 years of relative political stability it is an open question what the outcome of such an encounter of German democracy with collapsing world markets for financial credit, agricultural produce, raw materials, and especially manufactured goods would be.

Where James writes 'some of the causes of Germany's problems stemmed from the world economic setting, but many of them were endogenous', I would have offered just the opposite mix of causation. Most of Weimar Germany's economic problems – during the inflation period, the second half of the 1920s, and especially during the great depression – were caused mainly by international influences, which at times, as during the great depression, aggravated domestic political, social, and economic conflicts of rather normal dimensions into fundamental questions of life and death for the economic, social, and political order.

The notorious reparations issue with periods of extreme demands, fluctuating sums paid, and expectations of further reductions, a final settlement, or total cancellation is a first case in point.

Secondly, the hostile foreign trade environment, with the world's number-one creditor, the United States, playing a leading role in pressing for increased protectionism, is yet another international issue. It induced the American banker and economist B.M. Anderson to remark in 1930 on the US position: 'The debts of the outside world to us are ropes about the necks of our debtors, by means of which we pull them toward us. Our trade restrictions are pitchforks pressed against their bodies, by means of which we hold them off. This situation can obviously involve a very painful strain for the foreign debtor.'[2]

And, finally, the international issue that concerns us most here is the great depression. How much do we need in terms of 'internal weaknesses' as against the 'exogenous shocks' to explain Germany's economic problems during the last stage of the Weimar Republic? In contemporary political debate, Germany's depression was attributed by political parties or economic interest groups to whatever they didn't like about prior economic and social developments, such as the degree of taxation, spending, and intervention generally by the state, the collective bargaining results or government arbitration on labour markets, the welfare system, the concentration or cartellization of industry, misallocation of capital, protection of agriculture etc. The purpose always was to make use of the general anti-depression mood to support political action in favour of partial interests.

When Dingeldey, the German People's Party spokesman advocating industrial interests, complained in the Reichstag on 15 October 1931 that prior legislation had 'systematically chained the private economy' and had taken away its life and liberty to develop, he was interrupted from the audience three times with the same question: 'What about America?' And 'Who chains the American economy?'.[3] Indeed, only a comparative perspective makes it possible to determine in Germany's case to what degree the depression had domestic as against international causes. More research along these lines needs to be done.

Relatively low rates of savings and investment on the macroeconomic level constitute part of the established knowledge of the German economy's weaknesses between hyperinflation and the great depression. The low investment rates also mentioned by James are usually interpreted as a proof of the unfavourable business conditions contemporaneous German industrialists complained about. But a look at the structure of investment is revealing. The investment downturn occurred mainly in agriculture and home construction, while business investment, including industrial investment, kept up with the pre-war level.[4] This structural aspect should contribute to solving the puzzle of low macroeconomic investment ratios, on the one hand, and a rapid modernization of the German economy during the second half of the 1920s, on the other.

The positive results of 'rationalization' are, it seems to me, underrated by James. There was an unprecedented growth in labour productivity in the German economy during the second half of the 1920s, which contributed to the German economy's international competitiveness – as evidenced by an uninterrupted growth of German exports from 1924 to 1929 totalling about 100 per cent[5] – despite the considerable wage increases. The effects of rationalization still need further research, but the movement must have played a more positive role than the one acknowledged by James. It is significant that James fails to mention the machine-tool, the chemical, and the optical industries, i.e. three of Germany's best horses in the industrial export race.

The low savings rate indeed was a great weakness of the Weimar economy. It resulted mainly from the destruction of financial assets through inflation and thereby of the income of the *rentier* class, whose primary economic function in pre-war Germany had been to save. This function was *not* taken up by the wage and salary earners, who were the main beneficiaries of the income redistribution resulting from the great inflation. But it was partially taken up by the government sector. Macroeconomic data compiled by Dietmar Keese[6] reveal that this sector was by far the most important source of domestic savings from 1925 into the great depression, much more important than savings in the private sector (businesses and households). In 1928, for example, net domestic investment of 9.1bn Reichsmark was financed from the following sources: government savings 3.5bn, foreign savings (= capital imports) 3.2bn, private household savings 1.7bn, and undistributed profits 0.7bn Reichsmark. This structure was rather typical for the second half of the 1920s. Viewed from this perspective the government sector of the Weimar Republic did *not* live beyond its means, as is so often contended. The budget deficits of the late 1920s were an expression of the fact that only a part of the government's investment outlays was financed on credit. Therefore, the demand, by domestic industrial interests, the Reichsbank, and by foreign creditors of the Reich, to balance the budget, was a demand to finance not only public consumption and transfer expenditures out of ordinary current revenue, but also all public investment expenditure. This demand makes sense only when one takes into consideration the already mentioned scarcity of savings in the private sector (business and households). The growing government budget deficits after 1927 created financial and economic difficulties not because the government was living beyond its means, but because it contributed less and less to domestic savings, which were in any case low, and this precisely at the same time when the importation of foreign savings (= capital imports) was running down.

The Brüning government rejected the injection of French savings into the German economy immediately after the banking crisis had broken out in July 1931. The French government was willing to grant a long-term credit of two billion Reichsmark, the approximate amount that later surfaced in different work-creation proposals within Germany. But the German side was unwilling to meet the French peace and security concerns that were tied to the loan.[7] At this juncture, the revival of domestic savings would have had to be undertaken to stem the tide of deflation. An expansionary government programme, public investment financed by credit creation, would have been the *domestic* way out of the vicious circle of private income, public revenue, and private and public savings collapse. That the Brüning government, after the banking crisis, did not put up a political fight either for the acceptance of the French credit (albeit tied to the political demand of respecting French defence and national security concerns) or for the political acceptability of domestic credit expansion for work-creation purposes, makes it hard to believe that no room for manoeuvre existed. What we know for sure is that Brüning didn't try it out and that, when he was dismissed 'a hundred metres short of the finish line', the Weimar Republic was a shambles, economically and politically.

Notes

1. Harold James, *The German Slump, Politics and Economics 1924–1936* (Oxford, 1986), p.160.
2. Benjamin M. Anderson, in Chase National Bank (ed.), *The Chase Economic Bulletin* (New York), 14 March 1930. Cited from Gottfried Haberler, *The Theory of International Trade with its Applications to Commercial Policy* (London, 1936), p.80.
3. *Verhandlungen des Reichstags, V. Wahlperiode 1930*, vol.446 (Berlin, 1932), p.2131.
4. For data see my paper in this volume.
5. Institut für Konjunkturforschung (ed.), *Konjunkturstatistisches Handbuch 1933* (Berlin, 1933), p.78.
6. Dietmar Keese, 'Die volkswirtschaftlichen Gesamtgrößen für das Deutsche Reich in den Jahren 1925–1936', in Werner Conze and Hans Raupach (eds.), *Die Staats- und Wirtschaftskrise des Deutschen Reichs 1929/33* (Stuttgart, 1967), p.51.
7. Franz Knipping, *Deutschland, Frankreich und das Ende der Locarno-Ära 1928–1931. Studien zur internationalen Politik in der Anfangsphase der Weltwirtschaftskrise* (München, 1987), p.218. Hans Mommsen, *Die verspielte Freiheit. Der Weg der Republik von Weimar in den Untergang 1918 bis 1933* (Berlin, 1989), pp. 385, 397.

Comment on
Carl Holtfrerich's Paper

Harold James

Although over ten years have passed since Knut Borchardt's 1978 lecture to the Bavarian Academy on 'Constraints and Room for Manœuvre in the Great Economic Crisis of the Early Thirties: Towards a Revision of the Traditional Picture', this is surprisingly one of the first major English-language airings of the issues involved in the subsequent 'Borchardt debate': though a volume of essays, containing a statement by Borchardt on the state of the argument is shortly to appear.[1] Since much of the controversy inevitably consists of points of confrontation and refutation, it is worth pointing out some areas of consensus between some of the participants on each side. Holtfrerich and I disagree fundamentally in our characterization of the Brüning period, but we agree that:

1. Many voters believed that the government had a responsibility to deal with the economic crisis: either to alleviate its consequences, or (more radically) to end it. However, voters did *not* form a consensus on *how* to do this. The two parties to gain large numbers of votes during the depression – the Nazis and the Communists – offered different, not identical, solutions.
2. The perceived failure of Heinrich Brüning's government to act against the depression increased political polarization, and drove many voters 'into the arms of extremists' (Holtfrerich)

who held out 'unfulfillable promises to the German population' (James).

3. Thus the depression contributed to the erosion of democracy.

4. Some of the causes of the depression lay outside the government's control – for instance in the world economic slump, or in the demographic structure of Germany.

The differences between us concern the ease with which an alternative economic policy might have been possible within the framework of Weimar's constitutional and political system.

1. Holtfrerich regards the Weimar economy as less fundamentally sick than either I, or Knut Borchardt, who originally coined the term 'ill' for Weimar.

2. In particular he gives a different account of the contribution to economic catastrophe made by union demands, legislation on arbitration, Labour Ministry policy, and wage settlements.

3. Holtfrerich ignores completely the fiscal constraints on government that have figured heavily in the arguments of Theo Balderston and myself.

4. As a result of the more optimistic picture of what Brüning might have done, Holtfrerich is less inclined to see the period as a tragedy than as an era of mistaken policy carried out for ideological (conservative) reasons, or from a misplaced sense of the importance of removing Germany's reparation burden.

1. *Is an economy sick?* What was the state of the German economy in the later 1920s? We have to wrestle in the historical literature with clichés like the 'golden twenties'. When we use contemporary evidence on such issues, we should always bear in mind for what purposes that material was produced. Using, as Holtfrerich does, the public statements and reports of the Agent-General for Reparation Payments, will naturally yield an over-optimistic view: because the Agent saw it as his mission to extract surpluses from the German economy and to deny that Germany was too impoverished to pay. Equally, on the other side, it would be no good relying on business reports, which tend to be calculatedly gloomy:

again with the tactical purpose of showing that industry could not afford to pay high taxes and high wages. For both a domestic and an international audience, German banks and industry did not want to appear too prosperous even in the 'good years' 1927 and 1928. In 1927 the Deutsche Bank's Annual Report said: 'There can in fact be no question of any steady development of our economic life as long as the Reparation problem has not been solved definitively and in a manner favourable to us'. In 1928, the Report referred to 'the complete inner weakness of our economy. It is so overloaded with taxes required by the excessively expensive apparatus of state, with over-high social payments, and particularly with the reparations sum now reaching its "normal" level [as laid down by the Dawes Plan], that any healthy growth is constricted. Development is only possible to the extent that these restrictive chains are removed'.[2]

Fortunately, historians have other and independent ways of arriving at judgments. Was the depression of 1929–32 in Germany merely a consequence of world developments – the fall in primary product prices since 1926, or the US stock market boom and collapse? Germany suffered from higher unemployment and greater GNP decline than other European industrialized economies. Recent work on economic history – first by Peter Temin, and then by Balderston, Borchardt, James, and von Kruedener – has emphasized the domestic roots of Germany's problems. Dietmar Petzina justifiably speaks of a *Wachsttumsstau* ('blocked growth') in the Weimar Republic.[3] The particular economic weaknesses of Germany – which made Germany much more vulnerable to crisis – included the following: a discrepant development of labour productivity growth and real wages and an unstable financial system that was made more volatile by the large public sector debt incurred in the later 1920s.

2. *The Labour Argument*. A great deal of the discussion of labour productivity depends on the choice of time period for analysis. No one disputes that labour productivity per man hour rose rapidly in the later 1920s: but it rose from low levels, and the rise may not have been due to the 'rationalization wave' of the decade. Labour mobility was extremely high

during the inflation (up to 1923), and the return of stable circumstances and the reduction of job turnover rates appreciably raised productivity.

There is no doubt, either, on the basis of the figures supplied by Holtfrerich, that for the span 1925–9, and particularly in the latter part, real wages rose by more than productivity. From the 1925 base, by 1929 hourly wages exceeded productivity gains by 13.2 per cent.[4] Holtfrerich's argument does not deny the rapidity of the wage rise, but instead emphasizes that relative to pre-war levels, labour had gained little by 1929. It is not surprising that businessmen projected the development of 1925–9 forward into the future and saw declining profit opportunities, and that such a calculation reduced their willingness to invest and increased the volume of their complaints against the Weimar system. Again, we should discount much of this contemporary clamour, though Balderston notes, after surveying the 1927–8 combination of falls in real output per worker with wage rises: 'businessmen doubtless always complain of these things, but seldom with the intensity apparent in these years'.[5]

How much of the rise in real wages was due to institutional factors – the existence of the unions and their position in the Weimar polity? Of course it is true that union pressure is not the only determinant of the real wage level. In late 1920s Britain the real wage level was and is generally agreed to have been a problem, though unions were weak, and the responsibility for the development is most commonly laid at the door of the Bank of England's exchange rate policy (the return to gold at the rate of $4.86). In consequence real wages have entered the literature on the causes of British weakness in the 1920s without provoking any of the controversy which has followed from Borchardt's argumentation. Lionel Robbins's 1934 picture of Britain is still fundamentally undisputed: 'Wage rates in Britain were more or less constant from 1924 onwards. All that happened was that, in the face of a tendency to a decline in the demand for labour, wage rates were not lowered. The causes of the change in the conditions of the market did not originate with the trade unions. If the analysis given above is correct, they originated partly in monetary policy and partly in changes in world markets. But the effects were the same as would have been the case if they had'.[6]

A price weakness in agriculture should also raise real wages, although in Germany agricultural prices were to some extent insulated from the world market through tariff protection. Government regulation of housing also certainly helped to create shortages, reduce the geographical mobility of labour, and thus put upward pressure on wages. Pricing polices of cartels and syndicates did increase costs for the consumer and make it possible for business to pay higher wage rates (though some of the cartelized prices collapsed in the depression).

But in making this list of determinants of real wages levels, it would be difficult in the German case to ignore high nominal wage increases (unlike the case of Britain in the later 1920s: a commentator such as Robbins explicitly recognized the difference). The nominal rises do not appear in Holtfrerich's argument, yet they distinguish the German from the French or the British experience of the same time. The changes in nominal wage rates indicate that something was happening when wages were set in rounds of negotiation and occasionally arbitration and the imposition of legally binding pay awards. In explaining the German outcome, it would be hard to argue that the institutional framework of wage bargaining did not play a role. The awareness of the possibility of compulsory arbitration, and a Labour Ministry which until 1929 was openly sympathetic to wage increases, inevitably entered into the calculations of those undertaking wage bargaining, on both sides. Even in cases where there was no arbitration, the possibility encouraged a higher starting bid on the labour side, and greater willingness to make concessions on the part of the employers. When discussing the influence of cartels on the economy, many Weimar commentators, including Adolf Weber and Robert Liefmann but also the socialist Rudolf Hilferding, included unions when they spoke of market rigidities. Unions, indeed, may be considered as a special case of a cartel: a labour cartel.

Finally, Holtfrerich tries to explain the rising share of labour in National Income by reference to the shifting structure of employment, and the growing share of well paid white collar workers in the workforce. Such analysis appears convincing, but the higher skill levels he adduces should be reflected in higher productivity figures. Otherwise it would be fair to conclude, as does a recent scholar of the problem, that what had occurred was 'an uneconomic shift to white-collar employment in labour-force composition'.[7] The test of whether such a development was or was not 'economic' lies precisely in the productivity figures already examined: and they show a relatively poor development in Germany.

3. *Higher Interest Rates and Fiscal Constraints*. Holtfrerich considers the fundamental difficulty of the Weimar economy to be not the position of the trades unions, but rather the high level of interest, which notoriously affects house purchases and construction adversely, and may (although this is much more contested in economic theory) reduce investment levels. These high rates were a legacy of the destruction of the German capital market during the great postwar inflation. They had implications for policy formulation that Holtfrerich does not consider.

High interest rates followed not from any deliberate government decision to keep money dear, but from Germany's adherence to the gold standard after 1924, and from market-determined rates following from German integration in international capital markets. They represented the premium needed to attract in foreign loans (without which the Weimar economy would have faltered earlier). They also constituted a political necessity, in that they resulted from the gold exchange standard as imposed by the western powers in the international treaties of London (1924) and The Hague (1929–30). The choice in the mid-1920s before Germany's leaders was much larger than acceptance of the gold standard and capital inflows or rejection: it was a political matter of accommodation with the West or of confrontation. The latter would have meant a highly radical stance, and it could not be held to be a question of fine-tuning in economic policy.

The legacy of the hyperinflation made for an instability in public finance: it made it not only more expensive but, given the historical legacy, more difficult to borrow. In my arguments about Weimar's weakness, as well as in those of

Theo Balderston and William McNeil, this consideration constitutes a major part.[8] High public deficits in the later 1920s in turn played a part in pushing up German interest rates. A close modern analogy would be the role of the US federal budget deficit in raising world interest rates in the 1980s.

The fiscal constraint imposed by difficulties in funding the government debt became very apparent in the course of 1929, and at the end of the year caused a major political crisis when the SPD Finance Minister resigned. It led Brüning's predecessor Hermann Müller to begin the shift towards a deflationary budgetary position. It also was the greatest single limitation on Brüning's room for manœuvre. Yet it makes absolutely no appearance in Holtfrerich's argument.

The narrow capital market, the legacy of the inflation, and government funding difficulties in the later 1920s meant a high degree of vulnerability to the crowding out effects of public deficits if they were to appear in the depression, when the capital market narrowed yet further. Leading civil servants, and the German central bank (Reichsbank), took the position that the stimulating and expansionary effects of higher public spending would be outweighed by a negative effect on financial confidence: bank credits to non-bank borrowers would be cut; and business would be damaged by the rationing of credit through higher interest rates or through non-market credit allocation (administered through the fiat of the German Great Banks). This became the fundamental fiscal dilemma of government in the depression years: balanced budgets involved cutting aggregate demand, reduced profits and increased unemployment; unbalanced budgets meant credit withdrawals, credit rationing, interest rate rises, and for companies reduced liquidity of illiquidity. The latter option reduced demand and employment as surely as the former. It was not so much a question of either 'lack of choices' or 'lack of determination' as of weighing carefully each choice, and taking – as Brüning did – what he believed to be the least painful one.

In July 1931 the greatly feared bank collapse became a reality. Did this free the government from the fiscal dilemma? It was not clear to anyone that the bank crisis was a once and for all event. The financial collapse could have become a recurrent one – as was the case in the USA at the time, where between 1930 and 1933 wave after wave of bank failures constituted the transmission mechanism of an ever worsening depression.

In such a circumstance, the only room for expansionary policy lay not in fiscal activity (expanding government spending) but in monetary expansion.

Here, despite the appearance of rigid adherence to orthodoxy, the Reichsbank was quite willing to act in an innovatory way in order to remove the problems of illiquidity associated with the depression. In particular it founded an acceptance bank (*Akzept-und Garantiebank*) to provide an additional signature for bank bills, and in 1932 two institutions (the *Finanzierungsinstitut* AG, and the *Tilgungskasse für gewerbliche Kredite*) to allow banks gradually to write off their frozen or valueless assets. The Reichsbank also took a very active role in promoting trade credit for exports to USSR. By 1932 German banks provided, through consortia backed by the Reichsbank, 610m RM credit; and the Russian orders directly created some 150,000 jobs. More importantly, they allowed firms, particularly in engineering, which otherwise would have had to close down, to stay in business.[9] The Reichsbank also produced the plan for tax certificates given to employers creating additional jobs – the plan that later became the reflationary 'Papen programme' of September 1932.

These measures were not loudly trumpeted to the German public, and they did not form a coherent reflationary package. Which government in the early 1930s did have such an overall scheme for tackling the depression? Britain's National Government after 1931 reduced interest rates and applied higher external tariffs and Imperial Preference but remained fiscally conservative. Franklin Roosevelt's 'New Deal' administration imposed price stabilization for agriculture, devaluation of the dollar, new spending programmes, but also a cutting back of civil service pay.

The common international experience of the early 1930s was that the open advocacy of budget deficits, far from demonstrating political imagination, showed disregard for the preoccupations and priorities of voters. In his 1932 election campaign, Roosevelt had made the focal point of his attack on President Hoover *not* the policy of deflation, but an irresponsible and profligate attitude to the Federal budget. 'I regard reduction in Federal spending as one of the most important issues of this campaign', said Roosevelt. 'It is the most direct and effective contribution the government can make to business'. The (successful) Democratic platform in 1932 demanded a 25 per cent reduction of Federal expenditure and subsequently a balanced budget.[10] In Britain, Ramsay MacDonald made similar anti-inflationary statements during the 1931 general election, and to widespread public approval. When he paid his deposit in his constituency of Seaham in German inflation marks as a demonstration of the consequences of profligacy, he was, the press reported, 'cheered to the echo'.[11]

Germany combined public support for the 'verities' of fiscal orthodoxy with a tacitly experimental and new course already in 1931. The interest rate differential existed while Germany was integrated into the world economy in the 1920s, and followed inevitably from that integration.[12] After the summer of 1931, when the previous links were cut through exchange control and 'voluntary' standstill agreements in which creditors collectively agreed to leave some of their loans in Germany, a policy of interest rate reduction and credit expansion was possible, and was implemented – before 1933. Initially, the new measures may have been clumsy, and it might plausibly be argued that the decreed interest rate reduction of December 1931 proved counterproductive in that it sapped confidence in the integrity of the system. But something was happening.

4. *Politics and Tragedy*. What were the political possibilities for enacting a much grander expansionary programme during the twenty-six months of Brüning's chancellorship? It is important to note how far Borchardt's critics have tacitly given way here: they are now (in my view rightly) sceptical of the possibilities for alternative economic policies before the summer of 1931, or, in other words, before the banking collapse. July 1931 looks like the caesura of the Brüning period. Heinrich August Winkler says: 'Brüning could rely for a long time, until the autumn of 1931, on a broad consensus when he

made cutbacks the first priority in budgetary policy. . . . After the autumn of 1931, the policy of deflation stemmed not from economic necessities but from self-defined political priorities'.[13] Holtfrerich accepts in the second half of his contribution the position that only after the summer of 1931 did real alternatives exist.

This was late in the day: the clouds had gathered and the sun of democracy was setting. Total unemployment may have reached almost six millions in the first quarter of 1931. The Labour offices recorded 4,971,800 registered unemployed in February 1931, but their criteria excluded many unemployed.[14] The banking crisis made matters worse. Politics had become highly radicalized. Talking about changes in economic policy at this stage of the depression is very much a matter of shutting stable doors after bolted horses. Expansionary fiscal programmes have a notoriously long lead time before effects in increasing employment start to be visible.

Holtfrerich is specifically calling for a programme of higher public spending – perhaps public works – as the realistic 'alternative' to the Brüning policy of an orthodox facade with a more or less concealed monetary expansion. As evidence, he uses the attitudes of key figures in government whom he sees as sympathetic to reform: ministers (Dietrich, Warmbold, Stegerwald) and senior civil servants (Schäffer, Trendelenburg, Lautenbach, Wagemann). Readers of his and my contribution to this volume will be puzzled by the role played by Hans Schäffer, State Secretary in the Finance Ministry and without doubt the key figure in shaping fiscal policy under Brüning. In Holtfrerich's presentation, but not in mine, Schäffer appears to be a critic of Brüning. In fact he perceived more clearly than any other figure the fiscal dilemma, that unbalanced budgets might disequilibriate the financial sector and thus wreak general economic havoc. He formulated what Winkler has seen as the consensus policy of deflation until the summer of 1931. In the late autumn of 1931 (November) he pressed the clearly reluctant Finance Minister Hermann Dietrich for an increase in taxation. In early 1932 he criticized the Wagemann plan on the grounds that it did not tackle the issues involved in bank reform adequately, since the German weaknesses 'were consequences of the shortage of capital and not to be remedied by technical measures'. He attacked the publicity that Wagemann had mustered around his plan as representing 'advertisements for quack medicines or cleaning agents'.[15] In other words, he blocked most persistently exactly those public aspects of anti-cyclical policy which Holtfrerich *post facto* regards as constituting political 'leadership'.

It is clearly critical to know in what circumstances Schäffer was on 2 September 1932 prepared to argue for expansion. The possibility of a public works programme was discussed quite extensively in the summer of 1931, and a conference of the Friedrich-List-Gesellschaft met on 16–17 September 1931 to debate 'The Possibilities and Consequences of a Credit Expansion'. The session was to be attended by practical men and economists, and to meet in camera (for Schäffer, secrecy about economic policy remained a vital concern).

The weekend after the List-Gesellschaft conference showed that fear of financial crisis was still a realistic concern and not the hysterical product of a political ideology. On Monday 21 September a financial crisis in Britain forced the pound off the gold standard, and a new wave of financial instability gripped the world. Schäffer now abandoned this sort of plan, and criticized those who, like Dietrich and Stegerwald, wanted a more expansionary economic policy for political motives. Again, he pointed out the iron inexorabilities of the German fiscal dilemma. He attacked the Wagemann plan, not so much for its rather modest and limited content, but firstly because it seems to threaten confidence and financial stability, and secondly because it ran the risk of generating false hopes about what government policy might do.

A similar difficulty arises in the case of Wilhelm Lautenbach, who had already in 1930 argued that additional state orders could make up for the fall in demand caused by wage cuts. After the two major shocks to confidence in 1931, the bank crisis of July and the sterling devaluation of September, Lautenbach abandoned the idea of budget expansion financed through credit creation, since it 'would damage us in the eyes of foreigners and for that reason is in practice impossible'. He argued instead for cuts in cartel prices and in wages, and these then entered into Brüning's most deflationary decree of all, that of 8 December 1931. Borchardt has provocatively, but accurately, described his recommendations of 1931 as a blueprint for these components of Brüning's Emergency Decree.[16]

The discussion about 'alternatives' in government circles thus ran in a rather different direction to that described by Holtfrerich. Whereas ministers (including by the spring of 1932 Brüning himself) felt a need to 'do something' in order not to lose all political support, civil servants spelt out, coldly and dispassionately, why nothing could be done.

Industry's attitude to the Brüning policy is also problematical, and should not be described as simple opposition to deflationism. It is difficult to speak of industry, let alone business, as following one coherent course. Businessmen too were shocked by the crisis of July 1931, and indeed were among its first victims. Many nevertheless resented state assistance in reconstructing the banks, although this represented a necessary and unavoidable first step in the reconstruction of a market economy.

Until the summer of 1931, some businessmen had disliked Brüning's moderation in dealing with the trade unions, and felt that an open attack on the principles of wage contracts and compulsory state arbitration would be preferable. Nevertheless they had been held back from a too forward expression of their views by the calculation that a fall of Brüning would reduce foreign confidence in Germany and this would lead to a major credit crisis that would immediately harm business.[17] After 13 July 1931, such restraint no longer seemed necessary: there *was* a German credit crisis now, and business felt freer in the statement of its socially reactionary objectives. This accounts for part of the more hostile position towards the Brüning government.

It is, however, most doubtful whether business warmed to Hjalmar Schacht after his October 1931 speech to the meeting of the 'National Opposition' assembly in Bad Harzburg with its bitter attack on the policies of Brüning and Reichsbank President Luther. Schacht cast doubt on Germany's ability to repay her debts, and some of his industrialist friends felt alarm.[18] In addition, it is not clear what Schacht was calling for. He spent a great part of his Harzburg speech denouncing Brüning and Luther for allowing a currency to circulate without any real reserves or backing – in short, for being too inflationary. Throughout 1932, he repeated these charges, at greatest length in a speech in Kassel in June 1932, and as a book, 'The Principles of German Economic Policy'.[19] He boasted of his role in introducing the new stable currency in 1923–4; and he was treated, by his friends, as the guarantor of financial probity and orthodoxy during the depression. Hitler's appointment of Schacht to succeed Luther in the Reichsbank was generally taken as a demonstration that the new regime would not be irresponsible or inflationary. If Schacht had any policy recommendation in the midst of his heady demagoguery at Harzburg, it was economic nationalism in the form of repudiation of Germany's foreign debts accompanied by extreme fiscal orthodoxy.

Schacht's career shows how much political mileage might be extracted from an open stance against inflation. On the other side of the political spectrum, the reflationary proposals of Woytinsky, Baade and Tarnow were by the summer of 1932 submerged by the trade unions in a more general call for the socialist transformation of the economy: a demonstration of the political unacceptability on the left of a simple call for counter-deflationary policies on their own.

There is here a paradox: calling for reflation did not produce political gains for anyone; while on the other hand being associated with depression and deflation meant loss of popularity. Brüning recognized both sides of this paradox: and he was also quite well aware how unpopular he was in Germany. Public hostility was open and visible. When he visited the bankrupt farms in eastern Germany in January 1931, or when he came back from London in June through the port of Bremerhaven, he was faced by massive demonstrations. By February 1932, he was prepared to consider work creation plans – not so much because they might be effective against the depression, but because they would be a response to the call for government action.

Why had he not moved in this direction earlier? There is no sign in the historical record that Brüning welcomed the depression, or that he saw it as anything other than as a tragedy. That tragedy had causes: in German domestic politics, the expansion of state and local government spending, the size of the deficits, and the effect on the whole economy of the highly generous civil service pay award of 1927. In international relations, the world economic crisis had been made worse by the complex of reparations and war debts. If these matters were not corrected, the circumstances that had produced economic crisis would recur. It seems odd to describe someone who sees an unpleasant process, and takes steps to avoid that process happening again, as 'instrumentalizing' the process for his own ends.

In any case, what Brüning believed or did not believe may well actually be irrelevant to the question of policy choices: the fiscal dilemma, so persistently and carefully explained to the cabinet by State Secretary Schäffer and others, attached high costs – political and economic – to *any* course of action the government would take. Budgetary expansion risked financial collapse (economic) and public criticism for inflationism (political); budgetary restraint meant high unemployment and bankruptcy levels (economic) and public criticism from the victims of the depression.

It is certainly possible to follow Holtfrerich and convict Brüning retrospectively of 'disrespect for the electorate's primary concerns' – but how do we deal with the problem that those concerns were in practice unrealizable? Some, indeed most, expectations had to be disappointed in the Germany of the world depression. Peasants could not get complete debt relief, taxpayers lower rates and workers more employment by the stroke of any wand that economic management might supply. The National Socialists were able to appeal to these disparate voters not because Hitler had a better answer, or because he had greater respect for the electorate's primary concerns, but for one reason, and one reason alone. He was not in power in 1932.

Brüning's language at the time, and in his memoirs, is filled with words and phrases such as 'sacrifice' and 'courage to take unpopular steps'. In September 1930, he explains in his memoirs, he dissolved the Reichstag because he believed 'that the [economic] crisis would last for four years, and that a new government would have to take yet more unpopular measures and keep up those already in force, if it did not want to face the complete destruction of our finances and our economy'.[20] In his election speech to the Rhineland Centre Party in Cologne – in other words to his own supporters – on 8 August 1930, he said: 'I do not need to assure you that none of the members of the cabinet pressed to participate in this painful operation necessary for the preservation of life of the German people. Men could make their political reputation and assure their popularity in far better ways then by entering into this cabinet. The addiction and struggle for popularity can never save a people. We can only save it, if we have the courage to take responsibility in the darkest hour and to hold our heads high, come what may'.[21]

To me, Brüning's language does not seem inappropriate. It is that of a decent man, confronting an impossible situation and attempting to make responsible choices; and who, if he had remained in office for four rather than two years, would have had some successes as economic recovery set in. In the light of what happened after Heinrich Brüning fell, it is actually hard not to follow Borchardt and call the Chancellor's position 'tragic'.

Notes

1. The volume, edited by Jürgen von Kruedener, is scheduled to be published in 1989 by Berg, Leamington Spa, *Economic Crisis and Political Collapse: The Weimar Republic 1924–1933*.
2. Deutsche Bank, *Annual Report for 1927*, p. 8; *Jahresbericht für 1928*, pp. 19–20.
3. Dietmar Petzina, 'Zur Interpretation der wirtschaftlichen Entwicklung Deutschlands zwischen den Weltkriegen', in *International Economic History Association Congress Budapest 1982, B3: Long-Run Trends* (Budapest, 1982).
4. Stephen A. Schuker, *American Reparations to Germany 1919–1933: Implications for the Third-World Debt Crisis* (Princeton N.J., 1988, Studies in International Finance No.61), p. 85.
5. Theo Balderston, 'Cyclical Fluctuations in Germany 1924–1929' (Edinburgh PhD, 1979), p. 313.
6. Lionel Robbins, *The Great Depression* (London, 1934), p. 83.
7. Schuker, *American Reparations*, p. 11.
8. William C. McNeil, *American Money and the Weimar Republic: Economics and Politics on the Eve of the Great Depression* (New York, 1986).
9. Harold James, *The Reichsbank and Public Finance in Germany 1924–1933* (Frankfurt, 1985), pp. 311–13.

10. Kenneth S. Davis, *FDR: The New York Years 1928–1933* (New York, 1985), pp. 367, 371.
11. David Marquand, *Ramsay MacDonald* (London, 1977), p. 669.
12. Gerd Hardach, *Weltmarktorientierung und relative Stagnation: Währungspolitik in Deutschland 1924–1931* (Berlin, 1976).
13. Heinrich A. Winkler, *Der Weg in die Katastrophe: Arbeiter und Arbeiterbewegung in der Weimarer Republik 1930 bis 1933* (Berlin and Bonn, 1987), pp. 577, 579.
14. Winkler, *Der Weg*, p. 24; *Statistisches Jahrbuch für das Deutsche Reich*.
15. Schäffer diaries: memoranda of 19 and 28 Nov. 1931; and entry of 2 Feb. 1932. 28 Jan. 1932 Schäffer to Wagemann, Schäffer papers.
16. Knut Borchardt, 'Zur Aufarbeitung der Vor- und Frühgeschichte des Keynesianismus in Deutschland: Zugleich ein Beitrag zur Position von W. Lautenbach', *Jahrbücher für Nationalökonomie und Statistik 197* (1987), pp. 359–70.
17. Michael Grübler, *Die Spitzenverbände der Wirtschaft und das erste Kabinett Brüning: Eine Quellenstudie* (Düsseldorf, 1982).
18. Henry A. Turner, *German Big Business and the Rise of Hitler* (New York, 1985), p. 168.
19. Hjalmar Schacht, *Grundsätze deutscher Wirtschaftspolitik* (Oldenburg, 1932).
20. Heinrich Brüning, *Memoiren 1918–1934* (Stuttgart, 1970), p. 608.
21. Heinrich Brüning, *Zwei Jahre am Steuer des Reichs: Reden aus Brünings Kanzlerzeit* (Cologne, 1932), p. 15.

Comment on Dick Geary's Paper

Carl-Ludwig Holtfrerich

Dick Geary has produced a fine overview of employer and labour positions within and towards the Weimar Republic. He has most clearly illuminated the cleavages and factions within each of the two camps and the changes in positions over time.

It might seem self-evident, but I think Geary chose well to point out once more, that 'the Republic collapsed in a deflationary crisis characterized by falling prices and mass unemployment, not in the period of inflation or hyperinflation'. It means that the best chance to avoid the collapse of democracy in Germany lay in mitigating the effects of deflation.

Geary mentions one important economic sector in which the effects seem to have been stronger than in any other: the building trade, with 90 per cent unemployment. This labour-intensive domestic industry could have played a key role in government support for employment and stimulation of demand for other parts of the economy as well.[1]

Geary mentions 'high cartelized prices' and 'price-inflexibility' on the part of German coal and steel producers. As I argue in my paper, it might well have been this kind of rigidity that posed a more important barrier to full employment in the pre-depression Weimar economy than the wage level.

Finally, the data on low capacity utilization in German steel works, which Geary reports for 1925 to 1930, present a clue to where the way out of this economic problem lay. State Secretary Hans Schäffer's expansionary work-creation proposal of 2 September 1931, which I have presented in more detail in my paper, was based on the very insight that wage-cuts (and, I add, a reduction in taxes) were no solution to a profit squeeze resulting from a large underutilization of production capacities in capital-intensive industries such as steel. In such circumstances, the solution must be sought in a stimulation of demand.

Notes

1. See also J. Joseph Lee, 'Policy and Performance in the German Economy, 1925–35: a Comment on the Borchardt Thesis' in Michael Laffan (ed.), *The Burden of German History 1919–45. Essays for the Goethe Institute* (London, 1988), pp. 141–3.

Comment on
Dick Geary's Paper

Harold James

Dick Geary's paper fits well with the general themes of other
papers in this volume: that the disintegration of the Weimar
Republic can be viewed as a result of massive disaffection
caused by the collapse of initially high hopes. 'A large section
of the German working class ... expected more of the 1918
Revolution than just democratic reforms.' We have reached
a consensus that in 1919 a political system was created that
promised far more than it could deliver.

Geary is right at the same time to emphasize the role played
by authoritarian business interests in the movement away
from democracy. Two of the key steps on Germany's path
to dictatorship were the result, not of voting behaviour, but
rather of political manœuvre and intrigue: the fall of Hermann Müller in March 1930, and the dismissal of Heinrich
Brüning in May 1932. In the DVP, the business party *par
excellence*, Gustav Stresemann held the influence of heavy
industry in check, but after his death in October 1929 the
party launched itself on a more radical line, and tension
mounted in Müller's Great Coalition government. In the
spring of 1932 increasing business hostility to Brüning played
some part in President von Hindenburg's calculation that
Brüning no longer had the confidence of the German people,
though the hostility of the agrarians and the intrigues of
General von Schleicher played a greater role.

It is also correct to add that small business was more likely than the major industrial leaders to support Hitler. A substantial number of Hitler's intimates in the early 1930s indeed came from such a background: figures such as Wilhelm Keppler, Otto Wagener, Albert Pietzsch.

I am less convinced by the attempt to associate the precise political trajectory of business leaders with their economic fortunes, or to argue that 'dynamic industries' or export oriented trades (chemical or electrical) were more likely to stay committed to democracy than the more traditional heavy industries (coal, iron and steel) of the Rhine-Ruhr and Westphalia. To begin with, as Geary observes, by the 1920s extensive vertical integration meant that the divisions in industrial structure had become blurred. The large steel firms such as GHH or Krupp also owned great engineering and ship-building complexes which depended on the world market, and they fought desperately against protectionist plans that would help German agriculture but equally would invite certain retaliation from Germany's trading partners. At the same time coal producers began to move into chemical production.

The argument about different cost structures is scarcely compelling either: having a lower element of wage costs did not guarantee any immunity to depression, and high fixed costs rather increased vulnerability – particularly in the light of the exceptionally high interest rates during the financial crisis of the summer of 1931.

In general, moreover, there is a logical problem about the linking of business interests with political stances: the number of leading business men is so small that it is impossible to make the sort of statistical correlation that is essential in the case of our understanding of demoscopy in Weimar. We know that Catholics, or the unemployed, are less likely to have voted Nazi than were Protestants, or livestock farmers. These correlations refer to large groups of people, and they indicate the likelihood of certain forms of voting behaviour: they cannot be contradicted by finding individual cases of Protestant pig farmers who may not have voted for Hitler. When we speak of big business, however, we are speaking of a small elite, most of whom detested Weimar democracy and a few of whom supported Hitler. The size of the group is such as to permit no more confident statement than this. At this level of high political action, individual decisions and actions count for a great deal.

The political opinions of business also altered quite dramatically over the course of a few months: the most famous story, which has been well told by Henry Turner, sees Paul Reusch of the GHH, one of the most politically active of Weimar's steel and engineering industrialists, attempting in the spring of 1932 to win Hitler over to his view of the economy, but much more hostile to the Nazis by the autumn of that year. Reusch incidentally was not present at Bad Harzburg, and it makes little sense to see him as a part of a long-standing Nazi-Nationalist coalition: his absence from the Harzburg meeting was indeed bitterly criticized by Dr Schacht.

Schacht, another central figure in Geary's account, cannot be said to be a representative businessman, any more than say Schleicher could be claimed to be a typical German army officer. He had resigned as President of the Reichsbank in March 1930, complaining that he had been abandoned by his industrial friends in the struggle against the Müller government. By the end of 1932 the correspondence of Reusch and Krupp is filled with alarm about Schacht's autarkic economic plans. After 30 January 1933, Schacht delighted in bullying business into giving election campaign funds to the NSDAP; and four years later he lost a bitter clash with Hermann Göring over the reordering of the German steel industry, in part because the steel magnates would not stand behind him. Schacht was above all an unscrupulous political adventurer, almost universally held to be untrustworthy.

In retrospect it may seem plausible for Geary to claim that 'the fragmentation of the innumerable bourgeois parties and the electoral triumphs of the Nazis between 1930 and 1932 made the hope of an anti-socialist bloc *without the NSDAP* sheer fantasy.' Unfortunately German history is filled with occasions in which traditional elites, obsessed with strange fantasies, behaved in an unrealistic but often destructive way. The non-Nazi bourgeois bloc is not the only example in the Weimar Republic: throughout the 1920s, many businessmen spent large sums on the Ukrainian nationalist Hetman Skoropadski in the belief that he would bring down Russia's bolshevik rulers.

When assigning business responsibility for the collapse of Weimar it is easier to see an impact at the beginning of the depression – in bringing down Müller in 1930 – than two and a half years later, in actually putting Hitler into power in January 1933. Business's relentless opposition to democratic government – for the reasons well described by Geary – is nicely characterized by Richard Bessel as an 'abdication' of responsibility on the part of the old elite: a destructive activity rather than a subversive conspiracy. For that conspiracy, we need to seek other actors and motives; and at this level attempts to make connections between economics and politics work least well.

Comments on the Papers of Carl Holtfrerich, Harold James, and Dick Geary

Richard Bessel

If one divides historians of Weimar Germany into 'optimists' and 'pessimists', the pessimists have perhaps an unfair advantage: the troubled political history of the Weimar Republic does not give many grounds for optimism. Yet, considering the difficulties inherent in making the 'optimists'' case, it is noteworthy that until rather recently they have held sway. For years the overriding incentive for studying the Weimar Republic was to uncover the roots of the horrors which succeeded it. Understandably, historians have been ill-disposed to suggest that the path to dictatorship was a one-way street with all the detours closed off. Furthermore, there has been a strong desire – again understandable – to assign blame for what is probably the worst disaster in modern European history. Whether the aim has been to explain why Germany's 'experiment' in democracy ran aground, or to learn the 'lessons' of Weimar, or to castigate particular groups or individuals for allowing Hitler into the Reich Chancellory, historians of interwar Germany have been loathe to admit the possibility of a certain inevitability about the collapse of the Weimar Republic. Only in recent years, and stimulated in large measure by seemingly impersonal arguments about economic structures, have historians become more willing to think the unthinkable.

Yet we should not try to create disagreement where there is none. All the contributors to this volume share considerable agreement about the political and economic problems which faced the Weimar Republic. Furthermore, all would concur that the rise of the Nazi movement was more a consequence of than a pre-condition for the disintegration of Weimar democracy; all – whatever our assessment of the possibilities for its survival – would deny that the collapse of the Weimar Republic necessarily had to lead to the 'Third Reich'. The differences in our approaches involve the degree to which we believe that there were viable alternatives to the disastrous course pursued by politicians and interest groups in Weimar Germany, and how we conceive of the relation between economics and politics. In what follows I shall concentrate especially on Dick Geary's contribution to this volume, but before turning to Geary let me first make a few comments about the contributions of Carl-Ludwig Holtfrerich and Harold James. I do not want to enter into details of the debate between Holtfrerich and James, but there are a few points concerning the intersection of economics and politics where comment seems appropriate. Let me begin with some points raised by Holtfrerich.

Holtfrerich is concerned to demonstrate that reflationary economic policy was not necessarily a dirty word in the early 1930s and that the success of the Nazis proved this: 'If the Nazis were able to mobilize such tremendous political support for their promises to revive the economy, could Brüning and his political camp not have done better with actual measures in that direction?' But there were crucial differences between Hitler's position and that of Brüning. Brüning, despite his well-documented desire to recast the German political system in a more authoritarian mould, had to operate within existing domestic- and foreign-political constraints. Hitler, on the other hand, had built a huge, disparate and volatile political movement on the support of people who rejected the very basis of politics in which such constraints were recognized. As long as he was in opposition, Hitler did not have to face the consequences of the contradictory economic policy statements of the Nazi Party or the fears they might arouse. And once he got into power, he was willing and able to use repression (as James notes, to 'escape' from his 'unfulfillable promises') in a way Brüning, to his credit, never dreamt of.

Brüning as Chancellor constantly had to look over his shoulder, as Hitler the opposition politician and then dictator did not. While examining economic policy *per se* it may seem logical to posit that what was possible for Hitler should have been possible for Brüning. But this overlooks the fundamental differences in their political positions.

In conclusion, Holtfrerich asserts that the underlying problem of the Weimar economy stemmed not from excessively high wages but from insufficient savings, especially in the wake of the Inflation. Again, from a narrowly economic perspective this appears plausible. But would his closing suggestion – that 'the economic system and the social compromise of the Weimar Republic could have been viable, had it included an arrangement for the promotion of capital formation from wage and salary income in order to meet the requirements of the economic system as it emerged from the hyperinflation' – have been sustainable *politically*? After reading Dick Geary's discussion of working-class politics in Weimar Germany, it is difficult to answer in the affirmative. Could the trade unions or the SPD have advocated such a course? Wages may have been rising, but they were not high, and memories of the bitter distributional struggles of the inflation years were fresh. A policy of forced savings might have been virtuous, but in Germany during the 1920s, where many people had extremely low incomes and where the political system was excessively penetrated by narrow economic interests, there were few groups which could afford to display that kind of virtue.

Harold James approaches the question of economic policy options from a different angle and, to my mind, displays rather greater sensitivity to the interplay between economic and political constraints. My only comment here concerns reparations. The fate of the Republic was tied to the reparations question in a number of ways, and James is right to suggest that it may have had a stabilizing effect upon the political system. As long as reparations were outstanding, and the threat of foreign intervention (whether military or financial) to enforce payment hovered in the background, German domestic-political options remained circumscribed. (This, by the way, forms a significant contextual difference between the events of 1923 and those of 1933). And in a political climate where, as James points out, almost everyone 'relied on blaming other people for the crisis', it was extremely convenient to have an external target that all Germans could attack for their misfortunes. Reparations thus provided one of the few issues around which a popular consensus could form in an otherwise chronically divided polity. But the reparations consensus was a double-edged sword. It may have provided 'the unifying bracket that had clamped German politics together', but it also repeatedly undermined responsible politics. For example, how could a politician during the early 1920s propose sacrifices necessary to stabilize the currency when he would immediately face accusations that these sacrifices were being demanded of an impoverished German population in order to pay the French? The fearsome outcry directed against Stresemann in the autumn of 1923, when as Reich Chancellor (and armed with emergency decrees) he jettisoned the dead-end policies of confrontation with the French, clearly demonstrated how destructive the reparations issue could be. And the ways in which the reparations issue repeatedly split the parliamentary delegations of the bourgeois parties, from the DDP in 1921 through to the DNVP in 1924, to say nothing of the vitriolic right-wing campaign against the Young Plan in 1929, show how corrosive was this 'unifying bracket'.

Now, to turn to Dick Geary's contribution. Despite wide agreement on the reasons for the collapse of the Weimar Republic, there are two themes which Geary and I approach somewhat differently. The first concerns the weight assigned to labour relations in the demise of German democracy. In my contribution, the industrial relations are given a relatively minor role (alongside the economic constraints facing the Republic, the political, social and economic legacy of the War, and the disintegration of the bourgeois 'middle' ground of German politics before 1930); for Geary, this theme is more important – even though in places he concedes that industrial influence and labour politics were not the chief determinants of Weimar's collapse. The second is that Geary places greater emphasis upon the Depression, and appears to suggest that were it not for the Depression the tragedy might have been avoided. Labour's 'political isolation' (for which one could read 'political irrelevance') seems in Geary's account to have been in large measure a function of the Depression and the crushing unemployment which it brought; in my account, greater stress is placed upon deep political and economic problems which already were present before the Depression struck and which would have undercut the necessary basis for a healthy, functioning democracy, regardless of whether organized labour had been weakened by catastrophic unemployment or not.

The key question which arises from Geary's account is what relation the actions of employers and workers had to the collapse of the Weimar Republic. To this question, Geary gives no answer – I suspect perhaps because there is none. Opening his piece, he concedes that neither 'industry's increasingly hostile attitude to the (Weimar) political settlement' nor 'labour's impotence' form 'the key to the overthrow of the Weimar Republic'. He concurs with Henry Ashby Turner about the incoherence of industrialists' political interventions during the final years of the Republic and their inability to determine the course of political events. And he concludes his section on labour by stating that 'none of the above is intended to suggest that organized labour played a key role in the collapse of the Republic'. This would pose no real problem if the politics of industry and labour were examined against the background of what was going on elsewhere – where the political decisions were being made that destroyed the Republic. But it leaves Geary with a dilemma of what exactly to make of his subject.

His response, as I understand it, has two main components: first ('the crucial problem'), that largely as a result of Depression the German working class was isolated and therefore marginal to the politics of the collapse of Weimar; second, that the very real gains made by labour during the 1920s and within the framework of pluralist democracy seriously threatened established interests, which 'meant that the non-proletarian sections of community were not so tolerant' and that therefore 'the crisis of a welfare state in depression led to its destruction'. Let me take these in turn.

First, 'the political isolation of the German working class'. We certainly can agree that the German working class, or at least the parties of the Left which claimed to represent the working class, was politically isolated during the final years of the Weimar Republic. The Left never managed to gain anything like a majority of the popular vote; SPD participation on government, as demonstrated in 1928–30, was a red rag not only to the bulls in the *Reichsverband der deutschen Industrie* (RDI) but also to many in the bourgeois political parties on whose support any Weimar coalition was dependent; conservative concern about Brüning's dependence upon the toleration of the SPD proved an important cause of his government's fall in 1932; and the Communists, whose supporters were largely unemployed and marginalized socially and economically, simply were not players in the game of political power. But can this be described as 'the crucial problem'? I think not. The crucial problem lay elsewhere: in the fragmentation of the political middle, in the failure of the German liberalism, in the inability of the Weimar Republic to legitimate itself effectively among the mass of the German electorate (and not just among sections of the working class), and in the failure of Germany's traditional elites to maintain their grip on the political system. Labour was going to be marginal in any event, especially as the basis for old-style class-based politics was beginning to be eroded and fragmented by developments which both Geary and I mention. The only instance where the German working class was able to call the political tune had been in the quite exceptional circumstances of 1918–20. To expect that the working class should have been able to overcome its isolation thereafter and effectively manage a pluralist bourgeois democracy strikes me as rather unrealistic.

Second, the lack of tolerance by 'the non-proletarian sections of community'. Again, on the basics we agree. Labour's gains during the Weimar period cost money, and from the late 1920s industrial interests were becoming increasingly hostile and even hysterical about these gains. The Ruhr lock-out, the RDI's 1929 reform programme *'Aufstieg oder Niedergang?'* ('Rise or Fall?') and the behaviour of the industrialists' wing of the DVP after Stresemann's death were clear statements that tolerance no longer was regarded as an option. But did this make a real difference? Of course employers were going to be hostile towards developments which increased their costs. (And this is not really a matter of whether at any particular 'conjuncture' employers could or could not 'afford' a 'degree of latitude in their dealings with trade unions'; they complained about high labour costs regardless. They had done so during the Inflation, and they sought to drive down labour costs whenever the balance of the labour market allowed it.) We should not be surprised that employers criticized what they regarded as high taxation and 'political wages', that they took advantage of mass unemployment and political crisis to make what they regarded as economically necessary corrections, or that, as Geary notes, 'by 1933 industry wanted rid of the Weimar Republic'. But did the fate of Weimar democracy really hang on whether all industrialists were dissatisfied with it or not? I doubt it.

Of all interest groups, big businessmen had surprisingly little political clout as the Weimar Republic was being dismantled; indeed, Turner has argued convincingly that their major contribution towards undermining the Republic was not the result of a successful, coherent campaign to destroy it but the damage done when they withdrew financial support from the non-Nazi bourgeois parties in the early 1930s. Their main channel of influence – financing parties and candidates who would support policies to industry's liking – was limited for two reasons: first, their chosen vehicles, the bourgeois parties from the DDP through to the DNVP, could not retain mass support at the polls (and, as Larry Eugene Jones has shown, industrialists' support for a party such as the DVP could prove a considerable electoral liability); and second, the suspension of parliamentary government in 1930 meant that a Reich Chancellor armed with emergency decrees could ignore business interests and the Reichstag deputies they had bought. Geary notes that with the Depression 'it was the less progressive groups of capital which came into ascendancy'. Ascendancy in the RDI perhaps, but not in the political arena. There industrial interests were relatively powerless. It is a great irony of the final Weimar years that the government most to the liking of the most intolerant industrialists, von Papen's 'Cabinet of Barons', was also the government least dependent upon the representatives of business interests, since it rested entirely on the ability to call upon emergency legislation. The connection between the intolerance of employers and the destruction of the Weimar welfare state remains to be demonstrated.

No serious historian of Weimar Germany can be uncritical of the stances taken by spokesmen for big business, many of whom were hostile towards democracy and were convinced that restructuring the German political system in a more authoritarian mould was necessary for '*die Wirtschaft*'. But statements of intention, no matter how unpalatable and even when uttered by 'captains of industry', are not evidence of actual influence or of why specific political decisions were taken. Similarly, it is difficult not to be sympathetic towards labour, which paid more than its share of the costs of Germany's predicament and many of whose representatives made honourable if unsuccessful attempts to master a situation quite beyond their control. Geary asserts that 'had capital and labour united in support of the political order, it would certainly have been in a better position to survive'. Although rather less sharply focussed, this parallels the suggestion by Holtfrerich that 'instead of quarrelling over the level of wages and wage increases, the collective bargaining partners and the government should have addressed the issue of savings and capital formation'. But like Holtfrerich's suggestion that capital and labour should not have quarrelled over wages, Geary's retrospective prescription for industrial unity to save the Weimar Republic strikes me as rather unrealistic. (Would it be realistic in any capitalist country?) Furthermore, it ignores other, and in my opinion more important, factors contributing to the collapse of the Weimar Republic. To imply that, in the absence of a stable, robust, and responsible bourgeois middle and a broad base of popular legitimation, the Weimar Republic would have had rosy prospects even before the New York stock market crashed and even if German industrialists had been nicer and German labour leaders wiser, is to my mind wishful thinking. The problem perhaps is that we all wish things could have been different. It may be a cold comfort, but the real 'lesson' of Weimar is that there were, and are, no easy answers.

Comment on
Richard Bessel's Paper

Harold James

Richard Bessel gives an important and eloquent description of how a political system failed because it was overloaded with expectations. He convincingly traces these exaggerated hopes back to the World War, the loss of which severely limited Germany's capacity to deliver on her promises. 'Few Germans fully appreciated how much poorer their country had become'. In the light of 'the overwhelming and threatening character of the problems facing the governments which replaced the imperial system', traditional elites in the judiciary, the army, and in business 'abdicated their responsibilities', in the crises both of 1918–19 and 1930–3, and thus left a vacuum which only the Nazis could fill.

Readers of this volume will notice that this pessimistic interpretation of Weimar is shared – though with different emphases – by Dick Geary and myself.

Bessel is in my view right to be sceptical of the view that a more thorough-going social transformation in 1918–19 might have avoided later problems. But perhaps the overloading of the political system with expectations was made more acute by the form of the *constitutional* settlement of 1919. This is a theme that has been developed most systematically and clearly by the German historian Gerhard Schulz.[1] Throughout its existence the Weimar Republic was overshadowed by constitutional uncertainty. Under the Old Empire, the central state (Reich) controlled foreign policy, tariffs and the navy, but most authority in judicial, police, educational, and fiscal matters remained with the German states: the Empire was in reality a federation of states. In 1919, these states were renamed as *Länder*, but remained in existence. The Reich assumed a greater role in economic and fiscal policy; and throughout the 1920s a constitutional reform that would break up the largest *Land* (Prussia) was debated: but the idea of a more central and unified German state failed because of the attachment of the Catholic Centre party to the rights of the *Länder*, and because some of the most influential socialist leaders, in particular Otto Braun, remained committed to the existence of Prussia as a bulwark of the SPD.

The partition of governmental authority between three levels – Reich, *Länder*, and municipal or communal – encouraged political buck-passing, especially at moments of crisis. Brüning's constitutional changes were designed to make the *Länder* bear the unpopularity of raising taxes and cutting expenditure. The *Länder* responded by passing opprobrium further down the line – to municipal governments.

In 1919 liberals such as Hugo Preuss – the chief framer of the Weimar constitution, whose original drafts were substantially modified – and some socialists (mostly southerners such as Eduard David) had envisaged a unitary state: a settlement in which authority would be shared between the Reich on the one hand and local government on the other. Through an increased role of local authorities in political decision-making (and the destruction of the power of the intermediate *Länder*), people would be educated into political responsibility and awareness, rather in line with the intentions of the early nineteenth century Prussian reformers who had originally devised the system of local self-administration (*Selbstverwaltung*). While such a reform would perhaps not have reduced the expectations around Weimar's political system, or cut down the overload, it might have made buck-passing, the 'abdication of responsibilities', and thus the eventual political vacuum, more difficult. A democratic unitary state might in this way have been able to encourage the development of a new and healthy political tradition.

Such a proposition must remain a speculation, perhaps with little historical relevance or validity. But it may be a more realistic version of the 'lost opportunity' argument about Weimar than the case about the failure to establish genuine (or 'social') democracy through factory councils. Perhaps here too Ebert had few choices in 1919: he needed the Prussian SPD, which strenuously resisted, even in 1919, any attempt to end Prussia's historic role.

Notes

1. Gerhard Schulz, *Zwischen Demokratie und Diktatur: Verfassungspolitik in der Weimarer Republik*, 2 vols. (Berlin and New York, 1987). The first volume was originally published in 1963.

Comment on Richard Bessel's Paper

Carl-Ludwig Holtfrerich

I agree with Richard Bessel when he writes in his conclusion: 'Perhaps the remarkable thing about the Weimar Republic is not that it collapsed but that it lasted as long as it did'. The tensions and pressures to which Weimar democracy was subjected were not only numerous but extremely strong. And the democratic system for a long time displayed its mighty power of resistance. It was clearly more than a 'fair weather system', as Harold James suggests in this volume.

I also agree with his contention on the lack and final erosion of legitimacy, which left political elites in a vacuum of power, especially in 1932.

However, I do not share Bessel's opinion that the pressures of 'distributional conflict' undermined Weimar's democratic framework and led to the success of the Nazi Party's politics of propaganda. Distributional conflict was going on throughout the lifetime of the Weimar Republic, most acutely during the postwar inflation. Yet Nazism was not then successful. In my view, the Nazi rise to power was essentially linked to the great depression, which was a world-wide phenomenon and had little to do with domestic distributional conflict.

My major objection to Bessel is that he looks for *domestic* weaknesses of the Republic, where – in my view – the *foreign* pressures are as, if not more, important in explaining the collapse of democracy in Germany. Even the acuteness of domestic pressures cannot be explained without regard to the foreign situation: the war-guilt clause and the discriminating trade clause of the Versailles Treaty, the abortive security guarantee by the US and Britain for France, the reparations issue, world-wide protectionism etc. The Nazi propaganda capitalized strongly on freedom from the chains of the Versailles Treaty (replacing democratic freedom) and on freedom from the depressed world financial and goods markets (autarky). In this respect German democracy differed essentially from the Anglo-Saxon ones, indicating that the search for reasons for the collapse of the one and for the survival of the others should start in the field of international relations and foreign politics.

Comment on
Richard Bessel's Paper

Dick Geary

As Ian Kershaw points out in the Introduction, all contributors are agreed that the Weimar Republic faced innumerable
difficulties, although there are multiple disagreements about
the severity and timing of such difficulties. Richard Bessel
certainly goes furthest in both his account of such problems
and in his belief that the Republic was more or less doomed
from the start. One can only agree that the First World War
left a massive legacy of bankruptcy, that the new state was
rejected by many from the very beginning and that even in
the so-called 'golden years' of the mid-twenties all was far
from well: agriculture already had problems of indebtedness,
some sections of industry (coal, iron and steel) were already
locked in a crisis of profitability, rationalization was already
producing structural unemployment and an intensification of
labour for the industrial working class, and voters were
already deserting their traditional leaders. But to say all this
is *not* to explain the collapse, which did take place after all
in the early 1930s.

There is still the conundrum of why such a supposedly
'illegitimate' state was able to survive insurrections from left
and right in circumstances of humiliating defeat and massive
inflation between 1918 and 1923 and yet not control the deflationary crisis of 1930–33. The behaviour of Ruhr industrialists
in the lock-out of 1928 was not typical of industry as a whole
at that time and even gave Krupp sleepless nights. In fact,

as Carl Holtfrerich demonstrates, many industrialists in more buoyant sectors were prepared to pay above the union-negotiated wage rates in 1927/8. Only with a universalization of the crisis of profitability did the situation alter. The Nazis were restricted to the political sidelines in this period of stabilization; and coalition government did continue until 1930. Its breakdown, as Bessel himself points out, took place in the context of the collapse of the system of unemployment insurance, i.e. again in the context of depression and mass unemployment. Whether Germany's economic difficulties were as massive as either Richard Bessel or Harold James imagines is, of course, open to question, as Holtfrerich's contribution makes clear. There was, in any case, a sharp rise in man-hour productivity simultaneous with the oft-decried 'wages push'; and those same employers who complained about 'welfare taxation' and 'political wages' compounded their own difficulties with cartelized price-fixing. They were also to be found spending more on private, firm-controlled welfare schemes (associated with the re-emergence of company unions) at the same time as they denounced the extraneous imposition of 'financial burdens'.

In this context Bessel makes an important point: what made the Weimar situation so intolerable for so many businessmen was less the absolute nature of their difficulties than the fact that they measured their position against the benchmark of 1913, when profits were high, trade unions possessed no institutional support, and Social Democrats were excluded from government. This point seems to me to be absolutely crucial with regard to all those groups which came to reject the Republic: the army, the bureaucracy, some sections of industry, the agrarian lobby. They had known better, more privileged times under the Old Empire. Now they had to compete with unions, socialists, and urban consumers for influence, something which hit their pocket through new taxation and new forms of taxation. Significantly, those countries which possessed democratic structures and a relatively liberal national consensus before 1914 were able to negotiate quite massive economic crisis, most notably in the USA. Thus it was not the scale, or at least not only the scale, of economic crisis that undermined democratic government. Modern welfare states have been able to tolerate a much higher percentage of the national product accruing to wages or much higher welfare taxation than did Weimar. Yet in Weimar these things were measured against better days, when the army had power and influence and enjoyed a large percentage of state revenue, when workers were kept in their place, and when agriculture was even more protected than it was after 1918. Thus although the crisis of Weimar was in certain respects a very 'modern' crisis, the crisis of a welfare state in circumstances of acute financial distress, the reaction of various groups to that crisis was mediated by historical traditions and continuities.

This was true not only on the political right but also on the left. If the emergence of radical working-class politics were a simple function of economic distress, the history of Great Britain and the United States would look very different; for there mass unemployment, poverty, and agricultural crisis did not undermine the democratic polity. What mattered in the German case was that a significant section of the German working class was committed to socialist goals before 1914 and thus subsequently experienced the Weimar Republic as disappointment, even betrayal. Hence the emergence of mass support for the KPD long before the depression. The Weimar Republic was born into a Germany that was already remarkably polarized in class terms: bourgeois parties had only a small resonance amongst the industrial working class (unlike equivalent parties in the USA, Britain, or France), more workers voted socialist than in any other country, and little middle-class support found its way to Social Democracy before 1914. This meant that distributional conflicts were especially difficult to resolve, particularly in the context of depression and reductions in state expenditure. The close correlation between political parties and specific socio-economic interest groups, reflected in the division between the DVP and the SPD over unemployment benefits in 1930, further compounded the problem and rendered coalition government impossible at a time of financial crisis. (Significantly, as long as the coalitions were preoccupied with foreign-policy issues – Versailles, reparations – they tended to hold together.)

This raises a final point: Bessel states that a decline in specifically class issues may have formed the background to the Nazi victory and in particular may explain why some groups of workers found their way into Hitler's camp. One problem with such an argument is that a great deal of the barrage of National Socialist propaganda struck home at precisely middle-class values: anti-communism, anti-socialism, restoring the right of management to manage, restoring family values, getting rid of social-security 'scroungers'. Specific promises were also made to protect agriculture. Conversely those workers, and there were undoubtedly many of them who did turn to the Nazis, did not come from groups previously mobilized by communists, socialists, and the unions (the 'class-conscious') but mainly from groups that had previously voted National Liberal before 1914 and DNVP afterwards (company-union members at Krupps, for example), or and above all from groups with few traditions of previous socialist mobilization: rural labourers, artisanal workers, workers in domestic industry and small provincial towns, i.e. not the industrial proletariat of the large industrial towns but precisely groups of workers who had *never* previously given any organized expression to class loyalties. This makes the thesis of a breakdown of earlier class loyalties more than a little problematical and also casts doubt on the significance of working-class 'consumerism' in that process. Rural areas and small towns were the last places to be affected by such developments. Furthermore, those workers who were able to enjoy some of the fruits of this consumerism – the better-off, with small families, in superior housing – were precisely those who formed the backbone of the SPD. Again, for the unemployed in general and unemployed youth in particular, the problem remained that of survival.

In short, it is true that Weimar was afflicted by a host of problems from its very inception, including the expectations I have attempted to describe above. But the flouting of those expectations was likely to become disastrous in the context of a particular kind of crisis, namely a distributional one in the context of economic depression. (For reasons given in my own contribution, the inflation of the early years of Weimar did *not* produce such a crisis).

List of Abbreviations

I.   Political parties

BVP   Bayerische Volkspartei (Bavarian People's Party)
CNBL   Christlich-nationale Bauern- und Landvolkpartei
          (Christian National Peasants and Rural People's
          Party)
DDP   Deutsche Demokratische Partei (German
          Democratic Party)
DNVP   Deutschnationale Volkspartei (German National
          People's Party)
DVP   Deutsche Volkspartei (German People's Party)
KPD   Kommunistische Partei Deutschlands (Communist
          Party of Germany)
KVP   Konservative Volkspartei (Conservative People's
          Party)
NSDAP   Nationalsozialistische Deutsche Arbeiterpartei
          (National Socialist German Workers' Party)
SPD   Sozialdemokratische Partei Deutschlands (Social
          Democratic Party of Germany)
USPD   Unabhängige Sozialdemokratische Partei
          Deutschlands (Independent Social Democratic
          Party of Germany)
VB   Völkischer Block (Racial–Nationalist Alliance)
WP   Wirtschaftspartei des Deutschen Mittelstandes
          (Economic Party of the German Middle Class)
Z   Zentrum (Centre Party)

II. Other abbreviations

ADGB Allgemeiner Deutscher Gewerkschaftsbund (General German Trades Union Federation)

AEG Allgemeine Elektrizitäts-Gesellschaft (General Electricity Company)

DMV Deutscher Metallarbeiter-Verband (German Metal Workers Association)

GHH Gutehoffnungshütte Aktienverein (Good Hope Works Ltd – a major coal and steel combine)

IfK Institut für Konjunkturforschung (Institute for Business Cycle Research)

NSBO Nationalsozialistische Betriebszellenorganisation (National Socialist Factory Cell Organisation)

RDI Reichsverband der Deutschen Industrie (Reich Association of German Industry)

RGO Revolutionäre Gewerkschaftsopposition (Revolutionary Trades Union Opposition)

SA Sturmabteilung (Stormtroop)

ZAG Zentralarbeitsgemeinschaft (Central Labour Community)

Appendix of Statistical Data

Table I Elections to the National Assembly (1919) and the Reichstag (1920–33): Votes for Each Party (%)

	19 Jan. 1919	6 June 1920	4 May 1924	7 Dec. 1924	20 May 1928	14 Sept. 1930	31 July 1932	6 Nov. 1932	5 Mar. 1933
Turn-out	83.0	79.2	77.4	78.8	75.6	82.0	84.1	80.6	88.8
KPD	—	2.1	12.6	9.0	10.6	13.1	14.5	16.9	12.3
USPD	7.6	17.9	0.8	0.3	0.1	0.0	—	—	—
SPD	37.9	21.7	20.5	26.0	29.8	24.5	21.6	20.4	18.3
DDP[1]	18.6	8.3	5.7	6.3	4.9	3.8	1.0	1.0	0.9
Zentrum	15.9	13.6	13.4	13.6	12.1	11.8	12.5	11.9	11.2
BVP	3.8	4.2	3.2	3.8	3.1	3.0	3.7	3.4	2.7
DVP	4.4	13.9	9.2	10.1	8.7	4.7	1.2	1.9	1.1
DNVP[2]	10.3	15.1	19.5	20.5	14.2	7.0	6.2	8.9	8.0
NSDAP[3]	—	—	6.5	3.0	2.6	18.3	37.4	33.1	43.9
Others[4]	1.6	3.3	8.6	7.5	13.9	13.8	2.0	2.6	1.6

Source: J. Falter, T. Lindenberger, S. Schumann (eds.), *Wahlen und Abstimmungen in der Weimarer Republik* (Munich, 1986), p. 44.

[1] From 1930 Deutsche Staatspartei.
[2] In 1933 Kampffront Schwarz-weiß-rot.
[3] In 1924 part of Völkisch-Nationaler-Block.
[4] Includes more than 36 regional and small parties, the most significant of which were the Wirtschaftspartei, the Christlich-nationale Bauern- und Landvolkpartei, and the Christlich-sozialer Volksdienst (Evangelische Bewegung).

Declining Party-Political Support for Weimar Democracy

Election

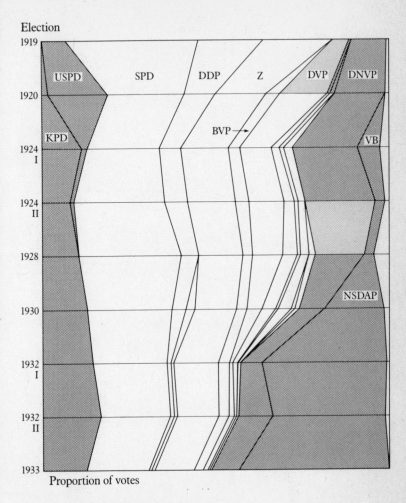

The unshaded sections represent those parties loyal to the Weimar constitution. The semi-shaded sections refer to parties whose loyalty was doubtful. Shaded sections denote parties hostile to Weimar democracy.

Source: H. Kaack, *Geschichte und Struktur des deutschen Parteiensystems* (Opladen, 1971), p. 106.

Table II Government Coalitions and their Parliamentary Support

Appointment of Reich Chancellor	Reich Chancellor[1] of new government	Coalition Parties	Per cent of Reichstag deputies in coalition parties
13.02.1919	Philipp Scheidemann (SPD)	SPD, Z, DDP	78.1 ⎫ National
21.06.1919	Gustav Bauer (SPD)	SPD, Z	60.3 ⎬ Assembly
27.03.1920	Hermann Müller (SPD)	SPD, Z, DDP	78.1 ⎭
25.06.1920	Konstantin Fehrenbach (Z)	Z, DVP, DDP	36.6
10.05.1921	Joseph Wirth (Z)	SPD, Z, DDP	44.6
22.11.1922	Wilhelm Cuno	DVP, Z, DDP, BVP	41.2
13.08.1923	Gustav Stresemann (DVP)	SPD, DDP, Z, DVP	58.8
30.11.1923	Wilhelm Marx (Z)	DVP, Z, DDP	36.6
03.06.1924	Wilhelm Marx (Z)	DVP, Z, DDP	29.2
15.01.1925	Hans Luther	Z, DDP, DVP, BVP, DNVP	55.6

Date	Name	Government / Coalition	%	Period
20.01.1926	Hans Luther	Z, DDP, DVP, BVP	34.7	
16.05.1926	Wilhelm Marx (Z)	Z, DDP, DVP, BVP	34.7	
29.01.1927	Wilhelm Marx (Z)	Z, DVP, BVP, DNVP	49.1	
28.06.1928	Hermann Müller (SPD)	SPD, Z, DVP, BVP, DDP	61.5	
30.03.1930	Heinrich Brüning (Z)	Presidential Government (incl. DDP, DVP, Z, BVP, WP, KVP)	(34.9) / (27.8)	To 14 Sept. 1930 / From 14 Sept. 1930
01.06.1932	Franz von Papen	Presidential Government (incl. DNVP)	(7.1) / (6.1) / (8.9)	To 31 July 1932 / 31 July to 6 Nov. 1932 / From 6 Nov. 1932
03.12.1932	Kurt von Schleicher	Presidential Government (incl. DNVP, CNBL)	(8.9)	
30.01.1933	Adolf Hitler	NSDAP, DNVP	42.5 / 52.5	To 5 Mar. 1933 / From 5 Mar. 1933

Source: Falter *et al.*, *Wahlen*, p. 45.

[1] Until 14 Aug. 1919 Minister President.

Table III   Economic Statistics

(a) Index of Industrial Production (1928 = 100)

	Total	Consumer Goods	Capital Goods
1913	98	97	99
1919	37	—	32
1920	54	51	56
1921	65	69	65
1922	70	74	70
1923	46	57	43
1924	69	81	65
1925	81	85	80
1926	78	80	77
1927	98	103	97
1928	100	100	100
1929	100	97	102
1930	87	91	84
1931	70	82	62
1932	58	74	47
1933	66	80	56

Source: D. Petzina, W. Abelshauser, A. Faust (eds.), *Sozialgeschichtliches Arbeitsbuch III. Materialien zur Statistik des Deutschen Reiches 1914–1945* (Munich, 1978), p. 61.

(b) Per capita net National Product at 1913 Prices (1928 = 100)

	Index	Yearly Growth Rate (%)
1913	93	
1925	89	
1926	88	− 1.0
1927	99	12.5
1928	100	1.0
1929	95	− 5.0
1930	91	− 4.2
1931	80	− 12.1
1932	76	− 5.0
1933	86	13.2

Source: Petzina *et al.*, p. 78.

(c) Wages as proportion (%) of
National Income

	National Income in mill. (Reich)marks	Wages as %
1913	45,693	46.4
1925	59,978	58.4
1926	62,673	58.1
1927	70,754	57.6
1928	75,373	59.5
1929	73,448	59.8
1930	68,524	60.1
1931	56,466	61.9
1932	45,175	60.7
1933	46,514	59.4

Source: Petzina *et al.*, p. 102.

(d) Employment Structure

Per cent of Earning Population Employed in:

	Agriculture and Forestry	Industry and Crafts	Total	Trade and Commerce	Tertiary Sector Public and Private Service	Domestic Service
1907	35.2	40.1	24.8	12.4	6.2	6.2
1925	30.5	42.1	27.4	16.4	6.6	4.4
1933	28.9	40.4	30.7	18.5	8.3	3.9

Source: Petzina et al., p. 55.

(e) Unemployment (Yearly Averages)

	Earning Population (in 000s)	Unemployed (in 000s)	Per cent of Trades Unionists Unemployed	Per cent of Earners Unemployed
1913	14,556		2.9	
1919	16,950		3.7	
1920	18,367		3.8	
1921	19,126	346	2.8	1.8
1922	20,184	215	1.5	1.1
1923	20,000	818	9.6	4.1
1924	19,122	927	13.5	4.9
1925	20,176	682	6.7	3.4
1926	20,287	2,025	18.0	10.0
1927	21,207	1,312	8.7	6.2
1928	21,995	1,391	8.4	6.3
1929	22,418	1,899	13.1	8.5
1930	21,916	3,076	22.2	14.0
1931	20,616	4,520	33.7	21.9
1932	18,711	5,603	43.7	29.9
1933	18,540	4,804	(46.3)[1]	25.9

Source: Petzina et al., p. 119.

[1] For the first six months.

(f) Indices of Economic Crisis (1928 = 100)

	1929	1930	1931	1932	1933
Production:					
Capital goods	103	86	61	46	54
Investment goods	103	84	54	35	45
Elastic demand consumer goods	97	91	87	74	80
Inelastic demand consumer goods	101	101	95	85	88
Employment:					
Employed persons	99	92	80	71	74
Prices and wages:					
Capital goods	102	101	96	86	83
Consumer goods	98	91	80	67	64
Cost of living	102	98	90	80	78
Real wages	101	97	93	87	91

Source: Petzina *et al.*, p. 84.

(g) Per Capita State Expenditure (all levels = Reich, Länder, and local government; at 1900 prices; 1913 = 100)

	1913 Mark	Index	1925 RM	Index	1929 RM	Index	1932 RM	Index
Defence and war-related (including military pensions)	25.1	100	21.9	87	27.7	110	14.2	57
Economy (including state concerns, industrial support, roads, transport)	17.0	100	15.8	93	22.1	130	18.2	107
Social sphere	20.5	100	64.7	316	101.6	496	106.3	519
of which:								
social insurance	12.2	100	23.2	190	49.2	403	50.0	410
health & welfare	7.9	100	31.4	388	39.2	496	51.8	656
public housing	0.4	100	10.1	2,525	13.2	3,300	4.5	1,125
Education	17.5	100	20.5	117	27.8	159	24.4	139
Public safety	7.7	100	12.1	157	13.7	178	14.6	190
Public administration and services	9.6	100	13.7	143	14.9	155	15.5	162
Debt	5.8	100	0.9	16	4.1	71	6.7	116

Source: Petzina et al., p. 147.

Further Reading

There is a vast literature on practically all aspects of the Weimar Republic written in German. In preparing the guides to further reading on the themes of their contributions to this volume, the authors have made every attempt to include English language material wherever possible. A full bibliography is provided in Eberhard Kolb, *The Weimar Republic* (London, 1988), which also offers a splendid introductory interpretative survey and commentary on the historiography. Further guides in English to historical writing on the Weimar Republic are: ABC-Clio Information Services (ed.), *The Weimar Republic. A Historical Bibliography* (Santa Barbara/Denver/Oxford, 1984), and – a little older – Peter D. Stachura, *The Weimar Era and Hitler 1918–1933* (Oxford, 1977).

An outstanding recent interpretative analysis, that of Detlev J.K.Peukert, *Die Weimarer Republik. Krisenjahre der Klassischen Moderne* (Frankfurt am Main, 1987), is so far available only in German, but will appear shortly in English. In the meantime, the flavour of the argument can be tasted in Detlev J.K.Peukert, 'The Weimar Republic – Old and New Perspectives', *German History*, 6 (1988), pp. 133–44.

I Economic Reasons for the Collapse of the Weimar Republic

Two very helpful English language articles giving an overview of the problems of the Weimar economy are by D.Petzina, in the *Journal of Contemporary History* 1969, and 'The Extent and Causes of Unemployment in the Weimar Republic' in P.Stachura (ed.), *Unemployment and the Great Depression in Weimar Germany*, London 1986. Some of the arguments set out in my article are expanded at greater length in my book, H. James, *The German Slump: Politics and Economics 1924–1936*, Oxford 1986 (paperback with a new conclusion 1987). There is a very useful brief survey of the origins of the depression in T.Balderston, 'The German Business Cycle in the 1920s', in *Economic History Review* 1977. Also see his longer piece, 'The Beginning of the Depression in Germany 1927–1930: Investment and the Capital Market', in *Economic History Review* 1983. In addition M.E.Falkus, 'The German Business Cycle in the 1920s', *Economic History Review* 1975; C.T.Schmidt, *German Business Cycles 1924–1933*, New York 1934; D.S.Landes, *The Unbound Prometheus: Technological Change and Industrial Development in Western Europe from 1750 to the Present*, Cambridge 1969. The essential background to the depression is the hyper-inflation of the early 1920s: on this see C. Bresciani-Turroni, *The Economics of Inflation: A Study of Currency Depreciation in Postwar Germany 1914–1923*, London 1953; and the more recent work of C.L.Holtfrerich, *The German Inflation 1914–1923: Causes and Effects in International Perspective*, Berlin/New York 1986. The links between politics and economics in the inflation period – and their implications for Weimar's future – are best examined through the work of Gerald Feldman: *Iron and Steel in the German Inflation 1916–1923*, Princeton 1977; and a forthcoming social and political history of the German inflation (Oxford and New York 1989).

The 'Borchardt debate' began with two articles, the first appearing in 1979 and the second in 1980. Both regrettably are available only in German: K.Borchardt, 'Zwangslagen und Handlungsspielräume in der grossen Wirtschaftskrise der frühen dreissiger Jahre: Zur Revision des überlieferten Geschichtsbildes', and 'Wirtschaftliche Ursachen des Scheiterns der Weimarer Republik'. Both are reprinted in his book: *Wachstum, Krisen, Handlungsspielräume der Wirtschaftspolitik* (Göttingen 1982). See the criticism by C.-L.Holtfrerich, 'Alternativen zu Brünings Wirtschaftspolitik in der Weltwirtschaftskrise', in *Historische Zeitschrift*, 235 (1982), and 'Zu hohe Löhre in der Weimarer Republik? Bemerkungen zur Borchardt-These', in *Geschichte und Gesellschaft*, 10 (1984). Borchardt replied with 'Noch einmal: Alternativen zu Brünings Wirtschaftspolitik' in the *Historische Zeitschrift*, 237 (1983); and I criticized Holtfrerich's arguments in 'Gab es eine Alternative zur Wirtschaftspolitik Brünings?' in *Vierteljahrschrift für Sozial- und Wirtschaftsgeschichte*, 70 (1983). A special issue of *Geschichte und Gesellschaft*, 11 (1985) on the Borchardt debate contains useful articles by J. von Kruedener, C.S.Maier, and B.Weisbrod, as well as a less than helpful piece by G.Plumpe.

II   Economic Policy Options and the End of the Weimar Republic

Theo Balderston, 'The Origins of Economic Instability in Germany, 1924–30: Market Forces versus Economic Policy', in *Vierteljahrschrift für Sozial- und Wirtschaftsgeschichte*, 69 (1982), pp. 488–514.

—, 'The Beginning of the Depression in Germany, 1927–30: Investment and the Capital Market', in *Economic History Review*, 36 (1983), pp. 395–415.

—, 'Links between Inflation and Depression: German Capital and Labour Markets, 1924–1931', in G.D.Feldman (ed.), *Die Nachwirkungen der Inflation auf die deutsche Geschichte 1924–1933* (Munich, 1985), pp. 157–185.

Knut Borchardt, 'Could and Should Germany Have Followed Great Britain in Leaving the Gold Standard?', in *The Journal of European Economic History*, 13 (1984), pp. 471–497.

—, 'Das Gewicht der Inflationsangst in den wirtschaftspolitischen Entscheidungsprozessen während der Weltwirtschaftskrise', in G.D.Feldman (ed.), *Nachwirkungen* (Munich, 1985), pp. 233–260.

Ursula Büttner, 'Politische Alternativen zum Brüningschen Deflationskurs: Ein Beitrag zur Diskussion über "okonomische Zwangslagen" in der Endphase von Weimar', *Vierteljahreshefte für Zeitgeschichte*, 37 (1989), pp. 209–51.

Harald Hagemann, 'Lohnsenkungen als Mittel der Krisenbekämpfung? Überlegungen zum Beitrag der "Kieler Schule" in der beschäftigungspolitischen Diskussion am Ende der Weimarer Republik', in H.Hagemann/H.D.Kurz (eds.), *Beschäftigung, Verteilung und Konjunktur. Zur politischen Ökonomik der modernen Gesellschaft. Festschrift für Adolph Lowe* (Bremen, 1984), pp. 97–129.

Carl-Ludwig Holtfrerich, 'Alternativen zu Brünings Wirtschaftspolitik in der Weltwirtschaftskrise', in *Historische Zeitschrift*, 235 (1982), pp. 605–631.

—, 'Zu hohe Löhne in der Weimarer Republik? Bemerkungen zur Borchardt-These', in *Geschichte und Gesellschaft*, 10 (1984), pp. 122–141.

Werner Jochmann, 'Brünings Deflationspolitik und der Untergang der Weimarer Republik', in D.Stegmann/B.-J.Wendt/P.-Ch.Witt (eds.), *Industrielle Gesellschaft und politisches System. Beiträge zur politischen Sozialgeschichte* (Bonn, 1978), pp. 97–112.

Henning Köhler, 'Knut Borchardts "Revision des überlieferten Geschichtsbildes" der Wirtschaftspolitik in der grossen Krise – eine Zwangsvorstellung?', in *Internationale wissenschaftliche Korrespondenz zur Geschichte der deutschen Arbeiterbewegung*, 19 (1983), pp. 164–180.

Wilhelm Lautenbach, *Zins, Kredit und Produktion*, ed. by W.Stützel (Tübingen, 1952).

J.Joseph Lee, 'Policy and Performance in the German Economy, 1925–35: a Comment on the Borchardt Thesis', in Michael Laffan (ed.), *The Burden of German History 1919–45. Essays for the Goethe Institute* (London, 1988), pp. 131–150.

Hans Mommsen, 'Staat und Bürokratie in der Ära Brüning', in G.Jasper (ed.), *Tradition und Reform in der deutschen Politik. Gedenkschrift für Waldemar Besson* (Frankfurt/M, 1976), pp. 81–137.

—, 'Heinrich Brünings Politik als Reichskanzler: Das Scheitern eines politischen Alleinganges', in K.Holl (ed.), *Wirtschaftskrise und liberale Demokratie. Das Erbe der Weimarer Republik und die gegenwärtige Situation* (Göttingen, 1978), pp. 16–45.

Reinhard Neebe, *Grossindustrie, Staat und NSDAP 1930–1933* (Göttingen, 1981).

Horst Sanmann, 'Daten und Alternativen der deutschen Wirtschafts und Finanzpolitik in der Ära Brüning', in *Hamburger Jahrbuch für Wirtschafts- und Gesellschaftspolitik*, 10 (1965), pp. 109–150.

Jürgen Schiemann, *Die deutsche Währung in der Weltwirtschaftskrise*

1929–1933. Währungspolitik und Abwertungskontroverse unter den Bedingungen der Reparationen (Bern, 1980).

Michael Schneider, *Das Arbeitsbeschaffungsprogramm des ADGB. Zur gewerkschaftlichen Politik in der Endphase der Weimarer Republik* (Bonn-Bad Godesberg, 1975).

—, 'The Development of State Work-Creation Policy in Germany, 1930–1933', in P.D.Stachura (ed.), *Unemployment and the Great Depression in Weimar Germany* (London, 1986).

Gerhard Schulz, 'Inflationstrauma, Finanzpolitik und Krisenbekämpfung in den Jahren der Weltwirtschaftskrise, 1930–33', in G.D.Feldman, *Nachwirkungen* (Munich, 1985), pp. 261–296.

—, *et al.* (eds.), *Politik und Wirtschaft in der Krise 1930–1932. Quellen zur Ära Brüning* (Düsseldorf, 1980).

Richard Tilly, 'Bemerkungen zur Kontroverse über die Wirtschaftskrise der Weimarer Republik', in H.Henning/D.Lindenlaub/E.Wandel (eds.), *Wirtschafts- und sozialgeschichtliche Forschungen und Probleme. Karl Erich Born zur Vollendung des 65. Lebensjahres zugeeignet von Kollegen, Freunden und Schülern* (St. Katharinen, 1987), pp. 347–374.

Udo Wengst, 'Heinrich Brüning und die "konservative Alternative". Kritische Anmerkungen zu neuen Thesen über die Endphase der Weimarer Republik', in *Politik und Zeitgeschichte*, vol. B 50 (13 Dec. 1980), pp. 19–26.

Heinrich A.Winkler, *Der Weg in die Katastrophe. Arbeiter und Arbeiterbewegung in der Weimarer Republik 1930 bis 1933* (Berlin, 1987).

Peter-Christian Witt, 'Finanzpolitik als Verfassungs- und Gesellschaftspolitik. Überlegungen zur Finanzpolitik des Deutschen Reiches in den Jahren 1930 bis 1932', in *Geschichte und Gesellschaft*, 8 (1982), pp. 386–414.

—, 'Die Auswirkungen der Inflation auf die Finanzpolitik des Deutschen Reiches 1924–1935', in G.D.Feldman, *Nachwirkungen*, pp. 43–95.

III Employers, Workers, and the Collapse of the Weimar Republic

1. *Big Business:* The most important work is Henry Ashby Turner Jr., *Big Business and the Rise of Hitler* (Oxford, 1985), which builds on Turner's earlier essays: 'Big Business and the Rise of Hitler' in *American Historical Review*, 75 (1969), 1, pp. 56–70; 'The Rurhlade' in *Central European History*, 3 (1970), pp. 195–228. Also important is the work of Gerald D.Feldman: *Iron and Steel in the German Inflation* (Princeton, 1977), and 'Big Business and the Kapp Putsch' in *Central European History*, 4 (1971), pp. 99–130. Much more controversial is David Abraham, *The Collapse of the Weimar Republic* (Princeton, 1981), which was attacked vehemently by both Turner and Feldman for inaccuracy and distortion. A revised second edition appeared in 1986. For a summary of the various arguments about big business and the Nazis, albeit one that was written

before the appearance of Turner's *magnum opus*, see Dick Geary, 'The Industrial Elite and the Nazis' in Peter D.Stachura (ed.), *The Nazi Machtergreifung* (London, 1983), pp. 85–100.

2. *Nazis, Workers and Voters:* Max Kele's *Nazis and Workers* (Chapel Hill, 1972) portrays the German working class as far from immune to Nazi propaganda. The same is true of several studies of the SA by Conan Fischer: *Stormtroopers* (London, 1983), especially ch. 6; 'The Occupational Background of the SA's Rank and File Membership' in Peter D.Stachura, *The Shaping of the Nazi State* (London, 1978); 'Class Enemies or Class Brothers' in *European History Quarterly*, 15 (1985), pp. 259–79. This is disputed in Dick Geary, 'Nazis and Workers' in *European History Quarterly*, 15 (1985), pp. 453–64. Detailed investigation of the electoral basis of Nazi support can be found in Richard Hamilton, *Who voted for Hitler?* (Princeton, 1983) and more thoroughly in Thomas Childers, *The Nazi Voter* (Chapel Hill, 1983). On both voting and party membership see Detlef Mühlberger, 'The Sociology of the NSDAP' in *Journal of Contemporary History*, 15 (1980), pp. 293–311. The most detailed analysis of NSDAP membership appears in Michael Kater, *The Nazi Party* (Oxford, 1983).

3. *Workers:* There is a massive literature on the revolutionary upheavals at the end of the First World War. See, for example, Werner T.Angress, *Stillborn Revolution* (Princeton, 1963); F.L.Carsten, *Revolution in Central Europe* (London, 1972); Richard Comfort, *Revolutionary Hamburg* (Stanford, 1966); Dick Geary, 'Radicalism and the German Worker' in Richard J.Evans (ed.), *Politics and Society in Wilhelmine Germany* (London, 1978), pp. 267–86; Wolfgang J.Mommsen, 'The German Revolution', in Richard Bessel and E.J.Feuchtwanger (eds.), *Social Change and Political Development in the Weimar Republic* (London, 1981); David Morgan, *The Socialist Left and the German Revolution* (Ithaca, 1971); Jürgen Tampke, *The Ruhr and Revolution* (London, 1979); A.J.Ryder, *The German Revolution* (Cambridge 1967).

On the German working class more generally see Richard J.Evans (ed.), *The German Working Class* (London, 1982); and Dick Geary, 'The Failure of German Labour in the Weimar Republic' in Michael Dobkowski and Isidor Wallimann (eds.), *Towards the Holocaust* (Westport, 1983), pp. 177–96. On the impact of unemployment see Peter D.Stachura (ed.), *Unemployment and the Great Depression* (London, 1986), and Richard J.Evans and Dick Geary (eds.), *The German Unemployed* (London, 1987). On the unions see Gerard Braunthal, *Socialist Labour and Politics in Weimar Germany* (Hampden, 1978), and John A.Moses, *Trade Unionism in Germany*, vol 2 (London, 1982). On Social Democracy and Communism there is Richard Breitman, *German Socialism and Weimar Democracy* (Chapel Hill, 1981); idem, 'Negative Integration and Political Parties' in *Central European History*, 13 (1980), pp. 175–97; Ossip K.Flechtheim, 'The Role of the Communist Party' in Theodore Eschenburg *et al.*, *The Road to Dictatorship* (London, 1964), pp. 93–110; Ben Fowkes, *Communism in Germany in the Weimar Republic* (London, 1984); W.L.Guttmann, *The German Social Democratic Party* (London, 1981); Erich Matthias, 'German Social Democracy in the Weimar Republic' in Erich Matthias and Anthony

Nicholls (ed.), *German Democracy and the Triumph of Hitler* (London, 1971), pp. 47–58; Richard N. Hunt, *German Social Democracy* (Chicago, 1970); Larry Peterson, 'From Social Democracy to Communism' in *International Labor and Working-Class History*, 20 (1981), pp. 7–30; Don Watts, 'Electoral Success and Political Failure' in *European History Quarterly*, 18 (1988), pp. 439–54; James Wickham, 'Working-class Movement and Working-class Life' in *Social History*, 8 (1983), pp. 315–43. An outstanding contribution to the history of communist street-fighters has been made by Eve Rosenhaft, *Beating the Fascists?* (Cambridge, 1983). See also A. McElligott, 'Street Politics in Hamburg' in *History Workshop Journal*, 16 (1983), pp. 83–90.

IV   Why did the Weimar Republic Collapse?

Richard Bessel and E. J. Feuchtwanger (eds.), *Social Change and Political Development in Weimar Germany* (London, 1981).

Martin Broszat, *Hitler and the Collapse of Weimar Germany* (Leamington Spa, 1987).

Jane Caplan, *Government without Administration. State and Civil Service in Weimar and Nazi Germany* (Oxford, 1988).

F. L. Carsten, *The Reichswehr and Politics* (Oxford, 1966).

Thomas Childers (ed.), *The Formation of the Nazi Constituency 1919–1933* (London and Sydney, 1986).

Michael N. Dobkowski and Isidor Wallimann (eds.), *Towards the Holocaust. The Social and Economic Collapse of the Weimar Republic* (Westport, Connecticut, and London, 1983).

Richard J. Evans and Dick Geary (eds.), *The German Unemployed. Experiences and Consequences of Mass Unemployment from the Weimar Republic to the Third Reich* (London, 1987).

Larry Eugene Jones, '"The Dying Middle": Weimar Germany and the Fragmentation of Bourgeois Politics', *Central European History*, 5 (1972), pp. 23–54.

Larry Eugene Jones, *German Liberalism and the Dissolution of the Weimar Party System 1918–1933* (Chapel Hill and London, 1988).

Eberhard Kolb, *The Weimar Republic* (London, 1988).

John A. Leopold, *Alfred Hugenberg. The Radical Nationalist Campaign against the Weimar Republik* (New Haven and London, 1977).

Rainer M. Lepsius, 'From Fragmented Party Democracy to Government by Emergency Decree and National Socialist Takeover: Germany', in J. J. Linz and A. Stepan (eds.), *The Breakdown of Democratic Regimes* (Baltimore/London, 1978), pp. 34–79.

Peter D. Stachura (ed.), *The Nazi Machtergreifung* (London, 1983).

Peter D. Stachura (ed.), *Unemployment and the Great Depression in Weimar Germany* (London, 1986).

Index